Upanisadas : The Real Truth

UPANISADAS
The Real Truth

D.D. Aggarwal

KALPAZ PUBLICATIONS
DELHI-110 052

PROTOCOL IN MAHABHARATA

Rs. 790

ISBN: 81-7835-177-3

Published in 2003 in India by
Kalpaz Publications
C–30, Satyawati Nagar
Delhi–110 052
E-mail: kalpaz@hotmail.com

Lasertypesetting by: Varsha Graphics, Delhi
Printed at: Chawla Offset Printers, Delhi

Contents

Preface

From the very term 'Upanisada', it is known that knowledge alone is the means of attaining the supreme human goal. Upanisada is said to be derived from the root 'sad' preceded by 'upa' and 'ni' conveying the sense of 'destroying', 'obtaining' or 'dissipating'. By the word 'Upanisada' is meant the knowledge of the subject matter intended to be presented by the book which is sought to be explained. Being meant for that purpose, the book also is an 'Upanisada'. In the case of seekers of liberation, who, having become dispassionate towards 'seen' or 'unseen' objects, pursue with diligence and determination the knowledge implied by the word 'Upanisadas'. The knowledge of Brahma destroys ignorance etc. that are the seeds of transmigration; it leads them to the supreme Brahma and dissipates the evils of being born in a womb, decrepitude, death etc. Thus in keeping with the very derivation of the term 'Upanisada', since it leads to the highest goal, which is superior to results achieved through all the means, the knowledge of Brahma is called 'Upanisada'.

Upanisadas contain discussion of various rishis on the subject leading to emancipation. In Mahabharata, Bhagvata, Ramayana etc. puranas, there is more preaching on bhakti, which can be had even by living in the universe. In upanisadas, on the contrary, it has been indicated that emancipation and absorption in Brahma is possible only by complete detachment from the universe, which can be possible only by leading a life of mendicancy because by involving in son, wealth and world, one cannot have full devotion towards Him and without full devotion, one cannot become Brahma. Also in upanisadas, there is no mention of incarnations as the philosophy of upanisadas recognises one Brahma. 'OM' only and the devotion to 'OM' is the only devotion of Brahma, which in turn is possible only if one thinks of Him whole-heartedly. This thinking and the reality has been arrived at by discussion between very learned rishis; Raja Janaka and Yagyavalkya rishi and others and indicated in the upanisadas.

The upanisadas speak of what is indicated in vedas but since it is in a very abstract form in vedas, one does not follow the same. Therefore, it has been indicated in the form of discussion and arriving at logical conclusion by the rishis with a view to convincing the readers.

There are several ways of reaching the almighty or attaining salvation. Vedas and upanisadas speak of reaching him by Gyan. For this purpose, the necessary requirements are Pranayam for purifying the body-system; restrain to get rid of all worldly involvements/pleasures/attractions; concentration to get rid of all sins and an effort to reach Him and finally the meditation to reach and get absorbed in Him. Such an effort is possible when one leaves the universe and lives in forests like mendicants because while living in the universe, one cannot get rid of the worldly involvements, which are impediments in attaining the goal of salvation. Another way is named Sankhya, in which one attains salvation by adopting Satoguna and absolving oneself of Rajo and Tamo gunas. Here it is said that such an attainment is possible while living in the universe but getting absolved from Rajo and Tamo gunas is not possible while leading a worldly (Grishasta) life. Next way is through yoga, in which through the system of Samadhi etc., one reaches Him and ultimately gets absorbed in Him. Such a method too is possible by leaving the universe. The last is through 'Bhakti', in which, one, while living in the universe, could reach Him (sagun) by absorbing oneself in Him through bhakti; thinking of Him only all the times and nothing else. Here too, though it is said that such a way could be adopted while living in the universe, yet one can get absorbed in Him when one bids good-bye to all worldly involvements. Such is the bhakti of sagun form of the God. In fact such a system came into being only after the incarnation of God as Rama, Krishna etc. and has been propounded by our rishis finding the human beings not in a position to resorting to the other methods. Bhagwat Gita/ Ram Charitmanas speaks of these all but says that one has to at first resort to 'Sagun Bhakti' and after reaching the climax in such a bhakti, one automatically shifts to 'Nirgun Bhakti' as propounded in upnishadas. So the attainment of the goal of getting rid of deaths and births by attaining salvation, is to reach Him in Sagun form first and then to get absorbed in Him in the Nirgun form, i.e., Brahma. This is what has been discussed in upanishadas by various rishis and narrated in this book.

There are several books written on vedas and upnishadas but I could not lay hand on any one, where the verdict is indicated in a narrative form having continuous flow of discussion in various upanishadas. I have tried to present the same in a continuous narration.

D.D. Aggarwal

1
Mundaka Upanisada

Upanisada means the closeness in realisation of self, devotion to almighty, knowledge of secrets of Brahma Vidya and the difference between the soul and the God. God has said in Rig Veda that there is no doubt in the fact that He is one, who never gets impaired and He (the Transcendental Reality) can be attained with spiritual knowledge and with His attainment, one attains all. So upanisadas lead us to the search and attainment of that almighty through their deep study. As a guru imparts knowledge to his pupils so do upanisadas to the readers. The ultimate aim of the upanisadas is to reach Him and attain salvation. Once, one indulges in such a search, he loses all his attachments with the universe or we can say one has to absolve oneself of universal attachments to reach Him. Krishna has, however, stated in Bhagwat Gita that even while living in the universe, one can reach Him through 'Bhakti', but here again absolvance is necessary from worldly instincts and once one has known Him, he becomes Him itself. This is easier in the case of a Sanyasi as he has already given up all his attachments and his only purpose now is to reach Him. This, however, is a constant effort. May be spread over several lives. It is, therefore, better one gives up all other attachments so that one is devoted to Him and remains in search of Him, all the time. Once, one is on that path, one is above the worldly decayings of aging, illness, animal instincts and so on.

Of all gods, Brahma came first. He is the creator, and maintainer of the universe. He is above all greatnesses, religions, knowledge, vairagya, and leisures and pleasures. He created the initial knowledge for the mankind. This knowledge (The Vedas) is the 'Brahma Vidya'. This Brahma Vidya has two parts—'Para Vidya' and 'Apara Vidya'. Apara Vidya is contained in all vedas and granthas and through the knowledge of Apara Vidya, one reaches Him, and that reaching is nothing else but the attainment of almighty, which is possible on getting absolved from worldly attachments and deep involvement in Apara Vidya and acting as per the path prescribed in vedas etc. On the contrary, if one thinks that he has gained everything while in the universe, he is mistaken as all that exists in the universe gets annihilated, sooner or later, and one cannot have satisfaction in attaining the worldly achievements as his desires go on increasing. It is, therefore, by their absolvance that one is able to achieve all in the universe as also the ultimate aim — the absorption in Brahma. That absorption in Brahma is the attainment of the 'Para Vidya'. Let us now understand Para Vidya. As many sparks arise out of fire and get submerged in fire itself, so many beings get created by the Brahma and they all get absorbed in Him ultimately. Various actions by the beings and their result is the field of Apara Vidya and after passing through those fields only one finds the path leading to Brahma, and that path only is the Para Vidya. Such a path is known by a few only and the rest get lost in this universe and on the expiry of life, one reports to Him for next job, and He, on the basis of his actions in the universe, ordains another life to him. He goes on in this cycle till ultimately he gets absolved in Him having known the path of Para Vidya. Those, who are in the cycle of the transmigration of soul, were not known to the universe till they came and shall not remain here when died. Therefore, coming and going from the universe is not a permanent arrangement but a temporary one. One has, therefore, to think of a permanent arrangement and that can be had only through the path of Para Vidya or the way to reach Him.

Now to understand the relation of the being and Brahma, one has to imagine that the Brahma comprises of this galaxy as sun as His head, and moon as His eyes, the directions as His ears, vedas as His tongue, air as His life, universe as His mind, and the earth as His legs. Since all these ingredients are available in the being as he is born, he should be taken as a mini-Brahma only. Subsequently, these mini-Brahmas, finish their jobs in this universe and report back to Him on death. He, either prescribes another job to be undertaken or keeps him with Himself, not assigning any other job. Getting the new assignment is getting new specie and retention by Brahma with Himself is salvation—No More Jobs.

The activities field of the people is this entire universe. The universe comprises of five ingredients — water, fire, air, earth and space and so is the being made of these five ingredients. Therefore, each being is a mini-universe within himself. In other words, the mini universe acts in the maxi universe and then reports to the creator of the universe. As the being, who is the mini universe, is non-existing, so is the maxi universe. Therefore, since both the mini and the maxi universes are annihilable, one has to think and reach the one, who is non-annihilable, and that is the creator of the annihilable. Further, since the creator is within oneself, one has to know oneself and if he has known himself, he has known the creator or the Brahma. Therefore, that Brahma is within everyone and refuge of every one; He is the life of everyone; He is the speech of everyone and the mind of everyone. One should accordingly concentrate on one's creator and with this exercise, shall sooner or later merge in Him. This is also explained in another way. Upasana be taken as bow, soul as the arrow and Brahma as the aim. The person should aim Brahma that is the soul, through upasana, or go and get merged in Brahma. Such merger only is the aim of life of a person. Brahma only is omniscient and earth, mountains, rivers, sun, moon, oceans etc., they all move on His orders within their limits so the persons too act as ordained by Him. It is here that one has to see beyond the ordained job to find out the 'One', who ordained and in this search attaining closeness to Him is the aim of life. Then one loses all worldly attachments and ultimately gets absorbed in Him. In other words, till one involves oneself whole-heatedly in that cause, leaving other assignments, one cannot reach Him and after reaching Him, one finds Him in front, in the back, on all sides and everywhere and then starts thinking himself as part of Him only.

One, who, even after realising the existence of Brahma, keeps indulged in worldly enjoyments, he loses all strings binding him with brahma, and as he goes deep in such indulgences, he is completely away from Him. Therefore, the worldly enjoyments take the person away from Him and absolvance from the same and then thinking of Him, takes a person closer to Him. One, therefore, has to decide if one wants to be away from Him, then one can enjoy the worldly luxuries, which infact are annihilable, and in these, one never gets satisfied, whereas on the contrary, indulgence in Brahma gives more and more satisfaction as one indulges in Him. Also, on absolving oneself from the worldly involvements and joys, one starts enjoying within oneself and ultimately the Brahma, who is within oneself. For this, one has to give up dependance on non-truth, indulgence in worldly enjoyments and above all the rage, as they all, as already stated, take a person away from Him. The mind is never without a job. It is, therefore, for the person to assign a job to the mind. If the assignment is relevant to the satisfaction of worldly enjoyments, then the mind sets in those enjoyments and if it is taken away from those enjoyments, then some assignment has to be awarded. Let that assignment be the thinking of Brahma. Although it is easier to involve in worldly enjoyments and difficult to involve in Him, yet one has to somehow adopt that difficult assignment and since the mind has to be busy somewhere, it may face some difficulty initially, but later, he shall start hating the worldly enjoyments and then the assignment of thinking about Him becomes easier for adoption and practice. That Brahma cannot be reached by tongue, as he is not related to any voice; he cannot be seen by eyes as he is without any shape; he cannot be felt by nose, skin, ears etc. too as he does not have these instincts. Therefore, he can be had only by 'Gyan' and 'Gyan' is nothing but the way of consigning the soul in thinking about Him and in course of time such continued thinking makes one assimilated in Him. Therefore, with the base of 'Truth', controlling all instincts, mind and brain and carrying them all with the soul in front to the almighty, is the 'thinking' of Brahma. Such an action gives pleasure to soul and through it to the mind and brain and then to all instincts. It is in this process that all instincts get satisfaction rather than in the indulgence in worldly pleasures. It is only the matter of constant thinking about Him only. It may, in this connection, be indicated that, as already stated, Brahma is all eyes, ears, nose etc. and the human being has all these instincts. Therefore, the human beings' instincts be considered as Brahma's ingredients, which should be all absorbed in Him rather than in the worldly pleasures relevant to these instincts.

Therefore, any one in the universe, who indirectly takes that "He himself is Brahma", he has known Brahma and infact becomes Brahma itself. Then, there is none in his family, who would not know Brahma. He becomes above all worldly instincts, ailments, worries, good or bad deeds, and it is definite that one who starts thinking that "He is Brahma", one shall not realise the feeling of any other instinct. He cannot even be influenced by gods as he then becomes Brahma, who is above all gods and worshipped by them all. This process can be through sacrifice, yagya, and recitation of mantras by heart.

Coming again to para and Apara Vidyas, when we read and understand vedas and other shastras, we attain Apara Vidya, and when we have known Brahma, through Apara vidya, then we have known Para Vidya. But knowledge of vedas and shastras cannot lead to the knowledge of Para Vidya (Brahmagyan). It has to be combined with Vairagya, i.e., the renunciation of worldly attachments/involvements/interests / feelings / enjoyments etc. So it is the study of vedas and shastras that leads to the Brahmagyan only when continued with Variagya. Now the question arises as to what kind of Brahma is He, who is known through Para Vidya. But to this question there is no reply except to say that he cannot be known by the human instincts (Gyanendriya and Karamendriya). He is not of any shape or figure as any shape or figure is annihilable whereas He is not annihilable. He is omniscient, omnipresent, and limitless. Such, therefore, is Brahma, who can be known through Para Vidya and can be realised and felt only by the person having known Para Vidya. He cannot explain the same as He is without any description. Then the question arises how from a non-describable, the world or the creature comes up, as also how many can arise from one and how inanimate can arise from animate. The answer can be found in the fact that like a spider, who without any other material, can weave a cobweb and gets lost in it, so without any figure or shape or material existence, Brahma created the universe. Thus the doubt arises that if Brahma becomes the universe, then he shall be annihilable and if he does not become universe then how universe can come up. The possible reply to this doubt is that animate Brahma does not become universe but by his 'Maya' only, he creates the universe as he is omniscient and knows all arts and through the knowledge of that art only, he is able to create the universe. One should only perform in this universe and such performance only grants him the pleasures of the universe and thereafter salvation. At first one should learn and then avail all pleasures in the universe and then engage oneself in the way told by vedas, i.e., Yagyas, Mantras and devotion to almighty otherwise one shall again come in next specie and so on. The performance towards Brahma is the thinking that the universe is not worth living. But to sanctify this thinking, one has to put commensurate devotion as small rivers can be crossed by boats but not the ocean. So small privileges can be had by echoes of mantras, sacrifices etc. these can lead to swarga but not to salvation (moxa) and such people after completing the shared period in swarga, again visit this universe. Such people have not fully come out of the ignorance of Brahma and, therefore, by dint of their thinking in attaining satisfaction in small performances, one has to cross one specie after another. But one, who performs with more devotion, he attains Brahmaloka from where again one has to come although after long interval. Therefore, for salvation one has to continuously strive with full devotion leaving all worldly involvements and after attaining full Vairagya. This can be attained by following the advice of a capable Guru. Availability of a capable Guru, therefore, is a must as the Guru only, after redressing all doubts tell the correct path leading to salvation and this process of imparting Para Vidya leads to the realisation of Brahma.

Brahma has created this universe through 'Maya', as already indicated. Therefore, the beings in this universe are under the influence of Maya only as with 'Maya', one has pride, ego, ignorance, raga, affection etc. and their removal is possible on attaining gyan, which is possible through a capable Guru on self-realisation. Once the curtain of 'Maya' is vanished, one sees soul or Brahma everywhere and that is the ultimate aim as this is the certain path to get absorbed in Him. When one is in 'Samadhi', he is away from worldly involvements and when 'Samadhi' is finished, then one is put in one of the two spheres—

indulgence in pleasures or absolvance from such pleasures. The latter leads to salvation. Therefore, samadhi too is not certain in leading to salvation and it has to be followed by absolving oneself from worldly involvements. This in turn is possible by adopting the way of truth, devotion and brahmcharya. One cannot have self realisation by speech, eyes, ears nor by 'tap' and other performances but by all together. Also one cannot realise the self by extra studies etc. It is, on the contrary, possible by God's grace, which can be had by belief in Him. So one has to devote oneself to the cause of almighty only by full devotion, forgetting all other involvements as diversion to or thinking of the worldly pleasures, cannot lead to realisation of self as such a person cannot be true to himself, cannot have purity of mind and unbiased, and unattached and such a person gets involved in the transmigration from one specie to another. Those, who are away from these ignorances, attain salvation by getting closeness to the almighty 'Om' Brahma and by such closeness only, the ignorance is completely destroyed.

'Om' Brahma, the creator of the universe and the protector of the world was the first among the gods to manifest Himself. To his oldest son Atharva, he imparted that knowledge of Brahma which is the basis of all knowledge. The word 'Brahma' means one, who is all surpassing great, i.e., excels all others in virtue, knowledge, detachment and splendour or the first in precedence among the shining ones, (Gods) such as Indra and others; became perfectly manifest that is to say, He was born independently unlike other worldly creatures, who take birth under the impulsion of virtue and vice. Samriti also says, He that is super-sensuous and cannot be grasped is this one-born independent, he is creator of whole universe and the protector of the world after it was created. The knowledge of Brahma that Brahma imparted to Atharva, Atharva transmitted to Angira in the days of yore. Angira passed on to Bhardwaj; Bhardwaj again passed on to Angiras. Saunik at that time told Angiras that there was two kinds of knowledge — Higher and lower. Higher is the knowledge of the supreme self and lower the knowledge of virtue and vice and their means and ends (i.e. the ignorance). The lower knowledge is that vedas, code of rituals, grammar, metre, astrology and higher is that by which that imperishable is attained. By higher knowledge, the wise realise everywhere that which cannot be perceived and grasped, which is without source, features, eyes, ears etc.; which has neither hands, nor feet; which is eternal multiformed, all pervasive, extremely subtle and undimishing and which is the source of all meaning thereby that it is only by the higher knowledge that the imperishable of this kind is realised, and that imperishable is the source of all creatures or the Brahma.

How it is the source of all creatures is narrated as a spider spreads out and withdraws its thread and as on earth glow the herbs and trees and as for a living man hair rise on the head and body, so out of the imperishable does the universe emerge here in this phenomenol creation—the entire universe, both similar and dissimilar. Through knowledge, Brahma increases in size and from that is born food (the unmanifested) from food evolves 'Prana' (Hiranyagarbha); then the cosmis-min; then the five elements (air, space, earth, fire and water) and from there the worlds and then the immortality that is merger with Brahma. So this is a cycle from Brahma to Brahma (Karmas are not eliminated even in billions of cycles). From Him, who is omniscient, the general and all knowing in detail and whose austerity is constituted by knowledge, evolve this derivative Brahma, man, colour and food.

Now we proceed to distinguish the solely matters — the state of bondage and freedom — of these two kinds of knowledge. The lower knowledge is the state of transmigration, which involves distinction in agents, actions and results. Such a state has to be eradicated wholly by each embodied being, because it consists of sorrow, and its inter-relation is like the unbroken current of a river and the subject matter of the higher knowledge is freedom, which consists in the elimination of that state and is beginningless, endless, ageless, deathless, immortal, fearless, pure, placid, and it is supreme bliss that is without a second and is nothing but remaining established in one's own self. In regard to lower knowledge again, it may be stated that the 'Karmas' that the wise men discovered in the mantras of vedas etc. are accomplished variously, where the three vedic duties prescribed by Rig, Yajur and Sam Vedas, get united. One performs them for ever with desire for the true results. This is one's path leading to the fruits of 'Karma' acquired by oneself. The first of the three vedic duties is Agnihotra, where the fire is set ablaze, the flame shots up, one should then offer oblation. This offering of oblation is the path of attainment of the results of 'Karma'. For agnihotra there is need of sacrifice; then the use of 'mantras' in the agnihotra; then the guests should be served; it should be performed at right time; should be performed in proper way with rites. The oblations thus offered turn into rays of the sun and take him up, who performs the rites in those flames at proper time, to where the single lord of the gods presides over all, i.e., to Swarga. Those engaged in sacrifice, on whom the inferior Karma rests, remain within the fold of ignorance and thinking they are wise and learned. Such fools, while buffeted very much, ramble about like the blind led by another blind alone. Moreover, continuing amidst the ignorance, the un-enlightened take airs by thinking that they had attained the goal. Since such men attained in their 'Karma', do not understand the truth under the influence of attachment, thereby they become afflicted with sorrow and are deprived of heaven on the exhaustion of the results of 'Karma'. Such deluded fools believing the rites inculcated by vedas and the samritis to be the highest, do not understand the other thing that leads to liberation. They having enjoyed the fruits of actions in the abode of pleasures in Heaven, enter this world as an inferior one. Contrarily, those who live in the forests, while begging for alms viz those forest-dwellers and hermits, who resort to the duties of their respective stages of life as well as to meditation—and the learned house holders, who have their senses under control, they after becoming freed from dirt, go by the path to the sun to where lives that 'Purusa', immortal and undecaying by nature. The course of transmigratory existence that is attainable through the lower knowledge culminate here alone.

Those, who become detached from this whole world of ends and means have competence for the higher knowledge. One should, therefore, resort to renunciation after examining the worlds acquired through 'Karma', with the help of the maxim, 'There is nothing here that is not the result of 'Karma', so, what is the need of performing 'Karma'. For knowing that reality, he should go, with sacrificial faggots in hand, only to a teacher well-versed in the vedas and absorbed in Brahma. Such a teacher, whose heart is calm and whose outer organs are under control, that man of enlightenment should adequately impart that knowledge of Brahma by which one realises the true and imperishable Purusa.

Now the subject matter of the higher knowledge of Brahma is that reality after knowing which, all becomes known. As from a fire fully ablaze, sparks fly off in thousands that are all in to the fire, similarly, from the imperishable, originate different kinds of creatures and they merge into it again. Amongst the imperishables too, the one Brahma is imperishable, which is higher than the other imperishables, which are the seeds of name and form, called unmanifested (Maya) and which is itself higher than its own modifications. This absolute imperishable, which is devoid of all differences created by limiting adjuncts, which is the very essence of the other immutables and which, like space is free from all forms and is describable by such expressions as "Not this, not this". If like the Purusha, (the all pervasive entity), the vital force etc. exist as such before creation, then by virtue of their coexistence with it, the all pervasive entity will be possessed of the vital force etc. But as a fact, unlike the all pervasive entity, the vital forces etc. don't exist there, as such, before creation, therefore, the supremely all pervasive entity is without vital forces, just as one is said to be without a son so long as a son is not born. Now in regard to how those vital forces don't exist, it may be stated that from Brahma originates the vital force as well as the mind, all the senses, space, air, fire, water and earth that supports everything. Further, the indwelling self of all is surely Brahma, of whom heaven is the head, the moon and sun are the two eyes, the directions are the two ears, the revealed vedas are the speech, air is the vital force, the whole universe is the heart and it is he from whom two feet emerged on the earth. He infact is the seer, hearer, thinker, knower, and the reality of all the senses in all beings. And the creatures too, that transmigrate through the five fires (heaven, cloud, earth, father and mother) are born from that very 'Purusa' and from him after emergence of fire i.e. heaven etc., of which the fuel is the sun, from the moon emerges cloud; from cloud the herbs and corn on the earth. A man sheds the semen into a woman and so from the supreme Purusa many creatures originate.

Then the auxiliaries of learners, as well as their fruits, emerge verily from him, through the sacrifices—whether with or without the sacrificial stake—offering to Brahmins, the year, the sacrificier, and the worlds, where the moon sanctifies (all) and where the sun shines, and from him emerge the gods in various groups, the sadhyas, human beings, truth, continence and dutifulness. Also from him emerge the seven sense-organs (two eyes, two ears, two nostrils and one tongue), the flames, fuel, oblations, seats—where sense-organs move and sleep in the cavity and one then deposited by God in groups in human beings. Also all mountains, oceans, rivers, foodgrains, juices etc. emerge from him by virtue of which the internal self verily exists in the midst of the elements. Thus all these emerge from the Purusa. Therefore, all modifications, are supported by speech and it is name only which is false, but only that which is the 'Purusa' is true. The Purusa alone is all this, comprising of 'Karma' and knowledge. He, who knows this Supreme, immortal Brahma existing in the heart, destroys here the knot of ignorance, even while living in the universe and not only after death.

Let us now see how the immutable can be known, though it is formless. It is effulgent, near at hand and well-known as moving in the heart and it is the great goal. All that move, breathe and wink or donot wink are fixed on it. It comprises of gross and subtle, which is beyond the ordinary knowledge of creatures, and which is the most-desirable and the highest of all. It is obviously Brahmna. He is subtler than the subtle and all dwellers of the world are fixed on him. This only is the speech, the mind, the vital force and is true, immortal, indestructible and can be shot at by the mind when concentrated on it. Therefore, one should try to shoot/fix one's mind on that imperishable. For shooting, one should hold the bow (as narrated in upanisadas) and fix on it, an arrow sharpened with meditation. Then drawing the string, one should hit that very target that is the imperishable with the mind absorbed in his thoughts. Here 'OM' is the bow; the soul is the arrow and Brahma is the target. It is to be hit by an unerring man meaning that one should become one with it just like an arrow. Just as the success of the arrow consists in its becoming one with the target, similarly one should bring about the result, consisting in becoming one with the imperishable, by eliminating the ideas of the body etc. being the self. Since the imperishable is hard to grasp, it is being presented over and over again so as to make it easily comprehensible. Then one should know that self (Purusha) alone that is one without a second and on which are strung heaven, the earth, the inter space, the mind, and the vital forces together with all the other organs and give up all other talks. This is the bridge leading to immortality. Having known the self, one should discard other talks that constitute the lower knowledge and give up also all 'Karmas' together with their fruits that one presented by the lower knowledge because this knowledge of the self is the bridge, the means of achievement of immortality and of liberation. It is comparable to bridge as it is the means of getting across the great sea of the world. Vedas also state that 'Knowing him alone, one goes beyond death, there is no other path to proceed by. Now within the heart in which nerves are fixed like the spokes of the hub of a chariot wheel, moves the aforesaid self by becoming multiformed. One should, therefore, meditate on the self thus with the help of 'OM' avoiding all hindrances on the way to reach the other shore beyond darkness i.e. to reach Brahma, who is free from ignorance. Here it is shown as to where he exists, who forms the subject matter of the superior knowledge, who is beyond ignorance and who has to be reached after crossing the ocean of the worldly involvements. That self, which is omniscient in general and all knowing in detail and which has such glory in this world — that self which is of this kind — is seated in the space within the luminous city of Brahma, the body. It is conditioned by mind and is the carrier of the vital forces and the body. It is seated in food (the body) by placing the intellect in the cavity of the heart and through their knowledge, the discriminating people realise that self as existing in its fullness every where — the self that shines surpassingly as blissfulness and immortality. The result of this knowledge of this supreme self is that when the self, which is both the high and the low, is realised, the knot of the heart gets untied; all doubts get solved and all one's actions become dissipated i.e. one becomes free on the eradication of the causes of the worldly state. In the supreme bright seathe (the self) is Brahma, free from taints and without parts. It is pure, and is the light of lights and it is that which the knowers of the self realise. There the sun does not shine, nor the moon or the stars nor do these flashes of lightning shine there. How can this fire do so? Everything shines according as he does so; by his light all this shines diversely. So the Brahma, which is the light of all lights is alone true and that everything else is its modification a modification that exists only in name, having speech alone as its support — is being restated at the end reaffirming whatever is said above. All that, which is in front is but Brahma, the immortal. Brahma is at the back, as also on the right and the left. It is extended above and below too and so this world is nothing but Brahma, the highest and the supreme truth.

Already the higher knowledge has been presented by which the imperishable truth, called 'Purusa' is attained and from his realisation, the causes of the worldly state as the knots of the heart are totally eradicated. Yoga, as the means for such realisation, has also been stated with the help of taking up a bow. Now we have to see the truth and the rest that are helpful auxiliaries to that yoga. A story of the two birds is relevant. The birds are ever associated and have similar names. They cling to the same tree. Of these, one eats the fruit of divergent tastes, and the other looks on without eating. Here the tree is the body; as it gets demolished like a tree; this tree sprouts up from its material cause, the unmanifested (merger) and is called the field and provides a support for all the results of the Karmas of all beings — God and the soul — as conditioned by the subtle body, which holds in itself the tendencies and impressions created by ignorance, desire and action — cling to it like birds. Of the two birds, one who hugs this tree, the individual soul and knower of the field, eats, enjoys the fruits consisting of happiness and misery brought about by actions, which are full of tastes, consisting in the experience of multifarious mental reactions. On the other hand there is God, who is by nature, eternal, pure, wise, and free and who is omniscient and has the totality of 'Maya' as his limiting adjunct, that God does not taste, as he is the director of both the enjoyer and the enjoyed. The other one merely looks on, without enjoying, for his dictatorship consists in mere observation, as in the case of a king. On the same tree, the individual soul remains drowned, as it were and so it moans being worried by its impotence. When it sees the other, the adored Lord, and his glory, then only it becomes liberated from sorrow and reaches the end of all desires.

When the seer sees the Purusa — the golden hue creator, the lord, and the source of the inferior Brahma — then the illumined one completely shakes off both merit and demerit, becomes taintless and attains absolute equality. This one is the vital force, which shines divergently through all beings and knowing this the illumined man has no further occasion to go beyond anything in his talk. He disports in the self, delights in the self and is engrossed in spiritual efforts. So this one is the chief among the knowers of Brahma. The bright and pure self within the body that is seen by the monks with habitual effort and attenuated blemishes, is attainable verily through truth, concentration, complete knowledge and continence, practised constantly. It can then be said that those in whom there is no crookedness, no falsehood, and no dissimulation, which is this self that is attainable through these disciplines, attain it through truth etc. constantly practised but not through inconstant truth etc.

Truth alone wins and not the untruth. By truth only is laid the path called Devayana by which the desireless seers ascend to where exists the supreme treasure, attainable through truth.

Question then arises as to what Truth is and what its attributes are ? It is great and self-effulgent; and its form is unthinkable. It is subtler than the subtle. It shines diversely. It is farther away than the far-off and it is near at hand in this body. Among sentient beings, it is perceived as seated in this very body, in the cavity of the heart. But it is not perceived by the ignorant because of its being covered by ignorance. Since it is not comprehended through the eye, nor through speech, nor through the other senses, nor is it attained through austerity or 'Karma', the unique means for its realisation lies in one becoming purified in mind through the favourableness of the intellect. Therefore, one can see that indivisible self through meditation, thinking of him with a concentrated mind.

Further, within the heart in the body, where the vital force has entered in five forms viz 'pran', 'apana' etc. is this subtle self to be realised through that intelligence by which the entire mind is pervaded as well as the motor and sensory organs of all creatures. And it is to be known in mind, which having become purified, this self reveals itself distinctly. For one, who attains as his own self that which is the self of all and which is possessed of the above characteristics, is being stated the result, consisting in the attainment of all, which follows from the very fact of his becoming one with all. The man of pure mind wins those worlds, which he mentally wishes for and those enjoyable things which he covets, Therefore, one desirous of prosperity, should adore the knower of the self.

The 'Purusa' knows this supreme abode, this Brahma, in which the universe is placed and which shines holy. Those wise ones indeed, who having become desireless, worship this enlightened person and transcends this human seed. Therefore, eschewing of the desires is the chief discipline for an aspirant of liberation. He, who covets the desirable things, while brooding on their virtues, is born amidst those very surroundings along with the desires. But for one, who has got his wishes fulfilled and who is self-poised, all the belongings vanish even in this universe. The purport is that desires do not crop up in his mind owing to the destruction of their causes. From this, some may be led to think that if the attainment of the self be the highest of all achievements, then for its realisation, one should practise extensively such processes as the study of the vedas. But this self is not attained through study only nor through the intellect nor through much hearing, the very self, which this one i.e. the aspirant seeks is attainable through that fact of seeking, this self of his, reveals its own nature, its own supreme nature, its reality, that was enveloped in ignorance. The idea is that when knowledge dawns, the self becomes revealed just like pots etc. on the coming of light. The purport being that the means of the attainment of the self consists in praying for this consummation to the exclusion of everything else. These spiritual disciplines too — viz strength, absence of delusion and knowledge — as associated with their signs coupled with monasticism are helpful to the prayer for the attainment of the self for the self is not attained by one devoid of strength, nor through delusion, nor through the knowledge unassociated with monasticism. But the self of that knower, who strives through these means, enter into the abode that is Brahma. Now having attained this, the seers become contented with their knowledge, established in the self, freed from attachment and composed. Having realised the all-pervasive one everywhere, these discriminating people, ever merged in contemplation, enter into the all, even at the time of falling of the body. They give up the limitations of the adjuncts created by ignorance, like space confirmed within a pot on the breaking of the pot. Thus the knowers of Brahma enter into the abode that is Brahma. Then, those to whom the entity presented by the vedantic knowledge has become fully ascertained, and who are assiduous and have become pure in mind through the yoga of monasticism — all of them, at the supreme moment of final departure, become identified with the supreme immortality in the worlds that one Brahma and they become freed on every side. But Brahma's attainment too cannot be determined in terms of limitation of space. Besides, the knowers of Brahma accept only that liberation, which consists in the removal of ignorance etc. which are the causes of mundane bondage and not that which is a product. Further more, at the time of liberation to their sources' repair the fifteen constituents of the body and to their respective gods go all the gods of the senses. The Karmas and the soul appearing like the intellect, all become unified with the supreme undecaying.

As rivers flowing down become indistinguishable on reaching the sea by giving up their names and forms, so also the illumined soul, having become freed from name, and form, reaches the self-effulgent 'Purusa' that is higher than the higher (Maya).

Anyone, who knows that supreme Brahma, becomes Brahma indeed. In his line no one is born, who does not know Brahma. He overcomes grief, and rises above aberrations; and becoming freed from the knots of the heart, he attains immortality. Then, there is the rule of transmission of the knowledge of Brahma. This rule has been revealed by the 'mantra', saying 'To them alone should one expound' this knowledge of Brahma, who are engaged in the practice of disciplines, versed in the vedas and devoted to Brahma, who personally sacrifice to the fire called 'Ekarsi' with faith and by whom has been duly accomplished the vow of holding fire on the head. The seer Angiras spoke of this truth in the days of yore. One that has not fulfilled the vow does not read this. Salutation to the great seers, salutation, starting with Brahma through whom that knowledge was successively handed down, the great seers being those, beginning with Brahma, who directly saw and realised Brahma. Salutation to those again.

2

Mandukya Upanisada

I bow to that Brahma, who after having enjoyed, all sorrows and happiness, during the waking state, of the gross objects by pervading all the human objectives through a diffusion of its rays (souls being reflection of Brahma) of unchanging consciousness that embraces all that moves or does not move, which again after having drunk (having merged in the unrealised self) during the dream state, all the varieties of objects, produced by desire as well as action and ignorance and lighted up by the intellect sleeps while enjoying bliss and making us enjoy through 'Maya', and which is counted as the fourth form (Besides sleep, dream and waking) from the point of view of 'Maya' and is supreme, immortal, and birthless. It is prayed that, the fourth one protect us which, after having identified itself with the universe, enjoys during waking state the gross objects created by virtue and vice, which again experiences through its own light the subtle objects of enjoyment that are called up by its own intellect, which further withdraws promptly all these into itself; and which lastly becomes free from all attributes by discarding every distinction and difference.

The letter 'OM' is all this. The phenomenal world of duality is a creation of ignorance and it can be eradicated through knowledge of Brahma. Veda says 'when there is duality, then one smells something, one sees something' and so on and when there is something else, then one can see and know something. But when to the knower of Brahma everything becomes the self, then what should one see and through what and what should one know ? 'OM' is the ramification of speech, which home for their contents such illusory, manifestations of the self as the vital force etc. and 'OM' is essentialy the same as the self, since it is devoted to the self.

So 'OM' is all this and all that is past, present or future is verily the same 'OM' and whatever is beyond the three periods of time is also verily 'OM'. The Supreme Brahma is known through the relationship subsisting between name and its object, it too is, but 'OM'. Further 'OM' is the superior as well as inferior Brahma, showing its proximity to Brahma by virtue of its being a means for the attainment of Brahma. So 'OM' is surely Brahma. This self too is Brahma. Self is possessed of four quarters starting from Vaisvanara, whose sphere of action is the working state, whose consciousness relates to things external, who is possessed of seven limbs and nineteen mouths — the five senses of perception and the five organs of action, the vital forces — Prana and the rest make up of five and mind (thinking power), intellect, ego and mind-stuff. These are mouths since they are the gates of experience. Since through the entrances Vaisvanara thus constituted, enjoys gross objects viz sound and the rest, therefore, he is an enjoyer of the gross. He is called Vaisvanara because he leads in diverse ways all 'viswa' being 'nara' to their enjoyment. This is the first stop to the knowledge of Brahma. Also this identity of Visva with Virat is suggestive of the unity with 'Hiranyagarbha' and the unmanifested as well.

The 'Taijasa' is the second quarter, whose sphere of activity is the dream state, whose consciousness is internal, who is possessed of seven limbs and nineteen mouths and who enjoys subtle objects. In this dream state the mind experiences greatness. The mind is internal in relation to the senses and he whose awareness in dream, takes the forms of the impressions in that mind, is aware of internal objects. He is called 'Taijasa' as he becomes the witness of the modes of cognition that is bereft of objects and appears only as a luminous thing. The third quarter is 'Prajna', who has deep sleep as his sphere, in whom everything becomes undifferentiated, who is a mass of mere consciousness, who abounds in bliss, who is surely an enjoyer of bliss, and who is the doorway to the experience of the dream and the waking states. Since sleep consists of the unawareness of reality, it is a common feature of the two states (of waking and dream) where there are the presence and absence, therefore, the adverbial clause, 'where the sleeper' etc. is used in order to keep in view the state of deep sleep. Or since sleep, consisting in the unawareness of Reality, is equally present in all the three states, deep sleep is being distinguished from the earlier two states, in which place or at which time, the sleeping man does not see any dream, does not desire any enjoyable thing for in deep sleep there does not exist, as in the two earlier states, either dream, consisting in the perception of things otherwise than what they are or any desire, this is that state of deep sleep. He, who has got this state of deep sleep as his sphere, is Susupta-Sthana (सुसुप्त स्थान). He is called Prajna, conscious par-excellence, since in him alone is there the knowledge of the past and the future and of all things. This Prajna, as described, is the third quarter. This is Lord of all, this one is omniscient, this one is the inner Director of all ; this one is the source of all; this one is verily the place of origin and dissolution of all beings. For the same reason, he gives birth to the universe together with its diversities, as described before, and hence this one is the source of all and since this is so, therefore, this very one is certainly the place of origin and dissolution of all beings. Thus gross satisfies Visva, and the subtle satisfies Taijasa and so also joy satisfies Prajna and know enjoyment to be threefold. He, who knows both these — viz the enjoyment that there is in the three states, and that which is declared to be the enjoyer there — does not become affected even while enjoying. In the three states there is one object of enjoyment that appears in triple form, known as gross, subtle and bliss and the entity known by the names of Vaisvanara, Taijasa and Prajna. Further, it is a well-established fact that origination belongs to all entities that have existence. Prana creates all objects, Purusa creates separately the rays of unconsciousness that are the living creatures.

Turia, the fourth quarter, which follows in order has to be stated, hence this is presented by the upanishada as not conscious of internal world etc. Since it is devoid of every characteristic that can make the use of the words possible, it is not describable through words and hence the upanisada seeks to indicate 'Turiya', merely through the negation of attributes. When 'Turiya' is realised as the self, it leads to the cessation of craving for the non-self, just as the hankering for silver ceases on recognising the nacre. Indeed there can be no possibility of such defects as ignorance, desire and the like, after the realisation of Turiya as one's self. Nor is there any reason why Turiya should not be realised as identical with one's self, in as much as all the upanishadas aim at this conclusion as is evidenced.

This very self, that is the supreme reality which has false appearances, has been spoken of as possessed of four quarters. Its unreal form has been dealt with which is a creation of ignorance and which is analogous to a snake superimposed as a rope and consists of the three quarters that are related mutually like the seed and its sprout. They consider the fourth to be that which is not conscious of the internal world, nor conscious of the external world, nor conscious of both the worlds, nor a mass of consciousness nor conscious nor non-conscious, which is unseen beyond empirical dealings, beyond the grasp (of the organs of action), uninferable, unthinkable indescribable, whose valid proof consists in the single belief in the self; in which all phenomena cease, and which is unchanging, auspicious and non-dual. That is the self and that is to be known. As the true nature of the rope is realised through the negation of the illusions of a snake etc., so the very self, subsisting usually in the three states is sought to be established as Turiya in the same way as is done in the case of the text, 'That thou art'.

The unchanging non-dual one is the ordainer, the Lord, in the matter of eradicating all sorrows. The effulgent Turiya is held to be the all-pervasive source of all objects. In the matter of eradicating all sorrows represented by Vaisvanara, Taijasa and Prajna, the self that is Turiya is the ordainer i.e., he is the Lord capable of ordaining the cessation of sorrow, for sorrow ceases as a result of his knowledge. Further, he is unchanging because he does not deviate from his nature, i.e., he is 'advaita' (non-dual). For determining the true nature of Turiya, the genetic and specific characteristics of Visva and the rest have to be ascertained. Visva and Taijasa are held to be conditioned by cause and effect and Prajna is conditioned by cause. But both these do not exist in Turiya. Prajna does not comprehend either himself or others, neither truth nor falsehood. But Turiya is for ever everything and the witness. Vedas say 'for the vision of the witness can never be lost' so there is no possibility of the darkness or shining in anyway other than that of the sun and so is the position of false perception in the absence of Turiya. Further, non-perception of duality is common to both Prajna and Turiya. Prajna is endued with sleep that is a casual state but in Turiya that sleep does not exist. Prajna consists in non-perception of Reality and that itself is the seed of the birth of cognition of varieties and Prajna is endued by this sleep that is a casual state. In Turiya, because of his being by nature a constant witness, therefore, in him there is no bondage of the casual state. Also the earlier two viz Taijasa and Prajnas are endued with dream and sleep but Prajna is endued with dreamless sleep. People of firm conviction do not see either sleep or dream in Turiya. Therefore, Turiya is not conditioned by the states of cause and effect (कार्य और कारण). It is being shown when one becomes firmly rooted in Turiya, Then dream comes to one, who cognises reality, falsity like the cognition of a snake on a rope, in the states of dream and waking, sleep belonging to one not cognising. Reality is equally present in all the three states. Dream and sleep, being the common features of both Viswa and Teijasa are treated as one and since in these two states sleep is of secondary importance owing to the predominance of false perception, the error is equated with dream. But in the third state, the error takes the form of sleep alone consisting in non-perception of reality. Therefore, when these two (Visva-Tejasa and Prajna) existing in the states of effect and cause, the two errors, consisting of false perception and non-perception, and consisting the two bondages in the form of effect and cause, are eradicated on the cognition of the Supreme reality, then one attains the state of Turiya. The idea is that as one does not perceive both kinds of bondages then one becomes firmly rooted in Turiya. Subsequently, when the individual, sleeping under the influence of beginningless 'Maya', is awakened then he realises the birthless, sleepless, dreamless, non-dual Turiya. Since it is beyond question that the phenomenal world would cease to be if it had any existence, all this duality that is nothing but 'Maya', is but non-duality in reality. The notable diversity in above concept shall disappear if it had been imagined by anyone. This kind of talk is for the sake of making instructions possible. Infact duality ceases to exist after the realization.

Coming back to 'OM', that very self considered from the standpoint of the syllable denoting it, is 'OM' and considered from the standpoint of the letters constituting 'OM', the quarters of the self are the letters of 'OM' and the letter are the quarters. The letters are 'a', 'u', 'm'. Vaisvanara, having the waking state as his sphere, is the first letter 'a' because of similarity of pervasiveness or being the first. He, who knows thus, does verily attain all desirable things and becomes the foremost. He, who is Taijasa with the state of dream as his sphere of activity, is the second letter 'u' because of the similarity of excellence and intermediateness. He, who knows thus increases the current of knowledge and becomes equal to all. None is born in his line, who is not a knower of Brahma. Then Prajna with his sphere of activity in the sleep state is 'm' the third letter of 'OM', because of measuring as barley is measured by the vessel called 'Prastha', so are Visva and Taijasa measured as it were because of their entry into and coming out of Prajna during dissolution and origination. Similarly too, at the end of the pronunciation, the letters 'a' and 'u' seem to enter into the last letter, 'm' to come out again from it. Similarly, Visva and Taijas merge into Prajna at the time of sleep. Because of this analogy too there is the identity of Prajna and letter 'm'. When the identity of Visva with the letter 'a' is intended, that is to say when Visva's identity with a letter is apprehended, the similarity of being the first, as well as the similarity of all-pervasiveness emerges in view. Similarly, in the matter of comprehending Taijasa, as identified with 'u', that is to say, when Taijasa's identity with a letter is apprehended, the similarity of excellence is clearly seen and intermediacy also is equally clear. In the matter of Prajna too, the identity with the letter 'm', that is to say when Prajna's identity with a letter is apprehended, the similarity of being a measure is seen to emerge plainly, and so also does the similarity of absorption. The idea is that in the matter of Prajna's identity with the letter 'm', measurement and absorption are excellent points of similarity. Then partless 'OM' is Turiya—beyond all conventional dealings, the limit of the negation of the phenomenal world, the auspicious, and the non-dual 'OM' is thus the self to be sure. He, who knows thus enters the self through his own self. The knower of Brahma, who has realised the highest truth, be entered into the self by burning away the third state of latency and hence he is not born again, since Turiya has no latency of creation. To those men of renunciation, however, who are possessed of dull or average intellect who still consider themselves aspirants, who tread the virtuous path, and who know the common features of the letters and the quarters, of 'OM' and the self, as presented above, when meditated on in the proper way, becomes helpful for the realisation of Brahma. Here one should know 'OM', quarter by quarter; for there is no doubt that the quarters of the self are the letter of 'OM'. Having known 'OM' quarter by quarter, one should not think of anything else what so ever. One should concentrate one's mind on 'OM' for 'OM' is Brahma, beyond fear. For a man, overfixed in Brahma, there can be no fear anywhere. 'OM' is surely the inferior Brahma and 'OM' is considered to be the superior Brahma. 'OM' is without cause, without inside and outside, and without effect, and it is undecaying. Also 'OM' is the beginning, the middle and end of everything. Having known 'OM' in this way indeed, one attains immediately identity with the self. Also one should know 'OM' to be God seated in the hearts of all meditating on the all pervasive 'OM. The intelligent man does not grieve at all and the 'OM', without measures and possessed of infinite dimension, is the auspicious entity where all duality ceases. He, by whom, 'OM' is known, is the real sage, and not so in any other man, even though he may be learned in the scriptures.

God is one only without a second. This is so because duality ceases to exist after the realisation. The wise men adept in the use of means of knowledge, say about the 'falsity' of all objects in a dream because of the location of the objects inside the body and by reason of the space, being small. Besides, One does not see places by going there, as the time is not long enough, Moreover, every dreamer, when awakened, does not continue in that place of dream. A man sleeping at night sees things as though in the day time. One does not dream by going anywhere outside the body for as soon as one goes to sleep, one sees as though one is dreaming in a place miles away from the body, where one could reach after several days. In fact one does not go anywhere in the dream. The things seen in a dream are unreal because the dream objects are unreal in a dream, so also, because of that very reason, the objects in the waking state are unreal. But objects in the dream state differ because of existence inside the body and because of the smallness of the space. In as much as diverse things are found to be similar in the strength of the familiar ground of inference, the wise say that the dream and the waking states are one as that which does not exist in the beginning and the end is equally so in the present i.e. in the middle. Though they are on the same footing with the unreal, yet they are seen as though real by the ignorant, who do not know the self. But their utility is contradicted in dream. Therefore, from the fact of their having a beginning and an end, they are rightly held to be unreal. The uniqueness that is supposed by a person to be seen in a dream is not so by its own right. This unique attribute is a mere attribute of the experience in a particular state, as it is in the case of the dwellers in Heaven. This he experiences by going there, just as one, well informed does, in this world. Just as the appearances of things in certain states, such as a snake or a rope or a mirage in a desert, are unreal, similarly, the novelties experienced in a dream are merely attributes of the dreamer in that state and, therefore, they are unreal. Accordingly, the analogy of the dream is not inapplicable. The assumption of uniqueness in the dream having been demolished, one proceeds by way of dilating on the similarity of objects of the waking and dream states. Even in the dream state itself, anything imagined by the inner consciousness is unreal, while anything experienced by the outer consciousness is real, but both these are seen to be false. Even in the waking state, whatever is imagined by the inner consciousness, is false and whatever is perceived by the outer consciousness, is true. It is reasonable that both these are unreal. It is also reasonable to say that both the so called true and false are unreal, for they are equally imagined either by the internal or external consciousness. But if all objects, in both the states be unreal, then who apprehends these objects and who indeed is their creator ? The idea is that if one does not want to adopt a theory of the non-existence of the self and wants to posit something behind phenomena, then who is the support of memory and knowledge ? The answer is that the self-effulgent self imagines itself through itself by the power of its own 'Maya'. The self itself cognises the objects and this is the conclusion of Vedanta. Imagining the way in which the self does so, the Lord manifests diversely the mundane things existing in the mind. Turning the mind outward, he creates the well-defined things as well as the undefined things. This is how the Lord imagines the things that exists internally as long as the thought lasts and things that are externally related to two points of time are all imaginations. Their distinction is not caused by anything else. The objects that appear indistinct inside the mind and those that appear vivid outside are all merely created by imagination. Their distinction is to be traced to the difference in the organs of perception. The fact that things in the mind, called up by mere mental impressions, have an indistinctness, while externally as objects of the sense of sight etc., they have a vividness. That fact is not due to the existence of the objects themselves, for this distinction is noticed even in dream. This is caused by the difference in the organs of perception. Hence it is proved that the things of the waking state are as much a creation of imagination as the dream objects. The root of imagining that the external and the mental objects are mutually related by way of causation that at first he imagines the individual soul and then he imagines the different objects, external and mental. The individual gets his memory in accordance with the kind of thought and impressions he has. As it happens in common experience that a rope, that is not well ascertained, in its true reality as 'This is so indeed', is imagined variously in hazy darkness, as a snake, a line of water, or a stick just because its real nature has not been determined earlier for if the rope had been ascertained earlier, there would not have been such imaginations as of a snake etc. as for instance, there is no such imagination with regard to the fingers of ones' own hands, similarly the self is imagined to be such countless diverse objects as an individual creature or the vital force etc., just because it has not been ascertained in its true nature to be pure intelligence, existence and non-duality and different from such evils on cause and effect, that are the characteristics of the world. Further, as the illusion on the rope ceases and the rope alone remains when the rope is ascertained to be nothing but the rope, so also is the ascertainment about the self. So if it be a well-ascertained truth that the self is but one, why is it imagined as so many of these infinite things like the vital force etc., that constitute phenomenal existence. This self is imagined to be the infinite objects like 'Prana' (The vital force) etc. This is the 'Maya', of that self effulgent one, by which he himself is deluded and those, who know 'Prana', consider 'Prana' to be the reality. The knowers of the elements consider the elements to be so (fire, earth etc.), the knowers of the qualities (gunas — Satto, Rajo, Tamo) cling to the qualities and the knowers of the categories swear by them viz the worshippers of gods stand by the respective gods. People conversant with the subtle, consider reality also to be so while others dealing with the gross consider it to be so. The worshippers of God with forms consider reality as possessed of forms whereas those who swear by formlessness call it a void.

The calculator of time (astrologer) call it time. The knower of the directions consider them real. The dabblers in theories (mantral etc.) accept these to be so and the knowers of the universe consider the fourteen worlds to be so. The knowers of the mind call it the self, whereas the knowers of intelligence take it for the reality and the knowers of virtue and vice attribute reality to them, while according to others they are infinite. Adepts in human dealings say that the people's pleasures are the real things. Persons conversant with the stages of life hold those to be the reality. The grammarians total the view that words belonging with masculine, feminine and neuter genders are the reality, while others know reality to be constituted by the higher and lower Brahmas. People, conversant with creation, call creation to be the reality, the knowers of dissolution call it dissolution. The knowers of subsistence call it subsistence; all these ideas, are for ever imagined on the self. Briefly stating, 'Prana' means 'Prajna', the self in the state of latency. Everything else, ending with subsistences is only his product and similarly all other popular ideas conceived by every being like a snake etc. on a rope are mere imaginations on the self that is devoid of all of them, and these are caused by ignorance consisting in the non-determination of the nature of self. This is the purport. Any one to whom a teacher may show a particular object as the reality, sees that alone and that thing too protects him by becoming identified with him. That absorption leads to his self-identity with the object of attention.

Through these things, which are really non-different from the self, this one (self identity) is presented as though really different, He who truly knows this, grasps the meaning of the vedas without any hesitation. It is said that the unreality of duality, that has been established logically, is also derived from the valid evidence of Vedanta. Just as dreams and magic seem to be unreal, or as is a city in the sky, so also this whole universe is known to be unreal from the upanisadas by the wisemen. Samritis say 'This universe is viewed by the wise as unreal like a crack on the ground that a rope appears to be in darkness or as always unstable like bubbles created by rain' devoid of bliss and ceasing to exist after dissolution. The highest truth about the self is that there is no dissolution, no origination, no bondage, none striving or aspiring for salvation and none liberated. All such conceptions as 'I am happy, miserable, ignorant, born, dead, worn-out, embodied, I see, I am manifest and unmanifest, emaciated and old, these are mine'— are all super imposed on the self. The self permeates all these ideas as it is invariably present in all of them just as a rope is present in all its different, illusory appearances as a snake, a line of water etc. Such being the case, the knowledge of the nature of the self has not to be generated by scriptures, since it is self-established and scriptures provide something that is not already known as if they restate something that is already known, they will lose their validity. Therefore, it is in the attributeless self that the distinct characteristics of being happy etc. are imagined. And as for the scriptural texts, speaking of the absence of happiness etc. in the self, it is proved that they are merely meant to remove the specific ideas of happiness etc. from it. This self is imagined to be the unreal things (like snake in rope) and also to be non-dual as these perceived things are also imagined on the non-dual self. Therefore, non-duality is auspicious.

This world, when ascertained from the stand point of its essential nature, does not exist as different nor does it exist in its own right nor do phenomenal things exist as different or non-different (from one another or from the self). This is what the knowers of truth understand. Further, this self, that is beyond all imagination, free from the diversity of this phenomenal world, and non-dual has been seen by the contemplative people, versed with vedas and unafflicted by desire, fear and anger. The idea is that the Supreme self is realisable only by the men of renunciation, who are free from blemishes, who are learned, and who are devoted to the purport of upanisadas, but not so by the logicians and others, whose hearts are tainted by attachment etc. and whose philosophies are prejudiced by their own outlooks. Since non-duality is auspicious and free from fear by virtue of its being, by nature, devoid of all evils, therefore, having known it, thus, one should fix one's memory on non-duality and having comprehended that non-duality etc. having realised directly and immediately that self that is beyond hunger etc., birthless, and above all conventional dealings—after attaining the consciousness, 'I am the supreme Brahma', one should behave in the world like a dull-witted man, that is to say, without advertising oneself as 'I am such and such.' So, the mendicants should have no appreciation or greetings for others and they should be free from rituals. He should have the body and soul as his support and he should be dependent on circumstances. Giving up all such activities as appreciation or greetings, and having given up all desires for external objects and having embraced the highest kind of formal renunciation, in accordance with the vedic text, "knowing this very self, the Brahmins renounce" and the samritis text 'with their consciousness, in that Brahma there self identified with that ever intent on that, with that for their supreme goal. The body changes every moment but the unchanging is the reality of the self. He should be dependent on circumstances that is to say he should merely depend on strips of cloth, coverings and food that come to him by chance for the maintenance of body. Examining the reality in the context of the individual and in the external world, one should become identified with reality, should have his delight in reality and should not deviate from reality. As the nature of the self is ever the same, and because it is impossible for it to change its nature, and one should be for ever unwavering from reality under the conviction, 'I am Brahma', that is to say, he should ever have the consciousness of the reality that is the self, in accordance with the samriti text as, 'the enlightened man views equally a dog or an outcast', 'He sees who sees the Supreme Lord existing equally in all beings', etc.

In the course of determining the nature of 'OM', in pre-pages, it was stated as a mere proposition that the self is the negative of the phenomenal world and is auspicious and non-dual. It was further said that 'duality ceases to exist after realisation. As to that; should non-duality be admitted only on the authority of scripture and tradition, or should it be accepted on logical grounds too ? In answer, it is said that it can be known on logical grounds as well. It has been narrated in previous pages that all diversity, comprising the worshipped, worship, and so on, is unreal and the absolute, non-dual self is the highest reality as the aspirant, taking himself to the devotional exercises, subsists in the conditioned Brahma. All this was but the birthless Brahma before creation. Such a man is considered narrow in his outlook. A worshipper, who resorts to devotional exercises like worship and meditation, as the means to his liberation, under the belief, 'I am worshipper and Brahma is to be adored by me'. Though I now subsist in the conditioned Brahma. I shall, through my devotion to it, attain the unconditioned Brahma, after the fall of my body. Before the creation, there was birthless Brahma and through my devotional exercises (Shall regain that which I essentially was before my birth, though after being born, I now subsist in the conditioned Brahma). Such an aspirant is cognizant of the partial Brahma, so that man is considered narrow in his outlook by those, who have seen the eternal and birthless Brahma. Since one becomes narrow by thinking oneself through ignorance to be unworthy and since on that account one comes to believe, I am born. I subsist in the conditioned Brahma and having recourse to its worship, I shall attain the unconditioned Brahma, therefore, I shall relate freedom from misery, limitlessness, the birthless Brahma, for that indeed is a source of limitation, where one sees another, hears another and knows another.'

Since the self is referred to as existing in the form of individual soul in the same way as space exists in the form of spaces confined within the jars and since the self exists in the form of the composite things just as space exists in jars etc., therefore, in the matter of birth, this is the illustration as it has been cited on the analogy of space. Further, as the space confined within the jars, etc., merges completely on the disintegration of the jars, etc., so do the individual souls merge here in this self, and just as all the spaces confined within the various jars are not darkened when one of the spaces thus confined becomes contaminated by dust, smoke, etc., so also is the case with all the individuals in the matter of being affected by happiness etc. As for the view of the vaisesikas and others, who assert that desire and the rest inhere in the soul, that too is untenable for the impressions of past experiences that generate memory cannot remain inseparably located in the self that has no location. And since according to them, memory arises from a contact of the soul with the mind, there can be no fixed rule regarding the rise of memory or there will be the possibility of the rise of all kinds of memories simultaneously. Furthermore, it is not a fact, though these others believe in it, that qualities like colour, or such categories as action, genus, species or inherence exist independently of the substances. If they were absolutely different from substances and if desires etc. were so from the soul, those qualities, etc., would not have any reasonable relation with substance (nor world desires etc. have any relation with the soul). Besides, if the self is possessed of such qualities as desires, etc., that are subject to increase and decrease, it will be open to the change of being impermanent like the bodies and the fruits of actions. On the other hand, if on the analogy of the sky, appearing to be blackened by dust and smoke, attributed to it through ignorance, it is supposed that the self appears to be possessed of the defects of happiness and sorrow generated by such limiting adjuncts as the intellect that are superimposed on it through ignorance, there remains no illogicality in its possessing bondage, freedom etc. in an empirical sense. Here it is being shown how through ignorance, there can be the possibility in the same self; of that same variety of actions become possible on the assumption of a multiplicity of souls. Though forms, actions and names differ in respect of difference in the space created by jars etc., yet there is no multiplicity in space. So also is the definite conclusion with regard to the individual beings. As in the same space, there is a difference of dimension such as smallness and bigness in respect of the spaces enclosed by a jar, a water bowl, a house, etc., so also there is a difference of functions such as fetching or holding water, sleeping, etc., and of names such as the space in a jar, the space in a water bowl, the space in a house, etc., which are all created by those jars, etc., but all these differences are not surely real that are implied in conventional dealings involving dimensions, etc., created in space, in reality, space has no difference nor can there be any empirical dealing based on the multiplicity of space unless there be the instrumentality of the limiting adjuncts.

As the space within a jar is neither a transformation nor a part of space as such, so an individual being is never a transformation nor a part of the Supreme self. In as much as the experience of birth and death etc., follows as a consequence of the differentiation among of individuals created by the limiting adjuncts constituted by the bodies, just as the experience of the forms, actions etc., are the results of the ideas of difference entertained with regard to the spaces within the jar etc., therefore, the association of the soul with such impurities as suffering and consequences of actions is caused by that alone, but not in any real sense. With a view to establishing this fact with the help of an illustration, the text goes on just as the sky becomes blackend by dust, etc., to the ignorant, so also the self becomes tarnished by impurities to the unwise. Further, the self is not dissimilar to space in the matter of its death and birth, as well as its going and coming, and existence in all the bodies. The idea is that one should realise that in the matter of birth, death, etc., the self in all the bodies is quite on a par with space in its relation to the space confined in a jar so far as origination, destruction, coming, going and motionlessness are concerned. The aggregates of bodies and senses are all projected like dream by the 'Maya' of the self. Be it a question of superiority or equality of all, there is no logical ground to prove their existence. By now, it has been amply elucidated on the analogy of space, that the individual living being that conforms to the soul of the seaths counting from that constituted by the essence of food, which have been fully dealt with in the Taittiriya Upanisada, (Brahma is truth, knowledge and infinite) is none other than the Supreme self 'Since self is referred to as existing in the form of individual souls in the same way as space', the idea is that unlike the self imagined by the logicians, the self is not to be established by the mere means of the human intellect. Now as it is demonstrated that space in the earth and the stomach is but the same, similarity in the Madhu Brahmin, the Supreme Brahma is revealed as the same with reference to the different dual contexts. The fact that the non-difference of the individual and the Supreme self is extolled by a statement of their identity and the fact that diversity is condemned, become easy of comprehension from this point of view alone, 'He, who still perceives multiplicity here, goes from death to death'. The separateness of the individual and the Supreme self that has been declared in the vedas earlier than the talk of creation in the upanisadas, is only in a secondary sense that keeps in view a future result viz unity for such separateness is out of place in its primary sense. Just like dream, the aggregates are created by the 'Maya' of the self and that birth, difference etc., of the individuals are analogous to birth difference etc., of the spaces within jars. Since falsity of these has already been dealt with, therefore, taking that very reason for granted, vedas dealing with creation are being adduced here from amongst the texts dealing with creation, difference etc., with a view to showing that they are meant for establishing the oneness of the self and the individual beings. The creation that has been multifariously set forth with the help of the examples of earth, gold, sparks etc. is merely by way of generating the idea of oneness, but there is no multiplicity in any way.

There are three stages of life — inferior, intermediate, and superior. The meditation is enjoined for them out of compassion. The three stages of life are varied possession of vision. They are induced with dull, medium and fine mental calibre. Meditation and rites have been prescribed accordingly for the persons of dull and medium intellect, who are affiliated to the stages of life and not for the people of superior intellect having the conviction that self is one without a second. So the perfect knowledge consists in the realisation of the non-dual self, since this is established by scriptures and logic, whereas any other view is false, it being outside the pale of these.

A further reason that the theories of the dualists are false is that they are based on such defects as likes and dislikes, the dualists, confirmed believers in the methodologies establishing their own conclusions, are at loggers-head with one another. But this (non-dual) view has no conflict with them. Non-duality is the highest reality, since duality heterogeneity is a differentiation, that is to say, a product of that non-duality, in accordance with the vedas, "In the beginning there was existence alone — only one, without a second—". It created fire. But for them, there is duality either way. Therefore, this view of ours does not clash with theirs. This point can be illustrated thus : A man sitting astride an elephant in rut does not goad his animal against a mad man standing on the ground and challenging him by saying, "I am also seated on an elephant in opposition, drive your animal against me", just because he has no inimical feelings towards the latter. Thus since in reality, the knower of Brahma is the very self of the dualists hence because of this reason, this outlook of ours does not clash with theirs. When it is asserted that duality is derived from the non-duality, someone may entertain the doubt that on that ground, duality, too, is real in the highest sense. Therefore, this birthless (self) becomes differentiated verily through 'Maya' and it does so in no other way than this. For should it become multiplied in reality, the immortal will undergo mortality. But those again, who talk of Brahma, who are garrulous interpretess of upanishadas; they vouch for the birth, in a real sense; of the one, which is birthless, which is by nature immortal, the reality that is the self. If the self be born, as they hold, it will undergo mortality, for a certainty. But that self, being by nature a positive entity, that is unborn, and deathless, how, can it undergo mortality. The idea is that it will in no way reverse its nature to embrace mortality which individuals are subject to. The immortal cannot become mortal. Similarly, the mortal cannot become immortal. The mutation of one's nature will take place in no way whatsoever just as fire cannot change its heat. Then how can an immortal entity continue to be changeless from the standpoint of one according to whom a positive object, which is immortal by nature, can pass into birth, it being a product. Vedic text are equally in evidence with regard to creation in reality and through 'Maya'. That which is ascertained by the vedas and is supported by reasoning can be the meaning and nothing else. All talks of creation in the primary or secondary sense, relate only to creation through ignorance and not to creation in reality as in denied in vedas. Since he is coextensive with all that is within and without and since he has no limit, therefore, that which is determined by the vedas to be one without a second, birthless and immortal and is supposed by reasoning, that alone becomes the meaning of vedas and nothing else. Since it is stated in the vedas, there is no diversity here, and the Lord, on account of 'Maya' is perceived as manifold the self without being born appears to be born in various ways, it follows that he is born on account of 'Maya' only. If creation had taken place in reality, the diverse things should have been real, and there should not have been any scriptural text showing their unreality. Since sense-knowledge is accepted as a kind of 'Maya', it being a product of ignorance, so means 'through different kinds of sense knowledge', are but forms of ignorance, as is proved by the vedas. Though unborn, it appears to be born in diverse ways.' Therefore, the self takes birth through 'Maya' alone. Besides, from the fact that realisation of unity is a fruitful thing as mentioned in vedas, "What delusion and what sorrow can there be for that seer of oneness". As per Upanisadas "He goes from death to death", who sees as though there is difference here, the idea of heterogeneity, implied by creation etc., is condemned. From the refutation of the worship of 'Hiranyagarbha', it follows that creation is negated. By the text 'Who should bring him forth' is ruled out in any case. So, since it is the individual soul itself, created by ignorance, and existing through ignorance alone, that attains its natural stature on the eradication of ignorance, therefore, in the highest sense, who should again bring him forth. For none indeed creates again a snake, superimposed on a rope through ignorance, once it is removed through discrimination. Similarly, none will create this individual. The idea is that a thing that was created by ignorance and later disappeared has no source of birth, in accordance with the vedas 'It did not originate from anything nor did anything originate from it'. Further, by taking into account the incomprehensibility of Brahma as a reason, all that has been explained above, as a means of the knowledge of Brahma, is negated by vedas' ultimate version, 'This self is that which has been described as "Not this, not this", the birthless self becomes self-revealed'. In a result of this, the reality of the self that is coextensive with all that is within and without and is birthless, gets revealed by itself to one, who knows that the means only serves the purpose of the end and that the end has ever the same changeless nature. Thus the definite conclusion arrived at by hundreds of vedic texts is that the reality of the self that is co-existence with all that exists within and without and is birthless is one without a second, and there is nothing besides. It is now said that, this very fact is established by reason as well. So the birth of a thing that already exists can reasonably be possible only through 'Maya' and not in reality. For one, who holds that things take birth in a real sense, there can only be the birth of what is already born. As the birth in the form of a snake etc. of an existing thing, a rope for instance, can reasonably be through 'Maya' but not in reality, similarly, though the self that exists is incomprehensible, it can reasonably have birth in the form of the universe through 'Maya' like the illusion of a snake in a rope, but the birthless self cannot have any birth in real sense. Hence it has to be accepted that what is already born, takes birth again and from this predication of birth from what is born, will follow an infinite regress. Therefore, it is established that the reality that is the self is birthless and one. So, there can be no birth for a nonexistent object either through 'Maya' or in reality, for the son of a barren woman is born neither through 'Maya' nor in reality. Now the question arises as to how again there can be birth for the existent through 'Maya' alone. The answer is as in the dream the mind vibrates, as though having dual aspects, so in the waking state, the mind vibrates as though two facets — the cognizer and the thing cognised, just like that in the waking state the mind vibrates as it were through 'Maya'. Then there is no doubt that in dream, the mind, though one, appears in dual aspects, so also in the walking state, the mind, though one, appears to have two aspects. The idea is that the case is similar in the waking state, as in dream, for in either state, there exists only the supremely real consciousness. The mind fancied on consciousness through ignorance, vibrates on the supremely real and constant consciousness in either state. Now all this that there is — together with all that moves or does not move — is perceived by the mind and, therefore, all this is but the mind, for when the mind ceases to be the mind, duality is no longer perceived. Like the illusory snake disappearing in the rope, the mind's activity stops through the practice of discriminating insight and detachment or when the mind gets absorbed in the state of sleep, duality is not perceived. From this non-existence, is proved the unreality of the duality. How then the mind cease to be mind is stated as when following the instruction of scriptures and the teacher, the mind ceases to think as a consequence of the realisation of the truth that is the self, then the mind attains the state of not being the mind, in the absence of things to be perceived, it becomes a non-perceiver. But if this duality be false, then how is the truth of one's own self realised is because they say that the non-conceptual knowledge, which is birthless, is non-different from the knowable Brahma, the knowledge that has Brahma for its content is birthless and everlasting. The limitless self is known by birthless knowledge.

It has been said that when the mind is divested of ideation by virtue of the realisation of the truth that is Brahma, and when there is an absence of external objects of perception, it becomes tranquil, controlled, and withdrawn like fire that has no fuel and it has further been said that when the mind thus ceases to be the mind, duality also disappears. The behaviour that the mind has when it is under control, free from all ideation, and full of discrimination, should be particularly noted. The behaviour of the mind in deep sleep is different and is not similar to that of the controlled mind when waking. Now since the behaviour of the mind in deep sleep is different, the mind then being under the deep cover of the darkness of delusion arising from ignorance, and it being still possessed of the latent tendencies that are the seeds of many evil actions, and the behaviour of the mind under control is surely different, since ignorance, the seed of evil activities, has been burnt away from that mind by the fire of the realisation of the truth that is the self and since from that mind has been removed the blemish of all afflictions, hence the sleeping mind's behaviour is not like that behaviour in the controlled state. Therefore, it is fit to be known. The reason for the difference of behaviour is that the mind losses itself in sleep, but does not lose itself when under control and that very mind becomes the fearless Brahma, possessed of the light of consciousness all around. It is all pervasive without a break. Brahma is birthless, sleepless, dreamless, nameless, formless, ever effulgent, everything and a knower. With regard to it there is not the least possibility of ceremony, the idea is that as Brahma is by nature eternally pure, intelligent, and free, there can be no possibility of anything to be done by the enlightened person, in any way whatsoever, after the destruction of ignorance. The reason for this is the namelessness as the self is free of all sense-organs, and is above all internal organs, it is supremely tranquil, eternal, effulgence, divine absorption, immutable and fearless, as he is devoid of all objects. Since Brahma itself has been described as divine absorption, immutable, and fearless, therefore, there can be no acceptance or rejection where all mentation stops. Then knowledge is established in the self and is unborn, and it becomes homogeneous. Everything else, apart from this realisation of the self, is within the sphere of misery, as is declared by vedas, 'O Gargi, he, who departs from this world without knowing this immutable, is miserable'. The meaning sought to be conveyed is that by knowing this, one becomes a Brahmin (knower of Brahma) and has one's duties fulfilled. Though this supreme reality is such yet the yoga that is familiarly referred to as 'contactless' is difficult to be comprehended by anyone of the yogis. For those yogis, who apprehend fear where there is no fear, are afraid of it. For those to whom the mind and sense organs, which are imagined like a snake on a rope, have no existence in reality when considered apart from this essence that is Brahma—for those who have become identified with Brahma—comes fearlessness, and for them naturally is accomplished the everlasting peace called emancipation which is not dependent on any other factor, as has been narrated earliar in, 'There is not the least possibility of ceremony'. But, for the yogis, who are other than these, who are still treading the path, who have inferior or medium outlook and think of the mind as something different from the self, though associated with it — for those who are not possessed of the realisation of the self that is the Truth, for all the yogis, fearlessness, the removal of misery, knowledge of the self, and everlasting peace are dependant on the control of the mind. Just as an ocean can be emptied with the help of the blade of kusa grass that can hold just a drop, so also can the control of mind be brought about by absence of depression. Even the control of mind comes about from the want of depression, for those yogis, whose minds are free from mental depression, and who are as relentless as in trying to empty an ocean with the help of that proper process, one should bring under discipline, the mind that remains dispersed amidst objects of desire and enjoyment, and one should bring it under content even when it is in full peace in sleep for sleep is as bad as desire. So far as that process is concerned, it is constantly remembering that everything is full of misery and one should withdraw the mind from the enjoyment arising out of desire. Remembering even the fact that the birthless Brahma is everything, one does not surely perceive the born viz the host of duality. For this purpose, one should wake up the mind merged in deep sleep, one should bring the dispensed mind into tranquility again, one should know where the mind is tinged with desire and is in a state of latency. One should not disturb the mind established in equipoise. This is possible with the help of the dual process of detachment and practice of knowledge. When the mind begins to move towards that goal, one should not disturb it from that course or in other words one should not turn it back towards objects and should not enjoy happiness in that state, but should become unattached through the use of discrimination and when the mind established in steadiness, wants to issue out, one should concentrate it with diligence. When the mind does not become lost nor is scattered, when it is motionless and does not appear in the form of objects, then it becomes Brahma or in other words the mind becomes identified with Brahma. That highest bliss is located in one's own self. It is quiescent, coexistent with liberation, beyond description and birthless. And since it is identical with the unborn knowable Brahma, they call it the omniscient Brahma. No individual being whichsoever, who is a doer or an enjoyer, takes birth. It has no source of birth. This Brahma is that highest truth where nothing whatsoever takes birth.

In the course of determining the meaning of 'OM', non-duality was advanced as a premiss on the basis of the scriptures, it was proved to be true on the basis of the fact that the differences found in things external are unreal, it was again directly determined with the help of scriptures and reason in the chapter on non-duality and that non-duality was summed up in the remark, 'This is the highest Truth'. Now begins the chapter on quenching the firebrand in order to show the detail how those are partial philosophies owing to their mutual contradictions and then after rejecting them, to sum up by proving the truth of the philosophy of non-duality with the help of the method of difference consisting in their rejection. The first verse is meant as a salutation to the promulgator of the school of non--duality by identifying him with non-duality itself, as it is desirable to worship one's teacher at the commencement of a scripture so that the result aimed at may be achieved. I bow down to the one, who is the chief among all persons, who has known fully the souls resembling infinite sky, through his knowledge that is comparable to space and is non-different form the object of knowledge. Here the effort is to establish the philosophy of the supreme reality that is devoid of the distinctions of knowledge, knowable and knower. For extolling the yoga taught in the philosophy of non-delusion, comes a salutation to it that is 'I bow down to that yoga that is well known as free from relationships, joyful to all beings, beneficial free from dispute, non-contradictory, and set forth in the scriptures'. Then there is contradiction in the dualists viz some disputants postulate the birth of a pre-existing thing. Otherwise ones, while disputing among themselves, postulate the birth of what does not pre-exist. Here it is being shown what is virtually asserted by them as they refute each other's point of view by talking otherwise. A thing that already exists does not pass into birth and a thing that does not pre-exist cannot pass into birth. These people, while disputing thus, are really non-dualists and they thus reveal the absence of birth. We too approve the birthlessness, that is revealed by them, we do not quarrel with them and say 'O disciples, understand this philosophy of the highest Reality that is free from dispute.' The talkers verily vouch for the birth of an unborn positive entity. But how can a positive entity that is unborn and immortal undergo mortality. The immortal cannot become mortal. Similarly, the mortal cannot become immortal. The mutation of one's nature will take place in no way whatsoever. How can an immortal entity continue to be changeless from the standpoint of one according to whom a positive entity, which is immortal by nature, can pass into birth, it being a product according to him. In as much as one's nature, even in the ordinary sense of the term, does not change, far less can the supreme nature change itself. It is now shown what the nature is. By the word 'nature' is to be understood that which is permanently acquired, or is intrinsic, instinctive, non-produced, or unchanging in its character. Then what is that nature, whose change is assumed by some and what is the defect in such an assumption. The answer is that all souls are intrinsically free from old age and death. But by imagining senility and death, and being engrossed in that thought, they deviate from their nature. The cause must undergo birth according to one who holds that the cause itself is the effect. How can a thing be birthless that takes birth, and how can it be eternal when it can be subject to partial disintegration. The meaning sought to be imparted is that it involves a contradiction on their part to say that a thing may be broken up partially and yet be birthless and eternal and if the effect be non-different from the cause, then on that account the effect too is birthless. And if that be so, how can the cause be still eternal, it being non-different, from its effect which is subject to birth as one half of a hen cannot be cooked, while the other half is reserved for laying eggs. Just as a father may be born of a son, so also may birth be a possibility according to those disputants, who admit that the effect is the source of the cause and the cause is the source of the effect. Those who assert that the cause originates from the effect, which is itself produced by the cause, get involved in a contradiction that is on a par with that implied in the birth of the father from a son. If it be contended that the contradiction pointed out above cannot be reasonably advanced then a sequence has to be found out in the births of cause and effect. For, should they originate together, there can be no causal relation, as between the two horns of a cow. Further, if the cause has to come out of an effect, it can have no right to recognition. Then how will a cause, which is not established as such, produce a result? And if the subsistence of the cause is dependent on the effect, and the subsistence of the effect is dependent on the cause, then which of the two has existence earlier, with relation to which the other may emerge ? If even after the dismissal of any causal relation between the so-called cause and the so-called effect by pointing out the defect that they cannot be inter-related, it is still contended that the cause and the effect subsist by mutual interdependence, then which one among the cause and the effect pre-exists, depending on the pre-existence of which the succeeding one may emerge into being. The inability to answer this will amount to the ignorance or there will be falsification of the sequence. Thus indeed is highlighted in every way the absence of birth by the learned ones. Causality is the kind of relation existing between the seed and the sprout. The answer is what is known as the illustration of the seed and the sprout is ever on an equal footing with the unproved major term. For an illustration that is as unprovoked as the major term is not applied for establishing the relation of the major term with the minor term. It is not that the causal relation between the seed and the sprout is without a beginning as it is admitted that the earlier ones have their beginning like the succeding ones. Just as separate sprout that has originated from a seed has a beginning and another seed born out of a separate sprout has also a beginning by the very fact of succession of birth, similarly the antecedent sprouts as well as the antecedent seeds must have beginning and thus since each one of the whole chain of seeds and sprouts has a beginning, it is illogical to assert eternity for any one of them. So also is the case with regard to causes and effects. If now it is argued that the chain of causes and effects is without a beginning, we say no; for any unity of such a series cannot be upheld. Indeed apart from the causes and effects, even those, who talk of the beginninglessness of such a series, donot, certainly vouch for a unitary entity called either a chain of seeds and sprouts or a procession of causes and effects. Therefore, it has been well said, 'How can beginninglessness be declared by them for cause and effect ?' Thus since such views involve an illogicality from a fresh point of view, it is not really avoiding the point at issue. Here it is being shown how birthlessness is highlighted by the wise. The ignorance of the precedence and succession is a pointer to beginninglessness itself. For if it be a fact that a thing takes birth, then why its cause cannot be apprehended. A thing, whatsoever it may be, is born neither of itself, nor of something else (nor both together). Nothing whatsoever is born that already exists, does not exist or both exists or does not exist. If a thing already exists, then just because it exists, it does not pass into birth like earth or a father and if a thing does not exist, then by the very fact of non-existence, it does not undergo birth like the horn of a hare etc. If it is both existent and non-existent then also it does not take birth as it is impossible to have a thing that is self-contradictory. Hence it is established that nothing whatsoever is born. As for those, who (Buddhists) assert that a product is nothing more than the mere act of birth, and by whom it is held accordingly that actions, accessories and results are but the same identical entity and that things are momentary, because a thing cannot be apprehended as 'This is so', since it ceases to exist for a second moment immediately after being perceived, and because memory of a thing not perceived earlier becomes impossible. Besides, by asserting that the cause and the effect are without beginning, one admits perforce that the cause and the effect are without birth because a cause is not born of a beginningless effect; nor does an effect naturally come out of a beginningless cause. Cause and effect are thus birthless for a thing that has no cause, has certainly no birth. In accordance with the perception of its cause, knowledge is supposed to be based on external objects. But from the standpoint of reality, it is held that the external cause is no cause. Consciousness has no contact with objects, so also it has certainty no contact with appearances of objects. For, according to the reasons adduced an object has no existence, and an illusory object is not separate from the awareness. Also consciousness does not ever come in contact with external objects in all the three states. There being no external objects, there cannot be any baseless apprehension of it too. Hence consciousness has no birth and things perceived by it do not pass into birth. Those, who perceive the birth of that consciousness, may as well see foot-marks in space itself. As for nihilists, who, while perceiving the non-existence of everything, asserts thereby the voidness of their own philosophy, they are even bolder than the idealists, in as much as they want to have the sky itself in their grasp. Through this reasoning, it is established that Brahma is one and has no birth and it is the birthlessness that, according to the disputants, takes birth. Since birthlessness is its very nature, therefore, the transmutation of this nature can take place in no way whatsoever. Here is another loophole discovered in the view of those who hold that the wordly state i.e. bondage and liberation of the soul are real. Moreover, if the world be beginningless, its termination will not be achieved and there will be no eternity for liberation that has a beginning. Then that which does not exist in the beginning and at the end, is equally so in the middle. Though they are similar to the unreal, yet they are seen as though real. Their utility is contradicted only in the dream. Therefore, from the fact of their having a beginning and an end, they are rightly held to be unreal. All entities are unreal in dreams since they are seen within the body. Then there cannot be vision of creatures within this narrow space here. It is, therefore, not proper to hold that dream objects are experienced by reaching them, since the requisite time involved in the journey is lacking. Moreover, nobody on waking up, continues in the place of dream. The idea implied is that there is no going over to any other place in dream for the time required for and the distance involved in coming and going, as validly settled in the waking state, have no corresponding fixity in the dream state. Further, having conferred with friends and others in dream, one does not get confirmation when awake and whatever one acquires in dream, one does not see it after awakening. Moreover, the body seen in a dream is unsubstantial since another body is seen to exist. As it is the case with the body, so is everything perceived through consciousness and is, therefore, unsubstantial. Things of the waking state, are unreal also because since a dream is experienced like the waking state, the former is held to be the result of the latter. In reality, however, the waking state is admitted to be true for that dreamer alone, it being the cause of his dream. Also since origination is not a well-established fact, it is declared by the upanisadas that everything is birthless. Moreover, there is no origination in anyway whatsoever, of any non-existing thing from an existing one. Having seen some unreal thing in the waking state and being emotionally affected, one sees it in dream also and having even seen some unreal thing in dream, one does not see it in the awaking state. In reality, however, it cannot be established that anything has any causal relationship with something in any way whatsoever. So, there is no unreal thing that has an unreality as its cause. Similarly, there is no unreal thing that has a reality as its cause. Moreover, there is no existing thing that has another existing thing as its cause. How can then there be an unreal thing that is produced out of something real ? Besides, there is no other kind of causal relationship possible or imaginable. So the idea implied is that, with discriminating people, causal relationship of anything whatsoever is really an unestablished fact. Again by way of removing any surmise about the causal relationship between the unreal waking and dream states, it is said that as some one, owing to lack of discrimination, may in the awaking state, be in contact with unthinkable objects, fancying them to be real, so also in the dream, one sees the objects in that dream alone, owing to want of discrimination.

Instructions about creation have been imparted by the wise for the sake of those, who from the facts of experience and adequate behaviour vouch for the existence of substantiating and who are ever afraid of the birthless entity, apprehending that this will lead to their annihilation. For those, who, being afraid of the unborn, deviate from the true path by relying on their experience of duality, the faults arising from acceptance of creation will not bear fruit, and the fault too will be insignificant. As an elephant confined by magic, up by magic is called an elephant by depending on perception and adequate behaviour, so from the facts of perception and adequate behavior, a thing is said to be existing. The purport is that the facts of being perceived and dealt with appropriately cannot be the tests establishing the existence of a thing. What again, is the absolutely real thing, which is the substratum of all unreal ideas of creation and the rest, it is consciousness — birthless, motionless and non-material, as well as tranquil and non-dual — which has the substance of birth, appears to move, and simulates a substance possessed of qualities. Thus, in accordance with the reasons addressed, consciousness does not undergo birth, thus are the souls considered—by the knowers of Brahma to be birthless. Since the non-dual self itself appears to be different in accordance with the multiplicity of bodies, those who, after renouncing old carvings for external things, know this indeed that the aforesaid consciousness, free from birth etc., is the non-dual reality which is the self, do not fall again into calamity, into the sea of darkness of ignorance, as is confirmed by the text of the vedic verse, 'What delusion and what sorrow can there be for that seer of oneness'. This realisation of self has been dilated upon by narrating that as the movement of a firebrand appears to be straight or crooked, so is it the vibration of consciousness that appears to be the knower and the known. As the firebrand, when not in motion, becomes free from appearance and birth, so consciousness, when not in vibration, will be free from appearances and birth i.e. the consciousness, which vibrates through ignorance, will, on the cessation of ignorance, become free from vibration, consisting in birth etc.—will remain free from appearances, birth and vibration. Moreover, when that very firebrand is in motion, the appearances of straightness, crookedness etc. donot come to be in it, from anywhere outside the firebrand, this is what is meant by non-adventitious, nor do they go out anywhere else from that firebrand, when it is at rest, nor do they enter into the motionless firebrand itself. Furthermore, they did not issue out of the firebrand, by reason of their unsubstantiality. With regard to consciousness also, the appearances must be of a similar kind, for as an appearance there is no distinction. It is being shown so how they are similar when consciousness is in vibration, the appearances do not come to it from anywhere else. Neither do they go anywhere else from consciousness when it is at rest nor do they enter into it. They did not issue out of consciousness by reason of their insubstantiality, for they are ever beyond comprehension, being without any relation of cause and effect with consciousness. Everything with regard to consciousness is similar to that of the firebrand; consciousness has this one distinction that it is ever unmoving. It is being pointed out as to what causes the appearances of creation etc., in the motionless consciousness. Just as the ideas of straightness etc. are perceived in the firebrand itself, although the appearances of straightness etc., are unreal, similarly the ideas of creation etc., in the absolute self, which appear even though there are no creation etc., must be false. Here it has been established that the reality which is the self, is one and unborn. Now, according to those who imagine causality, a substance can be the cause of a substance, and one thing can be the cause of another different from itself. But the souls can be considered neither as substances nor as something different from other things. Thus since self is neither substance nor different from anything, it is neither the cause nor the effect of anything. Thus according to the reasons adduced, consciousness is the very essence of the self that is identical with consciousness. Hence external entities are not the products of consciousness nor is consciousness a product of external entities as all entities are the mere appearances of that which is essentially consciousness, consequently, an effect is not produced from a cause nor is a cause from an effect. In this way, the knowers of Brahma, enter into, affirm, the birthlessness of cause and effect. The idea is that they arrive at the non-existence of cause and effect. Here it is being pointed out as to what will happen to those again, who cling to cause and effect, which spring into being so long as there is mental pre-occupation with cause and effect. There is no origination of cause and effect when the engrossment with cause and effect becomes attenuated. There is no origination of cause and effect. What is the harm even if there is the origin of cause and effect, since as long as there is mental pre-occupation with causality, so long does the worldly state continue. When engrossment with causality is exhausted, one does not attain the worldly state. Everything is produced by concealment, consisting in the empirical outlook within the domain of ignorance. Therefore, within the range of ignorance, there is surely nothing that is external. Hence it has been said that the world characterised by origin and destruction, remains outstretched. But from the standpoint of the highest reality, since everything is the birthless self, therefore, in the absence of birth, there is no annihilation of any cause, effect etc. The entities that are born thus are not born in reality. Their birth is as that of a thing through 'Maya' and that 'Maya' again has no reality i.e. the term 'Maya' relates to something non-existing. As from a magical seed grows a sprout equally illusory — it being neither eternal nor destructible — just so is the logic of birth or death applicable in the case of objects. The idea is that, from the standpoint of reality, there can be no real birth or death for the objects. But from the standpoint of absolute truth, the terms 'eternal' or 'non-eternal' do not apply to the birthless entities, the souls, whose essence consists in a mere eternal and homogenous consciousness. The term derivatively signifies those by which things are described and it means words and where, with regard to which souls, words do not apply, so far as their description or revelation is concerned, there is not uttered any categorical statement that 'This is so indeed' or in other words that 'It is either eternal or non-eternal', as is declared in vedas 'From where speech returns'.

As in dream, consciousness vibrates as though having dual functions, so in the watering state consciousness vibrates as though with two facets. There is no doubt that consciousness, though one, appears in dream in dual aspects, so also in the waking state, consciousness, though one, appears to have two aspects. That the absolute consciousness, which is realy non-dual, becomes, an object of speech, is due only to the activities of mind, but not so in reality. For this further reason, duality, describable by words, does not exist, The creatures, which the seer of a dream, ever sees, while moving in dream, in the place seen in a dream, as existing in all the ten directions, be they, those born from eggs or those born from moisture, those creatures are the objects of perception to the consciousness of the experiencer of dream. Therefore, they do not exist separately from the consciousness of the dreamer. It is, therefore, the consciousness alone that is imagined in the forms of diverse objects like creatures etc. Similarly, even this, which is the consciousness of the experiencer of dream, is surely an object of perception to that dreamer, meaning the experience of that dreamer. Therefore, such a thing as consciousness has no existence apart from the dreamer.

The creatures whether born from eggs or from moisture — which the experiencer of the waking state ever sees as existing in all the ten directions, while he is roaming in the places of the waking state, are but objects of perception to the consciousness of the man in the waking state, and they do not exist separately from that consciousness. Similarly, this consciousness of the waking man is admitted to be only an object of perception to the waking man. The creatures visible to a waking man are non-different from his consciousness, since they are perceived through consciousness, just like the creatures perceived by the consciousness of the dreamer. And that consciousness again engaged in the perception of creatures, is non-different from the experiencer, since it is perceived by the experiencer, like the consciousness in the dream state. They are both consciousness and the creatures — knowledge and its modifications — these two are objects of perception to each other. For the thing that is knowledge is what it is in relation to its objects such as the creatures; and the objects of perception, such as the creatures are so in relation to knowledge. Consequently, their awareness is mutually determined. Hence when it is asked, 'Does it exist', the answer made by the discriminating man is 'no' — nothing whatsoever, be it knowledge or the things perceived through knowledge, exists. For, in the dream neither an elephant nor a knowledge having an elephant as its content, exists. So also, in the waking state, these do not exist according to the discriminating people. Since, both knowledge and the objects of knowledge, are devoid of anything whereby they can be established, that is to say they are both without valid proof. Either is perceived merely because of a pre-possession with the other. There can be no knowledge of the pot by setting aside the idea of the pot nor can there be any comprehension of the idea of the pot by discarding the pot. The meaning implied is that in the case under consideration, no distinction of one being the knowledge and the other its object, can be made between the two.

As a creature seen in a dream undergoes birth and death, so also do all these creatures appear and disappear and as a creature conjured up by magic undergoes birth and death so also do all these creatures appear and disappear, no creature, whichsoever has birth, there is no source for it. This is that highest truth, where nothing whatsoever is born. It has been said that birth, death etc. of creatures within the range of empirical existence are like those of the creatures in dream etc., but the highest truth is that no creature undergoes birth. This duality possessed of subject and object is a mere vibration of consciousness and consciousness is objectless, hence it is declared to be eternally without relation. An object, a scripture for instance, which exists because of a fancied empirical outlook, it being called so because it is an empirical outlook that is imagined as a means for the attainment of the highest object; anything that exists by virtue of this, has no existence, from the standpoint of the absolute reality. And anything that may exist, on the strength of empirical outlook engendered by other systems of thought, that thing, when considered from the standpoint of the highest reality, does not exist, to be sure. Therefore, it has been well said, 'Hence it is declared to be without relations'. Further, since in accordance with the conclusion arrived at in the scriptures of the other schools, the soul undergoes birth from the empirical point of view, it is said by the non-dualists that the soul is birthless but from the standpoint of absolute reality, it is not ever birthless. There is in evidence a mere craving for false objects though no duality is in existence there. Realising the non-existance of duality, one becomes free from craving for false things, and one does not undergo birth and when one does not perceive the superior, medium and inferior causes, then consciousness ceases to have births as, if there is no cause, there cannot be any result too. The highest causes are those duties, which are enjoined in relation to castes and stages of life, which are performed by the people, free from hankering for results, which lead to the attainment of the states of gods and others, and which are purely virtuous. Those, that are mixed with irreligious practices and lead to birth among men etc., are the middling ones and the inferior causes are those particular tendencies that are known as irreligious and lead to birth among animals etc. when, after the realisation of the reality of self, which is one without a second, and free from all imagination, one does not perceive, all those causes that are fancied through ignorance just as the dirt seen in the sky by the children is not perceived there by a discriminating man, then consciousness is not born in the shape of gods and others that constitute the superior, medium and inferior results. It has been firmly asserted here that consciousness has no birth in the absence of causes. The birthlessness that consciousness attains, when freed from causes, is constant and absolute for all this viz duality — and birth was perceptible to consciousness that had been birthless and non-dual even before. Now since duality, the cause of truth, does not exist in accordance with the reasons adduced, one attains the state of fearlessness, which is free from desire, sorrow etc., and is without ignorance etc., that is to say, one is never reborn, after having realised causalness as the truth of the highest order and after not getting that is to say, not accepting any separate causes, such as virtue etc., which may lead to birth among the gods and others — after having renounced the desire for all external things. But since owing to a belief in the existence of non-realities, consciousness engages itself in things that are equally so, i.e., unreal, therefore, when one has the realisation of the absence of objects, consciousness becomes unattached and turns back from the objects that are the contents of the belief in the unreal. For, then, to the consciousness, which has got detached and does not engage in duality, there follows the state of inactivity. Since that is the object realised by the wise, therefore, that is the real equipoise and that is birthless and non-dual. The nature of the object of vision of the wise becomes birthless, sleepless, dreamless and self-luminous as this entity is ever effulgent by its very nature. But because of the passion for any object, whatever it be, that deity becomes ever covered up easily and then he is at all times uncovered with difficulty. When the passionate attachment of the learned to even such subtle ideas as the existence of the self or its non-existence ; becomes a covering of the Lord, the Supreme self, what wonder is there that the passion in the shape of the intellectual preoccupation of the dual should be much more so. Some disputants accept the idea that the self exists, another viz the believer in momentariness of things avers, it does not exist. Another half believer in momentariness, the naked one, who speaks of both existence and non- existence asserts it exists and does not exist. The absolute nihilist says, it does not exist. Of these states, that of existence is changeable, it being different from such impermanent things as a jar, and the state of non-existence is changeless, it being ever constant. The state of both existence and non-existence is of either kind since it relates to both the changeable and the changeless, and relates to an absolute non-existence. Each one of the fools, whether calling the self-existing or not, surely covers up the Lord by ideas of changeability, unchangeability, both changeability and un-changeability and non-existence — which all belong to the four alternatives. The idea implied is that when even a learned man, who has not realised the Supreme truth is but a fool, nothing need be spoken of one who is naturally stupid. Of what nature then is the supreme reality by knowing which one gets rid of stupidity and becomes enlightened, the answer is there are the four alternative theories viz it exists, it does not exist and so on as already mentioned, through a passion for which the Lord remains ever hidden. He, who sees the Lord as untouched by these is omniscient, or to put it otherwise, he is the truly enlightened man. Having attained omniscience in its fullness, and having reached the state of Brahminhood, as indicated in vedas, 'He who departs from this world after knowing this immutable Brahma is a Brahmin i.e. the knower of Brahma', this is the eternal glory of a Brahmin. It neither increases nor decreases through work while non-dual state of Brahminhood has no beginning, middle and end — that is to say, is devoid of origin, continuance and dissolution, does one make any effort and after this there is attainment of the self. The idea is that any effort becomes useless—in accordance with the samriti text, 'He has no end to achieve here either through activity or through inactivity.'

This is the modesty of the Brahmins, this is called their natural tranquillity, and this is their natural self-restraint resulting from spontaneous poise. Having known thus, one gets established in tranquility. Thus, since the philosophies of the sophists are at conflict with one another, they lead to the worldly state and they are the hot houses for such drawbacks as attractions and repulsions. Accordingly these are false philosophies. After having proved this fact by their own logic, the conclusion arrived at is that being free from all the four alternatives, the most perfect philosophy is the naturally tranquil philosophy of non-duality, which does not engender such faults as attachment etc. Now we shall think of arriving at truth. The empirical existence is that which co-exists with an empirically real thing; similarly is that which co-exists with experience. That is duality. That is the source of all behaviours, scriptural and others—and that is characterised by the subject—object relationship. It is the ordinary state, or in other words, the state of waking. In upanisadas, the waking state is admitted to be of such characteristics. That which is unsubstantial, there being an absence of empirical existence as well, which is associated with experience of things, as it were, though in fact there are no objects — that is admitted in the dream state to be pure, objectless, subtler than the gross objects of the waking state ; and it is ordinary, being common to all beings. It is traditionally held that the extraordinary is without content and without experience. Knowledge, object and the realisable things are for ever declared by the wise. When knowledge of the ordinary etc., is acquired and when after the knowable things of three kinds are known in succession — viz first the gross ordinary and in the absence of that again the extraordinary and then when the three states are eliminated and the supreme reality, the fourth, the non-dual, birthless and fearless has become known of its own accord, then for the man of great intellect, for such a knower, there emerges here in this world, the state of being all and enlightened, for ever since his realisation relates to what transcends the whole universe, that is to say if one's true nature is realised once, it never leaves him. For, unlike the knowledge of the sophists, there is no rise or decline of the knowledge of a man, who has realised the highest truth. From the fact that ordinary state etc. have been presented as objects to be known successively, some one may conclude that they have real existence. Hence it is said that the things to be realised, rejected, accepted, and made ineffective, are to be known at the very beginning. From among them, the three excepting the realisable are traditionally held to be only fancies resulting from ignorance. The idea is that those three — rejectable, acceptable and the fit to be made effective or ineffective — are admitted to be true from the highest standpoint. But from the ultimate stand-point, all the souls should be known as naturally analogous to space and as eternal. There is no plurality among them anywhere, even by a jot or title. As for the souls being objects of cognition, that too, is merely from empirical experience but not in reality. All the souls are, by very nature, illumined from the very beginning, and their characteristics, are well determined. He, to whom ensues is this way the freedom from the need of any further acquisition of knowledge, becomes fit for immortality. Similarly, there is no need for bringing about tranquility in the self. Since the souls are, from the very beginning, tranquil, unborn, and by their very nature completely unattached, equal and non-different, and since reality is thus birthless, uniform and holy, therefore, there is no need for any acquisition etc. Those, who have grasped the ultimate truth, as described, are the only people in the world who are not pitiable, but the others are to be pitied, since they have a proclivity for duality, follow duality that is to say confine themselves to the world — who are they ? Those who talk of multiplicity of things, or in other hands, the dualists, therefore, they are traditionally held to be pitiable. For there is no perfection for those, who are ever roaming about in duality, that is to say, for those who ever persist in the path of duality conjured up by ignorance. Consequently, it is proper that they should be objects of pity. This is the purport. This nature of the supreme truth is beyond the ken of those who have not the requisite expansion of heart, who are not learned, who are outside the pale of vedanta, who are narrow-minded and who are dull of intellect. They alone will be possessed of unsurpassable knowledge in this world, who will be firm in their conviction with regard to that which is birthless and uniform. But the ordinary man cannot grasp that reality. As in samriti, 'As it is possible to sketch the flight of birds in the sky, so even the gods get puzzled in trying to trace the course of one, who has become identified with the self of all beings, who is a source of bliss to all and who has no goal to reach'. Since it is traditionally held that the knowledge inhering in the birthless, steady, souls is truthless, steady — like light and heat in the sun, therefore, that knowledge, which is unassociated with any other object, is said to be unborn, since the knowledge does not relate to any other object, because of that reason, it is proclaimed to be non-relational like space. If in accordance with the schools of disputants, which differ from this, it be admitted that there is origination of any object of a different nature, inside or outside, howsoever, insignificant that origination be, then there can never be, any non-attachment for that non-discriminating man. What need one say that there is no destruction of covering souls, never had any veil, any bondage of ignorance etc., that is to say, they are free from bondage, and they are intrinsically pure, illumined and also free from the beginning since they are by nature ever pure, illumined and free. If they are so, why it is said that they know ? The answer is that they are masters ; have the power of learning that is to say, they are by nature endowed with the power of knowledge. This is just like saying, 'The sun shines', though the very nature of the sun is constant effulgence or like saying 'The hills stand', though it is the very nature of the hills to be perpetually motionless. The knowledge of the enlightened man, who is all pervasive, does not extend to objects, all the souls also, like knowledge, do not reach out to objects. This view was not expressed by Buddha. But the non-duality, the essence of ultimate reality, is to be known from the upanisadas only. After realising that state of non-duality, which is inscrutable, very profound, birthless, uniform and holy, we make our obeisance to it to the best of our ability, by bringing it within the range of empirical dealings, though it defines all relative experience.

In the end comes the salutation to the almighty. I bow down to that Brahma, who, though birthless, appears to be born through its inscrutable power; which, though ever quiescent, appears to be in motion ; which, though one, appears to be multiple to those whose vision has become perverted by the perception of diverse attributes of objects, and which destroy the fear of those, who take shelter in it. I salute by prostrating myself at the feet of my teacher, the most adorable among the adorables, who on seeing the creatures drowned in the terrible sea of the world infested with sea-monsters in the form of repeated births, extricated, out of compassion for all beings, this nectar, which is difficult to be obtained even by gods and which lies in the depths of the ocean called the vedas, which stirred up by inserting the churning rod of his illumined intellect.

I offer my obeisance with my whole being to those, sanctifying feet—the dispellers of the fear of transmigration—the fact of own teacher, through the light of whose illumined intellect, was dispelled the darkness of delusion enveloping my own mind, who destroyed for ever my fear of appearance and disappearance in this terrible sea of innumerable births, and having taken shelter at whose feet, others also get unfailingly the knowledge of the upanisadas, self control, and humility, which is fruitful and most worthy.

3

Prasana Upanisada

Rishis, Sukesha, son of Bhardwaj, Satyakama, son of Sibi, the grandson of Surya, born of the family of Garga, Kausalya, son of Asvala; a scion of the line of Bhrigu born in Vidarbha; and Kabandhi, descendant of Katya — all these, who were devoted to the inferior Brahma engaged in realising the inferior Brahma, and intent on a search of the supreme Brahma, approached with faggots in hand, the venerable Pippalada with the belief, 'This one will certainty tell us all about it'. To them, the seer said, 'Live here for a year in a fitting manner, with control over the senses and with Brahmacharya and faith. Then put questions as you please. If we know, we shall explain all that you are'. After that Kabandhi, descendent of Katya, having approached him asked questions :

Questions : From what indeed are all these beings born ?

Answer : As is well known, the Lord of all creatures, having become desirous of progeny, he deliberated on past vedic knowledge. Having brooded on that knowledge, he created a couple — food and Prana — under the idea, 'These two will produce creature for me in multifarious ways. After creating the cosmic egg, he created the sun and the moon, under the idea that these two viz fire and moon, which are the eaters and the eaten, will produce creatures multifariously for me'. The sun is verily Prana and food is verily the moon. Whatever is gross or subtle is but food. The gross, as distinguished from that subtle, is certainly food of the subtle. Now then the fact that the sun, while rising, enters into the eastern direction, thereby it absorbs into its rays all the creatures in the east; that it enters into the south, that it enters into the west; that it enters into north; that it reaches the nadir and the zenith; that it enters the intermediate points of Zodiac; that it illumines, all, thereby it absorbs all living things into its rays. That very eater, who is Prana, identified with all creatures, and who is possessed of all forms, being embodied in the universe, that is Prana and fire, that eater again rises everyday, absorbing into himself all the cardinal points. The realisers of Brahma knew the one that is possessed of all forms, full of rays, endowed with illumination, the resort of all, the single light of all and the radiator of heat. It is the sun that rises — the sun that possesses a thousand rays, exists in a hundred forms and the life of all creatures. Here it is being explained how this single pair — constituted by that which is the moon, the gross, the food on the one hand and that, which is the formless Prana, the eater, the sun on the other — could produce the creatures. There are two courses of the Lord — the southern and the northern. Those, who follow in that way the sacrifices and public goods etc. that are products of action, conquer verily the world of the moon, it is they, who come back. Hence these seers of Heaven, who, are desirous of progeny, attain the southern course. This, which is the course of the manes is verily food. Again, by searching for the self through the control cf senses, faith and meditation, they conquer the sun by proceeding along the northern course. This is the resort of all that lives. This is indestructible; this is fearless ; this is the highest goal, far from this, they do not come back. This is unrealizable to the ignorant. He, by whom the whole world is sustained, is called the year, the Lord of all creatures, and he is wholly evolved into the twelve months, which are his limbs. The month verily is the Lord of all creatures. The dark fortnight is his food and the brightness his Prana. Therefore, these seers perform the sacrifices in the bright fortnight. The others perform it in the other. Then the day and night are verily the Lord of all creatures. Day is his Prana and night the food. Those, who indulge in passion during the day, waste away Prana. That they give play to passion at night, is as good as celibacy. There is, therefore, an injunction enunciated in passing that it is one's duty to unite with one's wife in due time. It is the Lord of all creatures, who has evolved into day and night and exists identified with such food as rice and barley. Food is nothing but the Lord of all creatures. From that indeed issues that human seed and from that are born the beings. The question that was raised, 'From what indeed are the beings born' has, thus been answered by saying that the creatures are born by passing in succession through the pairs starting with the sun and the moon and ending with day and night and then by proceeding through food, blood and semen. This being so, those who undertake the well-known vow of the Lord of all creatures, beget both sons and daughters. From them alone is this world of the moon in whom there are that vow and continence, and in whom is found for ever avoidance of falsehood and from there is that taintless world of Brahma, in whom there is no crookedness, no falsehood and no dissimulation.

As for the Northern course marked out by the sun, which consists of self-identification with 'Prana', and is pure, not tainted like the lunar Brahmaloka, and not subject to waxing and waxing, that one is for them for those, in whom there is no fraud, no crookedness, unlike the householder in whom it becomes inevitable owing to the exigencies of many contradictory social situations. Also those in whom, falsehood does not become unavoidable, as it is, is with the householders in the course of play or merriment. Similarly, those in whom, unlike the householders, there does not exist any dissimulation, is a kind of false behaviour consisting in showing oneself publicly in some way and acting contrariwise. For those competent persons — the forest dwellers, and mendicants, in whom such blemishes as 'Maya' do not exist because there is no occasion for them, is this untainted world of Brahma, just in consonance with the disciplines they undertake. This is the goal for those, who undertake rites in conjunction with meditation. But the Brahmaloka indicated by the moon, mentioned earlier, is for those, who perform rites alone.

Question : How many are the deities that sustain a creature? Which among them exhibit the glory ? Which again, is the chief among them ?

Answer : Space is this deity and air, fire, water, space and earth are all elements that are the material causes of the body and speech, mind, eye and ear are organs of action and knowledge. The gods identifying themselves with the body and organs speak by way of exhibiting their own glory while vying for pre-eminence. It is we, who, like the pillars of a palace, hold together this aggregate of body and organs by holding it aloft, and not allowing it to be disintegrated. The idea of each one is this, 'It is indeed by me alone that this aggregate is upheld.' To them the chief Prana said, 'Do not be deluded. It is, who do not allow it to disintegrate by sustaining it by dividing myself five fold.' They remained incredulous. He appeared to be rising up from the body out of indignation. As he ascended, all the others, without exception, ascended immediately and when he remained quiet, all others too remained in position. Just as in the world, all the bees take to flight in accordance as the king of the bees takes to his wings, and they settle down as he does so, similarly, do speech, mind, eye, ear etc. behave. Becoming delighted, they began praising 'Prana'. How did they praise ? The 'Prana' burns as fire, this one is the sun, this one is the cloud, this one is Indra and air, this one is the earth and food. This god is the gross and the subtle as well as that, which is nectar. Like spokes on the hub of a chariot wheel, are fixed on 'Prana' all things — sacrifice, Kshatriya, and Brahmin (Kshatriya to protect all and Brahmin to perform sacrifice etc.). It is verily you, who move about in the womb as the Lord of creation and it is you, who take birth after the image of the parents.' 'O! Prana it is for you, who reside with the organs, that all these creatures carry presents. Since you are eater, so all else is food for you only'. The 'Prana' is the best transmitter to the celestials. He is the food offering to the manes that precede other offerings. He is the right conduct of the organs that constitute the essence of the body and which are known as the atharvas (essence of the body). 'Prana is Indra. Through its valour, he is Rudra, and he is the preserver on all sides. He moves in the sky — he is sun, the Lord of all luminaries. When the 'Prana' pours down as rain, then his creatures continue to be in a happy mood under the belief, 'Food will be produced to our heart's content'. 'Prana' is impurified, he is the eater; and he is the Lord of all that exists. We are the givers of his food in oblation. Air is our father. Hence it is established that Air's fatherhood is for the whole universe. One's aspect, which is lodged in speech, which makes the effort of speaking as a speaker, that which is in the ear and that which is in the eye. and that aspect which is pervasive in the mind, as acts of thinking etc., make that aspect calm. One should not make it inactive by ascending.

All this in this world, as also all that in heaven, is under the control of 'Prana'. It protects us first as a mother does her sons and ordains for us splendour and intelligence. In short, whatever enjoyable thing is there in this world, all this is verily under the control of 'Prana' and 'Prana' is even the ruler and protector of whatever is enjoyable in the universe. Thus in as much as the greatness of 'Prana' has been disclosed, his organs such as speech through his praise is the all pervasive entity. Therefore, 'Prana' is ascertained as the Lord of creatures and the eaters.

Question : From which is the 'Prana' born ? How does he come into the body ? How does he dwell by dividing himself ? How does he depart ? How does he support the external things and how does he support in the physical context ?

Answer : In view of the question having been put by a person, who is pre-eminently the knower of Brahma, the question appeared supernormal. Still the answer is that from the self is born this 'Prana'. Just as there can be this shadow, when a man is there, so this 'Prana' is fixed on the self. He comes to this body owing to the actions of the mind i.e. 'Virtue' results from virtue'. Vedas also say, 'Being attached, he, together with the work, attains that result to which the subtle body or mind is attached as it is the king alone, who employs the officers saying, 'Rule over these villages and these villages, just so this 'Prana' engages the other organs separately.' He places 'apana' in the two lower apertures. 'Prana' himself issuing out of the mouth and nostrils resides in the eyes and ears. In the middle, however, is 'Samana' which assimilates all that is eaten or drunk. Since this one distributes equally in all parts of the body, all this that is eaten or drunk, the food that is poured as a libation on one's bodily fire, therefore, from the burning of what is eaten and drunk, from the fire in the stomach, when it has reached the region of the heart, there issue, these seven flames that are lodged in the head (two eyes, two ears, two nostrils and the mouth). The idea is that the revelation of objects take form or colour etc., that constitutes what is known as seeing, hearing etc., is caused by 'Prana'. The self i.e. the subtle body is surely in the heart. There are a hundred and one of the chief nerves. Each of these has a hundred divisions. Each branch is divided into seventy two thousand such branches and among them moves 'Vyana' (the vital energy). 'Vyana' exists wholly pervading the body through the nerves, which like rays from the sun, issue in all directions from the heart, and by becoming particularly active in the joints, shoulders and vital parts, and in the interim between the functioning of 'Prana' and 'Apana', it becomes the performer of deeds requiring strength. Now then, 'Udana' (vital force, when it is in its upward trend through the nerves, it leads to a virtuous world, such as the world of gods, as a result of deeds, which are virtuous as enjoined by the scriptures ; it leads to a sinful world, to hell, to birth among beasts and so on, as a result of sins, which are opposed to those virtuous deeds and it leads to the human world as a result of both virtues and vices, when they predominate equally?

The sun is the external 'Prana'. It rises up favouring the 'Prana' in the eye. That deity that is in the earth, favours by attracting 'Apana' in a human being. The space (i.e. the air) that is in the middle is 'Samana'. The common air is 'Vyana' because of the similarity of pervasiveness and stays there helping the vital functions, That which is well known as common luminosity outside is 'Udana' in the body, that is to say, it favours the vital function called 'Udana' with its light. Since the 'Udana' that causes one's leaving the body is of the nature of luminosity and while staying in the body, it is favoured by external light, therefore, when an ordinary man gets his natural light extinguished, then it is to be understood that his life is exhausted and he is about to die. He attains another body (rebirth) together with the organs, counting from speech, which enters into the mind.

Together with whatever thought he might have had at the time of death, together with that very thought, and together with the organs, he (the creature) enters into 'Prana' the chief vital function. The purport is that at the time of death, the activities of the organs having declined, he continues to live only through the functioning of the chief, 'Prana' (vital energy). Then the relatives say, 'He breathes, he is alive.' That 'Prana' again, in association with the function called 'Udana' and along with the soul, the master that enjoys — that 'Prana', thus associated with the function called 'Udana'. leads that enjoyer of the fruits of work and make him reach, under the influence of virtuous and vicious actions, a world as was desired by him. Any illumined man, who known 'Prana', thus, as possessed of the description set-forth before viz. origin etc., for that man is being stated this result accruing in this world and the next. For that man of knowledge, the time of progeny consisting of sons, grandsons etc., certainly sustains no break and when this body falls, he becomes immortal, through his identity with 'Prana'. Pertaining to this idea, then occurs this narration in the form of being statement about this idea. Having known the origin, the coming, lodgement and five-fold overlordship and the physical existence of 'Prana', one achieves immortality.

Question : Which are the organs that go to sleep in this person? Which keep awake in him ? Which is the deity, who experiences dream ? To whom occurs this happiness and in whom do all get merged ?

Answer : Just as all the rays of the setting sun become unified in this orb of light, and they disperse from the sun, as it rises up again, similarly, all that becomes unified in the high deity, is the mind. Hence such a person does not then hear, does not see, does not smell, does not taste, does not touch, does not speak, does not grasp, does not enjoy, does not eject and does not move. People say, 'He is sleeping'. At that time it is the functions of the organs, resembling fire, of that 'Prana' that really keep awake, in the city of the body. That, which is this 'Apana' really resembles the Garhapatya. That can be so since the other, fire, called 'Ahavaniya' is obtained (extracted) at the time of the Agnihotra sacrifice. From the 'Garhapatya' fire which is the source of extraction, therefore, from the derivative sense of that from which, something is taken away, Garhapatya fire is the source of extraction (Pranayam). Similarly, for a man in sleep, 'Prana' moves from the mouth and nostrils, having been extracted, as it were, from the function called 'Apana'. Therefore, 'Prana' is comparable to 'Ahavaniya'. As for 'Vyana', since it moves out from the heart through the right orifice and is thus associated with the Southern direction, therefore, it is (the fire) called Daksinagni, known otherwise as 'Anvaharyapacana'. The two oblations, consisting or exhaling and inhaling, are the two oblations of the Agnihotra sacrifice, as it were, just because of the similarity of being two in number. Since these are oblations and since that vital function (called Samana) strikes a balance for ever, between these two oblations, so as to ensure the maintenance of the body, therefore, it is here verily the priest called the 'Hota', because of the similarity of carrying the oblation (like the priest) and this despite the fact that it is called a fire. It is 'Samana' and 'therefore' the sleep of an illumined man is verily a performance of the 'Agnihota' sacrifice. Therefore, the idea implied is that the illumined man is not to be considered a non-performer of rites. It is thus that in the 'Vajasaneyaka', it is said that all the component parts of the body and organs of this illumined man perform scarifies at all times, even while he sleeps. Such being the case, it is the mind that is the sacrificer, which keeps awake after having poured, as oblation, the external organs and their objects into the wakeful fires of 'Prana' and which seeks to reach 'Brahma' like an actual scarificer seeking to reach heaven, which is the result of Agnihotra. The mind is imagined to be the sacrificer because like the sacrificer it acts as the chief among the aggregate of body and senses, and because it sets out for Brahma, just as the sacrificer does for heaven. The result of the sacrifice is the vital function called 'Udana' because the achievement of the result of a sacrifice depends on 'Udana' as the 'Udana' every day leads the sacrificer, called the mind, to Brahma, the immutable as though to heaven, during the time of sleep, after causing the mind to cease even from the dream activities. Hence 'Udana' takes the place of the result of the sacrifice. Thus is praised the illumination of the enlightened person by showing that starting from the time of cessation from activity of the ears etc., till the time he rises up from sleep, he enjoy the fruits of all sacrifices, and his sleep is not a source of evil as it is in the case of an unenlightened man, and all this is meant as a praise, for on a contrary view, it cannot be held that in the enlightened man alone, the ears etc. sleep or that, the fires of the 'Prana' keep awake, or that his mind alone enjoys freedom in the dream and wakeful states and then goes to sleep everyday, for the fact of passing through the three states of waking, dream and sleep is similar for all creatures hence it is reasonable to say that this is only an analogy of enlightenment. As for the question, which is the deity who experiences dream, the answer is in this dream state, the mind experiences greatness. Whatever was seen it sees again, whatever was heard, it hears again, whatever was perceived in the different places and directions, it experiences again and again, it perceives all by becoming all that was seen or not seen, heard or not heard, perceived or not perceived, and whatever is real or unreal.

When the deity (the mind) becomes overwhelmed by the solar rays (called bile) then in this state, the deity does not see dreams. At that time, there occurs this happiness in the body. At this time, the body and organs that depend on ignorance, desire, and the result of past actions, become inactive. When these become quiet, the nature of the self, that appears distorted owing to the limited adjuncts, becomes non-dual, one, auspicious and calm. In order to indicate this state through a process of successively merging into it, the subtle forms of earth etc., that are creation of ignorance, the text cites an illustration. As the birds proceed towards the tree that provides lodging just so all these proceed to the Supreme self, to the immutable. What are all those things, the gross earth, possessed of the five attributes (sound, touch, colour, taste and smell), and its cause, the rudiment of earth and the fine form of smell as also water and the rudiments of water ; fire and the rudiments of fire; air and the rudiments of air; space and the rudiments of space. That is to say, all the gross and subtle elements ; so also eye, the organ, and the object of sight ; ear and the object of hearing ; the organs and the objects of smell; of taste ; of touch; speech and the content of speech ; the two hands and the object to be grasped ; sex and what is enjoyed; the organ of excretion and what is excreted; the two feet and the place walked over. Thus, it is to be understood, that the organs of knowledge and the organs of action have been enumerated. The mind, that has already been mentioned, and the object of the mind, what is the thought of understanding, the faculty of ascertaining and the object to be ascertained. The internal organ characterised by egoism and the object of egoism. The internal organ possessed of consciousness, and the object to be conscious of the skin, as distinct from the organ of touch, and possessed of lustre, the objects revealed by Prana and all that has to be held by Prana.

Next in order is that reality of the self that has entered here in the body like a reflection of the sun in water, etc., as the enjoyer and the agent of action. And this one is the seer, feeler, smeller, taster, thinker, ascertainer, doer the 'Purusa' (pervading the body and organs), who is a knower by nature. He becomes wholly established in the Supreme, the immutable self, which persists as the last resort of the universe and he, who realises that shadowless, bodiless, colourless, pure, immutable, attains the supreme immutable itself. He again who realises becomes omniscient and all. He who known that immutable, into which the cognising self (the 'Purusa' who is naturally a knower) — as also the organs and the elements together with all the deities merge, that omniscient one enters into everything.

Question : Which world does he really win thereby, who among men, intently meditates on 'OM' in that wonderful way till death ?

Answer : This very Brahma, that is both superior and inferior — the superior brings that which is truth and immutable and is called 'Purusa' and the inferior being the first born, called 'Prana', is but identical with 'OṂ' since 'OM' is its symbol. As the supreme Brahma cannot be directly indicated by words etc., and is devoid of all distinctions created by attributes and as it is on that account beyond the organs, therefore, the mind by itself cannot explore it. But to those who meditate on 'OM', which is comparable to the images of Vishnu and others and on which is fixed the idea of Brahma with devotion, that Brahma becomes favourable and reveals itself. This is understood on the authority of scriptures. Similar is the case with the inferior Brahma. Hence, it is said in secondary sense that, that Brahma, which is both inferior and superior is but 'OM'. Therefore one who knows thus attains either of the two — the superior or the inferior Brahmas — through this means alone, through this that is a means for the attainment of the self, consisting in meditation on 'OM' for 'OM' is the nearest symbol of Brahma. Now should he meditate on 'OM' as consisting of one letter, he becomes enlightened even by that and very quickly attains a human birth. Being endued there with self- control, continence and faith, he experiences greatness. Further, again, if he meditates on 'OM' with the help of the second letter (a u m), he becomes identified with the mind. By the vedic mantras, he is lifted to the intermediate space, the world of moon. Then having experienced greatness in the lunar world, he turns round again towards the human world. Again, anyone who meditates on the supreme 'Purusa' with the help of this very syllable 'OM', as possessed of three letters (a u m), becomes unified in the sun, consisting of light. As a snake becomes free from its slough exactly in a similar way, he becomes freed from sin, and he is lifted upto the world of Brahma (Hirnyagarbha) by the 'Sama' mantras. From this total mass of creatures (that Hiranyagarbha is), he sees the 'Purusa' who penetrates every being and is superior than the higher one (viz Hiranyagarbha).

The three letters in 'OM' by themselves are within the range of death. But if they are closely joined, one to another, are not divergently applied to different objects, and are applied to three courses of action—external, internal and intermediate—that when properly resorted to then the name of enlightenment does not shake i.e. remains undisturbed. Since a man, who is this enlightened, has become the self of all and one with 'OM', therefore, from where can he deviate and to where — no where. Only the intelligent, the enlightened, and not the ignorant, know this world associated with men, that is attainable through the Rig mantras. Intermediate space, presided over by the moon which is attainable through Yajurveda mantras and the third world of Brahma is attainable through Sama Veda : The enlightened one reaches the three-fold world indicative of the inferior Brahma through the aid of 'OM' and with the help of that very 'OM', he attains that which is Supreme — Brahma, the immutable, truth, called 'Purusa', the all pervasive, which is quiet, free, devoid of all such distinctions as waking, dream and sleep and is transcendental to the whole universe and is 'therefore' free from old age, beyond death, and since untouched by such changes as old age, and consequently fearless and just because it is fearless, it is unsurpassing. The idea is that he reaches this one also with the aid of 'OM', which is a vehicle of adorance.

Question : Where does he exist having sixteen Kalas (कला)?

Answer : He is here itself inside the body, in whom originate the sixteen Kalas (Prana and five senses, five knowledge senses and five action senses). The Purusha, who is partless appears through ignorance to be possessed of Kalas (limbs) as a consequence of his association with the sixteen parts that are his limiting adjuncts. But this 'Purusha' has to be shown as an absolute entity by eliminating through knowledge, those parts that condition him. That is why the parts are spoken of as originating from the Purusa. Since no empirical pronouncement as to attainability and the means of attainment can be made unless there be the superimposition of 'Prana' and the rest on the totally attributeless, non-dual, pure principle, therefore, the origin, existence and absorption of the parts that are within the domain of ignorance, are superimposed on the 'Purusa', for the parts are always seen to exist in identity with consciousness at the time of origin, continuation and dissolution and this is why some deluded people say, 'Just as ghee melts through contact with fire, so it is consciousness that originates every moment as pots etc., are created and gets destroyed. The nihilists say, 'When that consciouness stops, all things appear as void'. Still others (the logicians) say, 'The knowledge of pot and the rest arises and gets destroyed as a temporary phenomenon on the eternal self, which imparts consciousness'. The materialists say, 'Consciousness belongs to matter'. But consciousness that knows no increase or decrease, and yet appears diversely through the attributes of the limiting adjuncts, is nothing but the self, which fact is borne out by such vedic texts as 'Brahma is truth, knowledge, infinite'. 'Brahma is consciousness, knowledge, bliss, Brahma, the infinite reality is but pure intelligence'. Consciousness is proved to be invariable from the fact that consciouness remains unchanged even when objects change in their essence and because anything that is known in anyway, emerges to consciousness only as such an object of knowledge. It does not stand to reason to say that some external thing exists substantially and still remains unknown for this is like averring that colour is perceived while the eye is non-existent. A knowable thing may be inconsistent in relation to knowledge, but knowledge is never inconsistent in relation to objects for knowledge persists in relation to some knowable things even though a particular object may not be there ; indeed nobody can have such a thing as an object unless he has knowledge. As a description of 'Purusha', it has been said that 'Purusa' is one in whom originate those sixteen parts. Though that origination of the parts was stated there in the upanisadas, in another context, still the present text, dealing with creation, is meant to recount the order in which the origination occurred as also to show that creation is preceeded by intelligence. It is further deliberated 'As a result of whose departure shall I rise up ? And as a result of whose continuance shall I remain established ?' As for the illustration of an (officer, who does everything for the king and is called by courtesy a king or a master, that has no application here because it runs counter to the obvious primary meaning of the vedic text, 'He deliberated', which is meant to impart valid knowledge, for a secondary meaning of a word is called for only where the primary meaning is inadmissible. But here, it does not stand to reason that an insentient entity, viz., 'Pradhana' should engage in well-regulated activity for the purpose of bondage, liberation etc., in relation to the 'Purusa', keeping in view the difference between bound and freed should and taking note of such distinctions as of subject, object, space, time and causation. On the other hand this becomes justifiable from the stand-point already stated that omniscient God is the creator. By 'Purusa' alone, therefore, as by the king, is created 'Prana', the director of all and as he created 'Prana', from 'Prana' he created faith, space, air, fire, water, earth, organs, mind, food; from food he created vigour, self control, mantras (vedas), rites, worlds, and names in the worlds viz Dev Dutta etc. of the created beings. Thus, in conformily with the seeds constituted by such defects of the creatures as ignorance, these parts were created — like two moons, mosquitoes, bees etc., created by the blurred vision of a man suffering from the disease called 'Timira' or like all sorts of things created by a dreamer — and these again merge into that very 'Purusa' by giving up such distinctions of names, forms etc. How this happens is as illustrated. Just as the flowing rivers that have the sea as their goal, get absorbed after reaching the sea, and their names and forms are destroyed, and they are called merely the sea, so also these sixteen parts of the all seeing 'Purusas' that have the 'Purusa' as their goal, disappear on reaching the 'Purusa', where their names and forms are destroyed and they are simply called as 'Purusa' such a man of realisation becomes free from the parts and is immortal. When the names and forms are eliminated, the entity that remains undestroyed is called by the knowers of Brahma, as 'Purusa'. He, who has become thus enlightened after being shown by his teacher the process of absorption of the parts, becomes free from the parts, where the parts viz 'Prana' and the rest that are the creation of ignorance, desire and action are based through knowledge (and he becomes mmortal). Death is a creation of parts originating from nescience. When those parts are gone, one becomes immortal just because of one's partlessness. With regard to this matter, one should know that 'Purusa', who is worthy to be known and in whom are transfixed the parts like spokes in the nave of a chariot wheel, so that death may not afflict him anywhere. Having thus instructed, the disciples, Pippladu told them, 'I know thus far only, this, supreme Brahma, that is worthy to be known and beyond this there is not anything higher to be known'. He said this in order to remove from the disciples any doubt that there might still remain something unknown, and also in order to generate in them the conviction that they had attained the final goal. It is being stated that what those disciples did when they found no recompense for their knowledge after being taught by the teacher and getting their purpose fulfilled. While worshipping the guru by offering handfuls of flowers and saluting him with their heads, 'You indeed are our father, since you have generated through knowledge a fresh birth in Brahma that is eternal, ageless, deathless, and fearless. Since it is you, who, with the help of the raft of knowledge, have ferried us across ignorance or false knowledge — as though across an ocean itself, infested with birth, old age, death, disease, sorrow, etc., which are like sea animals — to the other shore of the boundless ocean of nescience, called emancipation, consisting in absolute cessation of rebirth, therefore, your fatherhood towards us is more justifiable than that of the others (i.e. our real fathers).' The other father that bigets the body alone, is yet the most worshipful in the world, what to speak of one, who guarantes absolute fearlessness. This is the purport. Salutation to the great-seers, the originator, of the line of traditional transmission of the knowledge of Brahma.' Om, Shanti, Shanti, Shanti.

4
Brhadaranyaka Upanisada

Because of its large size, this upanisada is named as 'Brhad' and since it was taught in forests (Aranya) it is Brhadaranyaka. The vedas are devoted to setting forth the means of attaining what is good and awarding, what is evil in so far as these are not known through perception and inference, for all people naturally seek these two ends. But in matters coming within the range of experience, a knowledge of the means of attaining the good and avoiding the evil ends is easily available through perception and inference. Hence the vedas are not sought for that and upanisadas come in for guidance. In one of the upanisadas we find, 'There is a doubt among men regarding the life after death.' Some say that the self exists and others that it does not exist and upanisada after narration of pros and cons on both sides concludes, 'It is to be realised as existing indeed' and so on.

At the start of the universe, there was nothing whatsoever here. It was covered only by death, (Hiranyagarbha, or hunger, for hunger is death, God created the mind and thinking, and then water and fire. Then what was there like froth on the water was solidified and became the earth. Then he was tired and when he was tired and distressed, his essence or lustre came forth. This was fire. God then desired to have a second form as his part 'Atma'. The God, death or hunger brought about the union of speech (the veda) with the mind. What was the seed there, became the year (Viraj). Before him there had been no year. The death reared him for about an year and after this projected him. When he was born, the death opened his mouth to swallow him but he cried 'Bhan'. That became speach. Death then thought that in case he killed him, he would be able to get not much of a food. Still he decided to eat him since the basic nature of death is to eat every thing. It is, therefore, called Aditi (Death) too. God then desired to hold sacrifice and to reborn out of it, having thus become ready for sacrifice. This was called Aswamedha too and since then 'Aswa' (Horse) is sacrificed. Then fire and sun again became God. Death further conquers death and death cannot overstall God as it becomes his self and the death becomes one with these deities. With death conquering death, there came into being two classes — the gods and Asuras. Gods were fewer in number and Asuras were more in number. They vied with each other for the mastery of the worlds. Gods said, 'Now let us surpass the Asuras in the sacrifice through the 'Udgitha'. That is the victory of gods and defeat of Asuras. Sometimes the reverse happened too. Accordingly, when the gods win, there is a preponderance of merit and the result is elevation up to the status of Prajapati. And when the Asuras triumph, demerit prevails and the result is degradation down to the level of stationary objects, while if there be a draw, it leads to human birth. When evil prevailed, the gods asked the deity identified with the organ of speech to chant (Udgitha) or perform the function of the priest called for them. This universe consists of three elements — the name, the form and the action and the Supreme self, which is, beyond the undifferentiated, does not consist of name, form and action and is the subject matter of knowledge and has been dealt with separately by denial of things other than the self with the words 'Not this, not this'. After speech, the gods asked the nose, to chant the 'Udgitha' for them. The nose chanted for them. The common good that comes of the nose, it secured for the gods by chanting, while the fine smelling it utilised for itself. The Asuras knew that through this chanting, the gods would surpass them. They charged it and struck it with evil. That evil is what we come across, when one smells improper things. Then the gods asked eyes to chant 'Udgitha' for them. The eyes accordingly chanted for them. The common good that comes of the eye, it secured for the gods by chanting, while the fine seeing it utilised for itself. The asuras thinking that through that chanting the gods would surpass them, they charged it and struck it with evil. That evil is what we come across when we see improper things Then the gods asked the ear to chant Udgitha for them too. Ear chanted but the common good that comes out of the ear, it secured for the gods by chanting while the fine hearing it utilised for itself. The Asuras with the fear of gods surpassing them changed it and struck it with evil. That evil is what we come across when we hear improper things. Then the gods asked mind to chant it for them and on the mind chanting, the Asuras, charged it and struck it with evil. That evil is what we come across when we think of improper things. Likewise, they also touched the other deities with evil and struck them with evil. In this way, they tried one by one the deities of the nose etc., thinking that they were each the deity referred to by the mantra enjoined for repetition and were to be meditated upon, since they too chanted the 'Udgitha' and the gods came to the conclusion that the deities of the organ of speech and the rest, whom they tried, one by one, were incapable of chanting the 'Udgitha' because they contracted evil from the Asuras owing to their attachment to utilising their power of doing fine performances for themselves. Hence more of them was the deity referred to by mantras, nor were they to be meditated upon, since they had been made impure. Likewise just as the organ of speech etc., the Asuras, also touched the other deities that have not been mentioned, the skin and the rest, with evil, that is to say struck them with evil and the gods were helpless. Similar is the human tendency — all organs having good and evil effect as they are put to use to.

Ultimately the gods asked the vital force (Pran) in the mouth to chant 'Udgitha' for them. The vital force chanted. The Asuras charged it and wanted to strike it with evil but the Asuras were shattered, flung in all directions and perished. Therefore, the gods became fire etc. and the Asuras were crushed. He, who knows thus and applies on self, becomes his true self and his envious kinsmen (the evil thinkings and actions) are crushed. Owing to this destruction of the Asuras i.e. dissociation from the evils due to natural attachment, which checked the manifestation of their divinity by virtue of taking refuge in the vital force in the mouth, which is ever unattached to gods, the organs, that are under consideration, became their own divine selves, fire or so forth, mentioned later on. Now having finished with the result of meditation on the vital force, the shruti resumes its allegorical form and goes on to explain why the vital force in the mouth be resorted to as one's self, to the exclusion of the organ of speech and the rest. It is because of the fact that the vital force is the common self of the organ of speech etc. as well as the body. The gods then searched for him, who had thus restored them to their divinity and discovered him in the mouth. That vital force is called 'Ayasha Angirasa' as it is the essence of the members of the body. The deity took away death, the evil of these gods such as the god of speech identified with the vital force. Everybody dies because of the evil due to the attachment of the organs to contact the sense objects, prompted by his natural ignorance. Hence this evil is death. The vital force is here spoken of as taking it away from the gods simply because they identified themselves with the vital force. Now the result of the act of meditation on the evil force as one's own self viz the identification of the organ of speech etc. with fire and so on, is being stated. This deity next carried them beyond death. Because death or the evil that limits one of the body, is removed by the identification with the vital force, therefore, the latter is the destroyer of evil of death. Hence that vital force carried the gods, that of speech etc., beyond death, the evil which is being discussed, and made them realise their respective unlimited divine forms as fire and so on. If the vital force, carried the organ of speech, the foremost one first, its importance consists in being a better instrument in the chanting of the 'Udgitha' than the other organs. When the organ of speech got rid of death, it became fire and that fire, having transcended death, shines beyond its reach. Then it carried nose and when it got rid of death, it became air. That air having transcended death, blows beyond its reach. Likewise, the eye became the sun and the sun having transcended death, it shines beyond its reach. Similarly, the ear became the direction and the direction having transcended death, remained beyond reach. Then it carried mind. It became moon and shined. Like this, the deity carries one, who keeps them beyond death. Next it secured eatable for itself by chanting as whatever food is eaten, is eaten by the vital force alone and it rests on that. Infact the food is not eaten by the vital force alone as it affords a share to all organs to make them vital too. Accordingly, gods said, 'Whatever food there is, is just this much and one secures it for oneself by chanting, now, let us have a share in the food.' Then the vital force asked them to sit around facing it. Then the gods sat down around it. Hence whatever food one eats through the vital force satisfies these, so do his relatives sit down around him facing him, who knows thus and he becomes their support, the greatest among them and their leader, a good eater of food and the ruler of them. That one among his relatives, who desires to rival a man of such knowledge, is powerless to support his dependents. But one, who follows him, or desires to maintain one's dependents bring under him, is alone capable or supporting them. The organs of speech etc., are called gods because they bring their respective objects to light, said to the vital force in mouth, 'Whatever food there is, is eaten in the world to sustain life, is just thus much and no more and one secures it all for oneself by chanting'. Thus the vital force is self of the body and organs. As already indicated it is called 'Ayasha (Angirasa)' for it is the essence of the members, of course it is their essence. For instance, from whichever member the vital force departs, right there it withers, therefore, it is of course the essence of the members. This alone in turn is Brihaspati (Lord of the Rig) being Lord of speech. This alone is Brahmanaspati (Lord of the Yujur) as Lord of Yujur. It is Saman (Sa and ama) as it is sa (Speech) and ama (vital force), therefore, it is Saman or it is equal to the ant to elephant, or equal to this universe, therefore, it is called Saman. He, who knows this Saman (Vital force) to be such, attains, union with it or lives in the same world as it is. Thus indeed is also 'Udgitha'. The vital force is 'UT' for all this is held aloft by the vital force, and speech alone is 'githa'. So this is 'Utgitha'. Regarding this, there is also a story. Brahmdutta, the great grandson of Chikitana, while drinking soma said, 'Let this soma strike off my head if I say that Ayasa Angirasa chanted the 'Uudgitha' through any other than this (vital force and speech)'. Indeed he chanted through speech and the vital force. The mention of his taking this oath shows that one must have a firm conviction of the knowledge, the purport being that he the chanter, called here Ayasa Angirasa, chanted through speech, which is subordinate to the vital force and the vital force which is his own self, meaning this is the significance of the oath.

He, who knows the wealth of this Saman (vital force), attains wealth. Tone is indeed its wealth. Therefore, one, who is going to officiate as a priest, should desire to have a rich tone in his voice, and he should do his priestly duties through that voice with a fine tone. Therefore, in a sacrifice, people long to see a priest with a good voice, like one, who has wealth. He who knows the wealth of Saman to be such, attains wealth and he, who knows the gold of this Saman (vital force) obtains gold. Tone is indeed gold. Further, he who knows the support of this 'Saman' (Vital force) gets a resting place. Speech and certain other parts of the body are its support, as resting on speech, the vital force thus chanted. Some call it resting on food (body). Now, therefore, there is edifying repetition (abhyaroha), only of the hymns called 'Pavamanas'. The priest called 'Prastotra' recites the 'Saman'. While he recites it, these mantras are to be repeated.' From evil lead me to good ; from darkness lead me to light ; from death lead me to immortality.' When the 'mantra' says 'From evil lead me to good', 'evil' means death and 'good' means immortality so it say 'from death lead me to immortality' i.e., make me immortal. When it says, 'From darkness lead me to light, darkness means death and light is immortality', so it say, 'From death lead me to immortality or make me immortal'. In the dictum 'From death lead me to immortality,' the meaning does not seem to be hidden. Then through the remaining hymns, the chanter should secure eatable food for himself by chanting. Therefore, while they are being chanted, the sacrificer should ask for a boon — anything that he desires. Whatever objects this chanter possessed of such knowledge, desires either for himself or for the sacrificer, he secures them by chanting. This meditation certainly wins the world (Hiranyagarbha). He who knows the Saman (vital force) as such, has not to pray lest be unfit for this world.

Thus it has been stated that meditation and rites together lead to identification with 'Hiranyagarbha'. There is no possibility of a doubt regarding this. Therefore, a doubt is being raised as to whether, in the absence of rites, meditation alone can lead to the result or not. To remove it, the text says, 'This meditation on the vital force certainly wins the world (Hiranyagarbha), even if it is disjoined from the rites. He has not to pray lest he be unfit for this world, for one, who has already realised his identity, with 'Hiranyagarbha' cannot possibly pray for the attainment of Him. He, who knows this 'Saman' as such, meditates upon the vital force, whose glories have been described above, till he realises his identity with it in the following way, 'I am the pure vital force, not to be touched by the evil characteristics of the Asuras, viz. the attachment of the senses to their objects. With these attributes, I am completely present in all bodies beginning with that of a white ant, being formless and all pervading'.

In the beginning this universe was but the Self (Viraj) of a human form. He reflected and found nothing else but himself. He first uttered, 'I am he'. Therefore, he was called 'Aham' (I). Hence to this day, when a person is addressed, he first says, 'It is I', and then says the other names that he would have known because he was first and before this whole (band of aspirants) burnt all evils, therefore, he is called 'Purusa'. He, who knows thus indeed burns one who wants to be 'Viraj' before him. Such a person was the product of vedic meditation and rites and this self was of a human form, with a hand, head, etc. i.e. Viraj. This Viraj in his past incarnation, when he was an aspirant by an inadequate practice of meditation and rites, was the first of those, who wanted to attain the status of Viraj by the same method, and before all his evils were burnt. Burning here means only the failure to attain the status of Viraj first due to deficiency in the practice of meditation. In order to show that the results meant to be extolled here of meditation and rites, enjoined in the ceremonial portion of the vedas, are not beyond the range of transmigratory existence. Such a Viraj was, therefore, afraid. Therefore, people still are afraid of being alone. He thought if there is nothing else but me, what am I afraid of ? From that thinking alone his fear was gone for what was there to be afraid of. It is only from a second entity that the fear comes from. Then the question arises as to what was Viraj's knowledge of unity due to ? If it came without instruction, the same might also be true of us. If, 'however', it was due to the impression of previous life, then the knowledge of unity would be useless. As Viraj's knowledge of unity acquired in his past life, although it was present, did not remove the cause of his bondage, ignorance — for being born with that ignorance, he was afraid — so the knowledge of unity would be useless in the case of everybody and should it be urged that the knowledge prevailing at the last moment only removes ignorance, then it cannot be laid down as a rule since ignorance may appear again just as it did before. Therefore, the knowledge of unity serves no useful purpose. Here it may be stated that the knowledge sprang from his perfected birth. As we see that when a person is born with a select body and organs as a result of his past merits, he excels in knowledge, intelligence and memory, similarly, Viraj, having burnt all his evils, which produce qualities, the very opposite of righteousness, knowledge, dispassion and lordship, had a perfected birth in which he was possessed of a pure body and organs ; hence he might well have the knowledge of unity without any instruction. As per samriti, the Lord of the universe is born with these four virtues — infallible knowledge, dispassion, lordship and righteousness.

He was not at all happy. Therefore, people still are not happy when alone. He desired a mate. He became big as man and wife embracing each other. He parted this very body into two. From that came husband and wife. Therefore, this body is one half of oneself, like one of the two halves of a split pea. Therefore, this space is indeed filled by the wife. He was united with her and from that union, men were born. But then the women thought as to how he could be united with her after producing her from himself. She thought of hiding herself. She became a cow, then the other became a bull and was united with her — and from that cows were born. The one became a mare, the other a stallion; the one became a she ass, the other became a he ass and was united with her and from that one hoofed animals were born. Thus did he project everything that exists in pairs, down to the anṭs. He knew that he indeed was the creator for he projected all this. Therefore, he was called creator. He, who knows this as such becomes a creator in this creation of Viraj. He rubbed back and forth thus and produced fire from its sources, the mouth and the hands. Therefore, both these are without hair at the inside. Where they talk of particular gods saying 'Sacrifice to him', 'Sacrifice to the other one', they are wrong since these are all his projections for he is all the gods. Now all this that is liquid, he produced from the seed. That is 'Soma'. This universe is indeed this much — food and the eater of the food. 'Soma' is food, and fire the eater of food. This is the super creation of Viraj that he projected the gods, who are even superior to him. Because he, although mortal himself, projected the immortals, therefore, this is the super-creation. He, who knows this as such becomes a creator in this super creation of Viraj. It is well- known from shrutis, and samritis that the Brahmins have fire as their deity, and their strength lies in their mouth. Similarly, from his arms, which are the abode of strength, he manifested Indra and other gods, who control the Kshatriya caste. Therefore, we know from the shrutis and samrities that the Kshatriyas and physical strength are presided over by Indra. Similarly, from his thighs, which are the source of effort, he manifested the Vasus and other gods, who control the Vaisyas. Therefore, Vaisyas are devoted to agriculture and other such pursuits, and have the Vasus etc. as their deities. Similarly, from his foot, he manifested Pusan, the deity of the earth and the Sudras, who have the capacity to serve — as we know from the Shrutis and Samrities. The aim of this narration is not to describe creation but to indicate that all the gods are but Viraj, as stated here, for manifested objects are not different from the manifestor and the gods have been manifested by Viraj.

This universe was then undifferentiated. It differentiated only into name and form — it was called such and such and was of such and such form. This self has entered into these bodies upto the tip of the nails — as a razor may be put in its case, or as fire, which sustains the world, may be in its source. People do not see it for it is incomplete. When it does the function of living, it is called the vital force ; when it speaks, the organ of speech; when it sees, the eye ; when it hears, the ears and when it thinks, the mind. These are merely its names according to functions. He, who meditates upon each of this totality of aspects, does not know, for it is complete, being divided from this totality by possessing a single characteristic. The self alone is to be meditated upon, for all these are unified in it. Of all these, this self alone should be realised, for one knows all these through it, just as one may get an animal through its foot prints. He, who knows it as such, obtains fame and association with his relatives.

Like the reflection of the sun etc. in water, the entrance of the self means only its living perceived like a reflection in the differential universe. Before the manifestation of the latter, the self is not perceived, but after it is manifested, the self is perceived within the intellect, like the reflection of the sun etc. in water and the like. This is self entering into the body. Piercing the dividing line of the head, it entered through that gate, and that deity (existence) thought, 'Well let me enter into these three gods, fire, water and earth, as this individual self etc. Then it knew only itself, therefore, it became all'. The knower of Brahma attains the highest and 'He, who knows that. Brahma becomes Brahma'. Upto the tip of the nails is the intelligence of the self perceived. As in the world a razor may be put in its case, the barber's instrument bag — the razor is perceived as being within— it or as fire, which sustains the world, may be in its source, wood etc. — as a razor lies in one part of the case or as fire lies in the wood pervading it, so does the self reside in the body pervading it in a general and particular way. People do not see it, realise the self that has thus entered into the body and does the above functions. The vital force etc. are merely its names according to functions, not describing the self as it is. Hence they do not express the entity of the self as a whole. Thus the self is differentiated by the activities of living etc. into name and form such as the vital force, which are engendered by those different activities and is manifested at the same time but not realised as a whole. He, who meditates through his mind upon each of this totality of aspects doing the functions of living etc., qualified as the vital force or the eye, without combining the other aspects doing particular functions — meditates that this self does not know Brahma, as this self is in complete living divided from this totality of aspects doing the functions of living etc. by possessing a single characteristics, and not including the other characteristics. As long as the man knows the self as such, a possessed of the natural functions, and thinks that it sees, hears, or touches he does not really know the whole self. Therefore, the self alone is to be meditated upon. Combining all the characteristics lies that the self as a whole possesses, it becomes whole (the Self). Further, for all the differences due to the limiting adjuncts such as the vital force and denoted by names arising from the functions of living etc., as described above, are unified in it, become one with the unconditioned self as the different reflections of the sun in water become one in the sun. Also the sentence, 'The self alone is to be meditated upon', is not an original injunction because except the knowledge that arises from the dictum setting forth the nature of the self and refuting the non-self, there is nothing to be done, either mentally or outwardly. An injunction is appropriate only where, over and above the knowledge that arises immediately from hearing a sentence of the nature of an injunction, activity on the part of a man, is easily understood, as in the sentences like, 'One, who desires heaven must perform the new and full moon sacrifices.' *In upanisadas, nothing is spoken of as a means to the attainment of the highest end of man except the knowledge of the identity of the self and Brahma.* The shrutis use the words 'knowledge' and attainment as synonymous. The non-attainment of the self is but the ignorance of it. Hence the knowledge of the self is its attainment too. The attainment of the self cannot be, as in the things other than it, the obtaining of something not obtained before, for here, there is no difference between the person attaining and the object attained. Where the self has to attain something, other than itself, the self is the attainer and the non-self is the object attained. This, not being already attained, is separated by acts such as producing, and is to be attained by the imitation of a particular action with the help of particular auxiliaries, and that attainment of something new is transitory, being due to desire and action that are themselves, the product of a false notion, like the birth of a son etc. in the dream. But this self is the very opposite of that. By the very fact of its being the self, it is not separated by acts such as producing. But although it is always attained, it is separated by ignorance only. Just as when a mother of pearl appears through mistake as a piece of silver, the non-apprehension of the former, although it is being perceived all the while, is merely due to the obstruction of the false impression and its subsequent apprehension is but knowledge for this is what removes the obstruction of false impression, similarly, here also the non-attainment of the self is merely due of the obstruction of ignorance. Therefore, the attainment of it, is simply the removal of obstruction by knowledge, in no other sense it is consistent. Therefore, the shruti, wishing to express the indubitable identity of meaning of knowledge and attainment, says after introducing knowledge, 'May get', for the root 'vid' also means to get. He, who knows the self as described above, obtains 'Kirti' or the knowledge of unity coveted by seekers of liberation and sloka or liberation, which results from that knowledge, get these primary results of knowledge.

There is another reason why the self should be known to the exclusion of every thing else. This self is dearer than a son, dearer than wealth, dearer than everything else, and is innermost. Should a person (holding the self or dear) say to one calling anything else dearer than the self, 'What you hold dear will die' — he is certainly competent to say so — it is indeed true. Therefore, one should meditate upon the self alone as dear. Of him, who meditates upon the self alone as dear, the dear ones are not mortal. Therefore, giving up all other dear things, one should meditate upon the self alone as the dear, who knows that self alone is dear and nothing else and thinks of it with the full conviction that the other things commonly held dear are really anything, but dear — of one possessed of this knowledge, the dear ones are not mortal. Still people say that men think that through the knowledge of Brahma, they shall become all. This self was indeed Brahma in the beginning. It knew only itself as, 'I am Brahma.' Therefore, it became all, and whoever, among the gods knew it, also became that ; and the same happened with sages and men. The sage Vamdeva, while realising this (self) as that, knew 'I was Manu, and the sun', and to this day, whoever is like-manner knows it as 'I am Brahma', becomes all this universe. Even the gods cannot prevail against him, for he becomes their self. While he, who worships another god thinking, 'He is one, and I am another', does not know. He is like an animal to the gods. As many animals serve a man, so does each man serve the gods. Even if one animal is taken away, it causes anguish, then what should one say of many animals. Therefore, it is not liked by them that men should know this. On the basis of scriptural statements, meditation is only an idea and knowledge only removes the false notion, it does not create anything as it is an accepted principle that the scriptures are only informative and not creative. Further, all things spring from definite causes and we also see variety in the universe. Both these shall be inconsistent if things happen spontaneously. Since it is the accepted view of the vedas, samritis, reasoning and tradition that happiness, misery, and the like, are the outcome of one's past work, the gods, or God or time by no means upset the results of work for these depend on requisite factors. Work, good or bad, that men do, cannot come into being without the help of factors such as the gods, time and God and even if it did, it would not have the power to produce results for it is the very nature of work to spring from many causes such as the different factors. Therefore, the gods, God and others being auxiliaries to work, there is nothing to shake one faith in the attainment of its results. Nor can the gods check the result of knowledge as the realisation of Brahma, which is this result, consists in the mere cessation of ignorance. Also it has been suggested that the gods may thwart the attainment of Brahma, which is the result expected from the knowledge of it, but they do not have that power, because this result (the attainment of Brahma), immediately follows the knowledge. As in the world, a form is revealed as soon as the observer's eye is in touch with light, similarly the very moment that one has knowledge of the Supreme self, ignorance regarding it must disappear. Hence the effects of ignorance being impossible in the presence of knowledge of Brahma, like the effects of darkness in the presence of a lamp, whom should the gods thwart and by what means as the knower of Brahma is the self of gods. Since it is so, therefore, the gods can thwart as well as help an ignorant man. As in the world many animals, such as cows or horses serve a man, their owner and controller, so does each ignorant man, equivalent to many animals serves the gods, manes and others.

In the beginning the Kshatriya and other castes were indeed one Brahma only. Being one, he did not flourish. He specially projected an excellent form, the Kshatirya — those, who are Kshatriyas amongst the gods, Indra, Varun, Moon, Rudra, Parjanya, Yama, Death and Isana. Therefore, there is none higher than the Kshatriyas. Hence the Brahmin worships Kshatriya from a lower position in the Rajsuya Sacrifice. He imparts that glory to the Kshatriya. The Brahmin is the source of Kshatriya. Therefore, although the king attains supremacy in the sacrifice, at the end of it, he resorts to the Brahmin, his source. He, who slights the Brahmin, strikes at his own source. He becomes more wicked as one is by slighting one's superior. Even after projecting the Kshatriyas, he (Viraj) did not flourish in his work, as before, for want of someone to acquire wealth. He then projected the Vaish, in order to acquire wealth, which is the means of performing the rites. The Vaisyas are those species of gods, who are designated in groups. The Vaishyas abound in groups, for they succeed in acquiring wealth, mostly in combination, not singly. He still did not flourish, so he projected the sudra caste. In the word 'shudra', there is projected meaning 'Pusan', i.e. who nourishes. This earth is 'Pusan', the shruti itself gives the derivation. For it nourishes all this that exists. Yet he did not flourish. He specially projected the excellant form, righteousness (Dharma) meaning an action approved by scriptures. This righteousness is the controller of the Kshtriyas. Therefore, there is nothing higher than that. So even a weak man hopes to defeat a stronger man through righteousness, as one contending with the king. That righteousness is verily truth. Therefore, they say about a person speaking of truth. 'He speaks of righteousness,' or about a person speaking of righteousness, 'He speaks of truth,' as both of these are but righteousness. Therefore, it is the controller of Kshatriyas. Hence an ignorant man identified with righteousness, in order to practise its particular forms, identifies himself with one or the other of the castes — Brahmin, Kshtriya, Vaish or Shudra — which is the precondition of that practice, and these are naturally the mans that qualify one for the performance of rites.

Now this self (the ignorant man) is an object of enjoyment to all beings. That he makes oblations in the fire and performs sacrifices is how he becomes such an object to the gods. That he studies the vedas is how he becomes an object of enjoyment to the rishis. That he makes offering to the manes and desires children is how he becomes such an object to the manes. That he gives shelter to men as well as food is how he becomes an object of enjoyment to men. That he gives fodder and water to animals is how he becomes such an object to them. And that beasts and birds, and even the ants, fed in his home is how he becomes an object of enjoyment to these. Just as one wishes safety to one's body, so do all beings wish safety to him, who knows it as such. This indeed has been known and discussed. This aggregate of desirable objects, was but the self in the beginning — the only entity. He then desired to have a wife, so that he could born as a child and desired to have wealth, so that he could perform rites. This much is the range of desires. Until he obtained each one of these, he considered himself incomplete. His completeness also comes thus. The mind is his self; speech his wife, the vital force his child; the eye his human wealth, for he obtains it through the eye ; the ear his divine wealth, for he hears of it through the ears and the body is its instrument of rite, as he performs rites through the body. So this sacrifice has five factors, the animals have five factors, the men have five factors, and all that exists, has five factors. He, who knows it as such, attains all this. The desirable objects are wife, son, wealth and rites and the results of the above are the three worlds of men, manes and the gods and the desire for the means viz wife, son etc. is to attain these only. Further, since all undertakings are for the sake of results, the desire for the worlds, being implied for the former desirer is taken as mentioned.

In ancient times, an ignorant man possessed of desires, wished like this, and others before him had also done the same. Such is the way of the world. This creation of Viraj has been like this. It has been said that he was afraid on account of his ignorance; then, prompted by desire, he was unhappy in being alone, and to remove that boredom, he wished for a wife, and he was united with her, which led to this creation. Because it was like this, therefore, to his day in his creation a man being single, before marriage he desired to have a wife so that he be born and to have wealth to perform rites and so on. Then these rites, which represent the activity of the vital force etc. are performed with the help of wealth that is visible to the eye. Hence the eye is human wealth. Wealth is of two kinds — human and other than human. Hence the qualifying word human is to keep out the other kind. Human wealth such as cattle, which is used in ceremonies is seen by the eye, hence the eye stand for it and is called human wealth. The other kind of wealth is ear, which is divine wealth since meditation is concerning the gods, it is called divine wealth as he hears the divine wealth or meditation through the ear. Hence meditation being dependent on ear, it is called divine wealth. The body is the rite. Atman (Self) here means the body and the body stands for the rite because it is the cause of the rite as one performs rites through the body. Although men are also animals and both animals and men have five factors, yet men are qualified for rites and are distinguished from the others. In short, all this, the means and the results of rites that exists, has five factors. He, who knows it as such imagines himself to be the sacrifice, consisting of five factors, attains all this universe as his own self.

Now ignorance has been discussed. It has been said in that connection that an ignorant man worships another god, thinking he is different from himself, and that prompted by desire, he, identifying himself with a particular caste and order of life and being regulated by a sense of duty, performs rites such as making offerings in the fire, which help the gods and others and make him an object of enjoyment to them. And as all beings by their rites individually projected him as their object of enjoyment, so did he by his performance of rites with five factors, such as making offerings in the fire, and projecting all beings as well as the whole universe as his object of enjoyment. Thus every one according to his meditation and rites is both the enjoyer and the object of enjoyment of the whole universe. That is to say, everyone is alternately the cause as well as the effect of every one else. The universe, which the ignorant man, in question, projected as his object of enjoyment through his meditation and rites with material ends having five factors, such as making offerings in the fire, being divided in its entirity into seven parts as causes and effects, is called the seven kinds of food, being an object of enjoyment. Hence he is the father of these different kinds of food. The father produced seven kinds of food through meditation and rites means that the father indeed produced them through meditation and rites. 'One is common to all eaters', means the food that is eaten is the common food of all eaters. He, who adores this food, is never free from evil, for this is general food. Secondly, he apportioned to the gods' means making oblation in the fire and offering presents otherwise to the gods. Therefore, people perform both these. Some, however, say, these two are the new and full moon sacrifices. Therefore, one should not be engrossed with sacrifices for material ends. The third was given to animals — it is milk, as men and animals first live on milk alone. Therefore, they first make a new born baby lick clarified butter or suckle it. And they speak of a new born calf as not yet eating grass. 'On it rests everything, what lives and what does not', means that on milk indeed rests all this that lives and that does not. It is said that by offering milk in the fire for a year, one conquers further death. One should not think like that. The father produced them through meditation and rites means that the ignorant man is the father of the means, beginning with wife and ending with the rites, whereby the worlds are achieved as the result and it has also been stated in the passage. 'Let me have a wife, etc.' Then it has been said that meditation, which is divine wealth, rites and son are the means whereby father projects the worlds which are the results. Hence it is right to say when the father produced them through meditation and rites, why are the foods not exhausted although continuously eaten, because the being is the cause of their permanence. Just as in the beginning, the father was the producer of the different kinds of food through his meditation and rites with five factors, such as wife etc. and their eater too, so those to whom he gave the foods, although they are their eaters, are their fathers as well, as they produce them through meditation and rites. Thus The being, who eats the food, is cause of this permanence, he himself being permanent. The remaining three he designed to himself means; the mind, the organ of speech and the vital force, these he designed for himself. Some people say, 'I was absent-minded, I did not see it', 'I was absent minded. I did not hear it'. It is through the mind that one sees and hears. Desire, resolve, doubt, faith, want of faith, steadiness, unsteadiness, shame, intelligence, and fear — all these are but the mind. Even if one is touched from behind, one knows it through the mind ; therefore, the mind exists and any kind of sound is but the organ of speech as it serves to determine a thing, but it cannot itself be revealed. Prana, Apana, Vyana, Udana, Samana and Ana — all these are but the vital forces. This body is identified with these — with the organ of speech, the mind and the vital force. The three be designed for himself means : the mind, the organ of speech and vital force are the three kinds of food. Thus the father after producing them at the beginning designed for himself. Regarding absent-mindedness, it may be stated that there is something other than eye or ear who see and hear and it is mind. It joined itself to the objects of all organs; exists in the absence of which the eye and the other organs fail to perceive their respective objects such as form and sound, although they have the capacity to do so and in the presence of which, they succeed in it. Hence it is through the mind that everybody sees and hears for vision, hearing etc., are impossible when the mind is engaged. Then what is the nature of mind is desire, sex, attraction and the like, resolve, deciding about a thing which is before us that it is white or blue and so as, doubt, notion of uncertainty, faith, belief in the efficiency of rites directed to invisible ends as well as in the existence of gods and the like, want of faith, the opposite notion, steadiness etc. when they droop, shame, fear etc. are all but the mind. They are forms of the mind or the internal organ. As already stated, another reason for the existence of mind, is knowledge when one is touched from behind. The sound is uttered of creatures through organ of speech, i.e., the function of the organ of speech is to reveal.

Now the vital force is described 'Prana', the function of which is connected with the heart and is capable of moving to the mouth and nostrils, so called because it moves forward. 'Apana', which functions below the heart and extends upto navel, is called 'Apana', because it helps excretion. 'Vyana' is which regulates the 'Prana' and 'Apana' and is the nexus between them as also the cause of actions requiring strength. 'Udana' causes nutrition, rising up and so on, it extends from the sole of feet to the head and functions upwards. 'Samana' assimilates, what we eat and drink, it has its seat in the belly and helps the digestion of food. 'Ana' is the generalisation of these particular functions and is concerned with the general activities of the body. Thus all these functions of the 'Prana' and the rest, as described above, are but the vital force (Prana).

The organs of speech, the mind and the vital force are the three worlds called the earth, sky and heaven. The organ of speech is this world ; the mind is the sky and the vital force is that world (Heaven). Also there are three vedas ; the organ of speech is Rig veda. The mind is Yajur Veda ; and the vital force is Sama Veda. These are also three (lokas) — the gods, the manes and the men. The organ of speech is the gods; the mind, the manes and the vital force, the men. These are father, mother and son too. The mind is father, the organ of speech, the mother and the vital force is the child. These are what is known, what is desirable to know and what is unknown. Whatever is known is a form of the organ of speech, for it is the knower. The organ of speech protects him, who knows this by becoming that which is known. Whatever it is desirable to know, is a form of the mind for mind is what it is desirable to know ; the mind protects him, who knows this by becoming that which it is desirable to know. Whatever is unknown is a form of the vital force, as the vital force is what is unknown. The vital force protects him, who knows this by becoming that which is unknown. Now since the organ of speech, the mind and the vital force, have been divided into forms of what is known, what it is desirable to know and what is unknown, the statements, 'These are the three worlds' and so on are to be accepted solely on the authority of the shruti. Since we see these three forms viz what is known etc. are applicable to every thing ; It is from the statement of shruti that we are to understand that the meditation is to be confined to the particular objects as indicated. The vital force protects him by becoming that i.e. becomes his food in the form of what is unknown. We often see that the teachers and parents, for instance, help their pupil and children, barely suspected by or unknown to them. Similarly, the mind and the vital force can be the food of the sage, barely suspected by and unknown to him respectively.

Now regarding the manifestation of the speech, mind and vital force relating to the gods is that the earth is the body of that organ of speech, and the fire is its luminous organ. And as far as the organ of speech extends, so far extends the earth and so far does the fire. Heaven is the body of the mind and sun is its luminous organ and as far as the mind extends, so far extends heaven and so far the sun. The two were united and from that the vital force emanated It is the Supreme Lord. It is without a rival. The second being is indeed a rival. He, who knows it as such has no rival. Water is the body of this vital force, and that moon is its luminous organ. And as far as the vital force extends, so far extends water and so far does the moon. These are all equal and all infinite. But, he who meditates upon these as finite, wins an infinite world.

The Prajapati (Hiranyagarbha) has sixteen digits and is represented by the year. The nights and days are his fifteen digits and the constant one is his sixteenth digit. He, as the moon, is filled as well as wasted by the nights and days. Through the sixteen digits, he permeates all the living beings on the new-moon night and rises the next morning. Therefore, on this night, one should not take the life of living beings, not even of a chameleon in adoration of this deity alone. Further, the Prajapati, who has sixteen digits and is represented by the year, is his fifteen digits and the body his sixteenth digit. He is filled as well as wasted by wealth. This body stands for a nave, and wealth is the felloe. Therefore, if a man loses everything, but he himself lives, people say that he has only lost his outfit. It has thus been expanded how a man by the performance of rites with five factors, combined with meditation, the divine wealth, becomes the Prajapati consisting of the three kinds of food. And it has also been said that wealth such as the wife stands for the outfit. In the previous portion, it has only been known in a general way that sons, rites, and meditation lead to the attainment of the worlds, but not that there is a very definite relation between them and those results. This relation between the means such as the son and the particular results has to be stated. There are indeed three worlds, the world of men, the world of manes and the world of the gods. The world of the men is to be won through the son alone and by no other rites ; the world of manes is to be won through rites and the world of the gods through meditation. The world of the gods is the best of the worlds. Therefore, they praise meditation.

Thus the three means called the son, rites and meditation, have been connected with their respective results, the three worlds. A wife, being an aid, to the obtaining of a son and the performance of rites, is not a separate means, and has, therefore, not been separately mentioned. Wealth too, being an aid to the performance of rites, is not a separate means. It is a well-known fact that meditation and rites lead to the winning of the worlds by merely coming into existence. But one does not know how a son, not being of a nature of an activity, can help to win them. Now, therefore, follows the entrusting. This is the name of the rite, because a father in this manner entrusts his own duties to his son. Where a man, a father, on account of some omen or otherwise, thinks, he will die, he says to his son, 'You are Brahma, you are the sacrifice and you are the world'. The son replies, 'I am the Brahma, the sacrifice and the world'. Thinking the meaning of these sentences to be hidden, the ṣhruti proceeds to explain them. Whatever is studied or remains to be studied, is all unified in the word 'Brahma'. That is 'Let the study of vedas which so long was my duty, be henceforth done by you for you are Brahma'. Similarly, whatever sacrifices there are, that were to be performed by me, whether I have performed them or not, are all unified in the word 'Sacrifice'. That is 'Let whatever sacrifices I was to perform, be henceforth performed by you, for you are the sacrifice and whatever worlds there are that were to be won by me, whether I have won them or not, are all unified in the word 'World'. Henceforth you should win them as you are the world. From now onwards I entrust to you the resolve, which was mine of dutifully undertaking study, sacrifices and the conquest of the worlds and I am freed from the resolve concerning these ties of duty'. All this the son accepted as it was, having been instructed to that effect. When a father, who has entrusted his resolve about his duties to his son departs from this world, he penetrates or pervades his son together with the organ of speech, the mind and the vital force, which are under consideration. Should anything, any duty, be left undone by the father, through any slip or omission, the son exonerates him from all that unfulfilled duty of his standing as are obstacles to his attainment of the world, by fulfilling it himself. Therefore, because he saw his father by fulfilling his duties, he is called a 'Putra' (a son). Divine and immortal speech, mind and vital force, pertaining to Hirnyagarbha, permeat him (the father), who has entrusted his duties to his son. The son, rites and meditation lead respectively to the world of men, of the manes and the gods. If one has a son and at the same time performs rites and meditation together, one turns away from the three worlds and through the knowledge of the Supreme self, attains liberation. Hence the means such as the son, lead indirectly to liberation itself. Similarly, the divine mind from heaven and the sun permeats him and that is the divine mind, being naturally pure, through which only, he becomes happy and never mourns not being connected with the causes of grief. Likewise, the divine vital force from water and the moon permeates him. That is the divine vital force, which, when it moves or does not move, feels no pain nor is injured. He, who knows as above, becomes the self of all beings. As is this deity (Hiranyagarbha) so is he. As all beings take care of this deity, so do they take care of him. However, these beings may grieve, that grief of their's is connected with them. But only merit goes to him. No demerit ever goes to gods.

It has been said above that he becomes the self of all beings, hence being identified with the bodies and organs, he may be affected by their joys and sorrows. In this connection, it may be stated that it is not so as his understanding is not limited. It is those, that identify themselves with limited objects, who are seen to be affected by sorrow when, for instance, they are aroused by anybody, thinking he has abused them. But this sage, who is the self of all has no particular notion of identity with either the object that is abused the agency that abuses and cannot, therefore, be miserable on that account.

Let us now consider about the 'Vow'. Prajapati projected the organs. These, on being projected, quarrelled with one another. The organ of speech took a vow 'I will go on speaking'. The eye 'I will see'; the ear, 'I will hear' and so did the other organs according to their functions. Death captured them in the form of fatigue — it overtook them, and having overtaken them, it controlled them. Therefore, the organ of speech invariably gets tried, and so do the eyes and the ears. But death did not overtake the vital force in the body. The organs resolved to know it, 'This is the greatest among us that when it moves or does not move, feels no pain nor is injured'. Well, let us all be of its 'form'. So they all assumed its form. Therefore, they are called by this name of 'Prana'. That family in which a man is born, who knows as above, is indeed named after him and he, who competes, with one, who knows as above, shrivels, and after shrivelling, dies at the end. This is with reference to the body. Here is concluded the subject of meditation on the vital force as identical with oneself in so far as it relates to the body.

Now with reference to gods : Fire took a vow ' I will go on burning'. The sun 'I will give heat'. The moon, 'I will shine'. And so did other gods according to their functions. As is the vital force in the body among these organs, so is 'Vayu' (Air) among these gods. Other gods sink, but not air. Air is the deity that never sets. The gods observed the vow of that from which the sun rises and in which it sets. It is followed today and it will be followed tomorrow. The sun indeed rises from the vital force and also sets in it. What these gods observed then, they observe to this day. Therefore, a man should observe a single vow — do the functions of the 'Prana' and 'Apana' (Respiration and excretion), lest the evil of death (fatigue) should overtake him and if he observes it, he should seek to finish it. Through it, he attains identity with this deity or lives in the same world with it. But the vow of the organ of speech etc. and of fire and the rest is broken as we see that at the time of setting and when one falls asleep, they sink in air and the vital force respectively. Similarly, when a man sleeps, his organ of speech is merged in the vital force, and so are the mind, the eye and the ear. And when he awakes, these again arise from the vital force. This is with reference to the body. With reference to gods when fire goes out, it sets in air, then it is said to have set. It indeed sets in the air and when the sun sets, he enters air and so does the moon ; the quarters too rest on air, and they again arise from the air. Infact, the vocal and other organs in all beings as well as fire and other gods are but a part and parcel of vital force (Prana or air) and the self, (vital force) initiates all movements. He attains identity with this deity, the vital force, or lives in the same world with it. The latter result takes place when the meditation is not up to the mark.

This universe indeed consists of three things — name, form and action. Of these names, speech (sound in general), the source for all names, spring from it. It is their 'Saman' (common feature) as it is common to all names. It is their

Brahma (self) for it sustains all names. The forms like eyes (anything visible), the source for all forms, spring from it. It is their 'Saman' (common feature) as it is common to all forms. It is their Brahma (self) for it sustains all forms. Of action, the body (activity), is the source as all actions spring from it. It is their common feature as it is common to all actions. Also it is their Brahma as it sustains all actions. These three together are one — this body, and the body though one, is these three. This immortal entity is covered by truth (the five elements). The vital force is the immortal entity and name and form are truth, so this vital force is covered by them.

Now of all particular actions, the body i.e., activity in general is the source. Hence action or activity in general, having its seat in the body, is designated as body. The whole differentiated and undifferentiated universe is this much — consists of name, form and action and the body although one viz the aggregate of body and organs, yet existing in different forms in its aspects relating to the body, the elements and the gods, is these three — name, forms and action. This entity is covered by truth.

The self alone is to be meditated upon and to search after it, is to search after everything and that self being dearer than everything else, is to be searched after. The passage, 'It knew only itself,' as 'I am Brahma', shows that the self alone is the subject matter of the knowledge. And what is concerned with seeing differences is the subject matter of ignorance, indicated in the passages, 'He is one and I am another', does not know. 'It should be realised in one form only'. 'He goes from death to death who sees difference as it were in it'. In such passages, as these, all upanisadas differentiate the subject matter of knowledge from that of ignorance. Here the great abstruseness of Brahma is set forth in elaborate detail in the conversation between Saklaya and Yajnavalkya. Hence the attempt to present the truth in the form of a story comprising a prima facic view and a conclusion is quite reasonable. Moreover, the story is meant to teach rules and conduct. The story also forbids the use of mere argumentation as given out in shruti, and smriti passages 'This understanding is not to be attained through argument', and 'To one who has been burnt by logic-chopping, this instruction is not to be given'. Therefore, 'One, who has faith, attains knowledge', says samriti. There was in ancient times a man holding the prima facie view and knowing only the conditioned Brahma, which is the subject matter of ignorance. Of the Garga family, descended from a Proud Balky. 'Proud because of his very ignorance about the real Brahma and Balaki the son of a Balaka. Who was a speaker is one skilled in expounding eloquent. He said to Ajatshatru, the king of Banaras, after approaching him 'I will tell you about Brahma' and Ajatshatru undertook to give one thousand cows for this. Gargya said, 'The being, who identifies himself both with the seen and the eye and who, having entered the body through the eye, resides in the heart as the ego — the experiencer and agent — that being I meditate or look upon as Brahma in this aggregate of body and organs. Therefore, 'I ask you to meditate upon that being as Brahma'. Ajatshatru said, 'Please do not talk about him, this Brahma, as something to be known.' 'When both of us know the same Brahma, you insult me by trying to make me out as ignorant. If you know of any other Brahma, you should tell me of that and not of what I already know. If, however, you think that I know only Brahma, but not his particular attributes nor the result of meditating upon them, please donot think so as I know all that you speak of. As, all surpassing, who exists surpassing all beings, also the head of all beings, and resplendent, being endowed with resplendence. I Meditate upon the Brahma with these attributes as the agent and experiencer in this aggregate of body and organs'. And one, who meditates upon such conditioned Brahma, obtains results accordingly. He, who meditates upon him as such, becomes all-surpassing, the head of all beings and resplendent, for the results must correspond with the particular attributes meditated upon. As shruti says, 'one becomes exactly as one meditates upon him'. 'Gargya said, 'that being, who is in the moon. I meditate upon as Brahma'. Ajatshatru said, 'Please do not talk about him, I meditate upon him as the great, white - robed radiant Soma, and he, who meditates upon him as such has abundant Soma pressed in his principal and auxiliary, sacrifices every day and his food never gets short.' Then Gargya said , 'I meditate upon lighting as Brahma. Ajatshatru said, 'I meditate upon him as powerful and he, who meditates upon him as such becomes powerful and his progeny too becomes powerful. Then Gargya said there is one God in the ether, enclosed by heart and in the heart. Ajatshatru said, 'I meditate upon him as full and unmoving, and he, who meditates upon him, as such, is filled with progeny and cattle and his progeny is never extinct from this world. Likewise, there is one god in air, the vital force and the heart. The Lord irresistible and the unvanguished army one that has never been defeated by enemies, are the attributes. 'Army' because the Maruts (the air god) are known to be a group and the result of the meditation is that he ever becomes victorious and invincible by enemies and conquers his enemies. Gargya then said he meditates upon fire as Brahma. Ajatshatru said he meditates upon him as forbearing and he who meditates upon him as such becomes forbearing and his progeny too becomes forbearing, tolerant of others. Gargya then said he meditate upon water as Brahma but Ajatshatru said he meditate upon water as agreeable and so has only agreeable things coming to him and not contrary ones and also from him are born children, who are agreeable i.e. obeying the scriptures. Gargya said he meditates upon the being in the looking glass as Brahma.

Ajatshatru said he meditates upon him as shining and who meditates upon him as such becomes shining. The progeny too is included in the result because there are many shining objects. Gargya said he meditates upon the sound that issues behind a man as he walks as Brahma. Ajatshatru said he meditates upon him as life and attains his full term of life in this world and life does not depart from him before the completion of that term. Gargya said he meditates upon quarters (directions) as Brahma. Ajatshatru said he meditates upon him as non-separating and who meditates upon him gets companions and his followers never depart from him i.e. he is never deserted by his men. Gargya said he meditate shadow as Brahma. Ajatshatru said, he meditates upon him as death. And he who meditates upon him as such attains his full term of life within world and death does not overtake him before that term. Gargya said, he meditates upon self as Brahma. Ajatshatru said he meditates upon him as self-possessed and its meditator becomes self-possessed and his progeny too becomes self possessed.

When his conceptions of Brahma were thus rejected, one by one, owing to the king having already known them, Gargya, with his knowledge of Brahma, exhausted and had nothing more to say in reply and remained silent with his head bent down. Ajatshatru said by knowing this much, one cannot know Brahma. Then Gargya approached him as his student. But Ajatshatru said that it was contrary to usage that a Brahmin should approach a Kshatriya for teaching about Brahma. Still he undertook to instruct him. He took Gargya by hand and rose and came to a man, who was asleep in a certain part of the palace. He addressed the sleeping man by names 'Great, white robed, radiant Soma.' The sleeping man did not get up. The king then pushed him with the hand till he awoke. From this, it is evident that the being, whom Gargya wanted to convey, was not Brahma, the agent and experiencer in this body. Further, if the Brahma meant by Gargya were the experiencer by its very nature, it would perceive objects whenever it came in contact with them. For instance, fire, whose nature it is to burn and illumine, must always burn any combustible it gets, such as straw or tender grass and also illumine things. If it does not, we cannot assert that fire burns or illumines. Likewise, if the vital force advocated by Gargya were by nature such that it would perceive sound and other objects that came within its range, it would perceive the words great, white robed, etc. which are appropriate objects for it. It can, therefore, be said that it is not by nature, an experiencer, for a thing can never change its nature, and, therefore, it is conclusively proved that vital force is not the experiencer. Similarly, none of the organs can be put forward as the experiencer, for in that case it would be impossible to connect memory, perception, wish etc. in the same subject as in the case of different bodies. What one person has seen, another cannot recollect, or perceive, or wish or recognise. Therefore, none of the organs can by any means, be the experiencer. Nor can mere momentary consciousness be such. Moreover, the vital force, being a compound, must be for the benefit of some other entity. Like the post etc. of a house, it is the internal supporter of the body and is combined with the body etc. It is also as a felloe is to the spokes. And in it, which is comparable to a nave, everything is fixed. Therefore, we understand that like a house etc. it has been compounded for the benefit of some entity, categorically different from its parts as also its aggregate. Since the deity (called the vital force) is conscious, it is equal in status to the self, then how can it be subordinate to the other. In this connection the position is that the relation of principal and subordinate is only for the dealings of the differentiated or conditioned Brahma, and not the opposite one, whereas the whole upanisada seeks to teach about the unconditioned Brahma for it concludes with, 'This self is that which has been described as "Not this, not this", etc. Therefore, it is proved that there is a conscious Brahma other than and different from these types of unconscious Brahmas, such as sun etc.

Ajatshatru said, 'When this being full of consciousness (identified with the mind) was thus asleep, where was it, and whence did it thus come' ? Gargya did not know that. He told that when the being, full of consciousness is thus asleep, it absorbs at the time the function of the organs, their capacity to perceive their respective objects, through its own consciouness, the particular manifestation in its limited adjunct, the mind caused by its material, ignorance and lies in the space (Akasa) that is in the heart. Space here means the Supreme self, which is identical with its ownself. It lies in that Supreme self, which is its own nature and transcendent, not in the ordinary ether, for there is another shruti in its support : 'With existence, my dear, it is then united'. The idea is that it gives up its differential forms, which are created by its connection with the limiting adjunct, the subtle body, and remains in its undifferentiated natural, absolute self. During sleep, the organs of speech, eye, ear and the mind are absorbed. Therefore, the organs being absorbed, the self rests in its own self, for then it is no more changed into action, its factors and its results.

When it thus remains in the dream state, these are its achievements. It then becomes an emperor, as it were, or a noble Brahmin, as it were, or attains states high or low, as it were. As an emperor, talking to his citizens, moves about as he pleases in his own territory, so does it, thus taking the organs, move about as it pleases in its own body. Further, since in dream, which is a kind of experience, the impressions of past experiences are objects, we know that they are not attributes of the self, and that for this reason, it is pure. Now in the passage, 'Hence it moves about as it pleases', movement at pleasure has been spoken of. It may be urged that the relation of the seer to the objects is natural and that, therefore, it becomes impure. Hence to establish its purity, the shruti says, 'Again when it becomes fast asleep when it does not know anything it comes back along the seventy - two thousand nerves called HITA, which extends from the heart to the pericardium (the whole body), and remains in the body. As a baby, or an emperor, or a noble Brahmin lives, having attained the acme of bliss, so does it remain.' The heart is in the seat of the intellect, the internal organ, and the other or external organs are subject to that intellect abiding in he heart. Therefore, in accordance with the individual's past actions, the intellect in the waking state extends, along those nerves, interwoven like a fish net, the functions of the organs such as the ear to their seats, the outer ear etc. and then directs them.

The questions raised by the shruti are 'Where was it then and whence did it come ? Now that in which a thing exists, is its container and what is there is the content, and the container and content are observed to be different. Similarly, that from which a thing comes is its starting place and that which comes is the agent, which is observed to be different from the other. Therefore, one would be apt to think, in accordance with convention, that the self was somewhere, being different from that place and came from somewhere being different from it and the means by which it came is also different from it. That idea has to be removed by the answer. So, this self was not in any place different from itself nor did it come from any place different from itself, what then is the import ? That the self was in its own self. This is born out by shruti passages, 'It merges in its own self', 'With existence, my dear, it is then united'. 'Fully embraced by the Supreme self', 'Rest on the Supreme self' etc. For the same reason, it does not come from any place different from itself. This is shown by the text itself. 'From this self', etc. for there is no other entity besides the self. As a spider moves along the thread, it produces, and as from a fire, tiny sparks fly in all directions, so from this self emanate all organs, all worlds, all gods and all beings. Its secret name is the 'Truth of truth'. The vital force is truth and it is the truth of that. The secret name in upanisada of this self or Brahma etc. means that which brings one near 'Brahma', that is a word denoting it a name. That this capacity to 'Bring near' is a speciality of this particular name, is known on the authority of the scriptures alone. What is this secret name, 'The truth of truth'. Since this secret name always has a transcendental import, it is difficult to understand. Therefore, the shruti gives its meaning : The vital force is truth and it is the truth of that. The text says the origin of the universe from a self, which awoke on being pushed with the hand, which perceives sound etc., and which is possessed of a distinct state, profound sleep. To be explicit there is no Supreme self devoid of the desire for food etc., which is the ruler of universe because the shruti mentions the rousing of the sleeping man by pushing with the hand — thereby showing him to be the perceiver of sound etc. — and describing his transition through the dream state to that of profound sleep, shows the origin of the universe from that very self, possessed of the state of profound sleep by the illustrations of spider and the fire. Therefore, 'Self alone is to be meditated upon'. This self is dearer than a son, dearer than wealth etc. It knew only itself as "I am Brahma" etc. would be consistent if there were no Supreme self. It will also be said further on to be the self. Moreover, in all vedanta, it is the inner self which is put forward as the entity to be know as 'I am Brahma' and never any external object like sound etc. saying "That is Brahma". Similarly' in upanisada "Do not seek to know about speech, know the speaker" etc. it is the agent, the individual self using speech etc. as instruments, which is put forward as the entity to be known. Hence one should wish to worship Brahma with flowers, water, folding of the palms, praises, prostration, sacrifices, pursuits, repetition of its name, meditation, yoga etc. Knowing it through worship, one becomes Brahma, the ruler of all. But one should not think of the transcendent Brahma as the relative self; it would be like thinking of fire as cold and the sky as possessed of form. The scriptural passages too that teach the identity of the self with Brahma, should be taken as merely eulogistic. This interpretation will also harmonise with all logic and common sense.

If the individual self be a modification of Supreme self, there may be the following alternatives :

1. The Supreme self may be an aggregate of many things and consist of parts, like the substance earth, and the individual self may be the modification of some portion of it like a jar etc., or
2. The Supreme self may retain its form, and a portion of it be modified like hair or a barren tract, for instance ; or
3. The entire Supreme self may be modified like milk etc.

Now in the first view according to which, a particular thing out of aggregate of a great many things of the same category, becomes the individual self since this particular thing is only of the same category, the identity is but fugitive, not real. In that case it would be a contradiction of the verdict of the shruti. If, however, as in the second view, the Supreme self is a whole, eternally consisting of part inseparably connected together, and while it remains unchanged in form, a portion of it becomes the relative individual self, then since the whole inheres in all parts, it is affected by the merit or defect of each part ; hence the Supreme self shall be subject to the evil of transmigration attaching to the individual self. Therefore, this view also is inadmissible. Now the view that holds that the whole of the Supreme self is transformed disregards all the shrutis and samritis and is, therefore, unacceptable. Therefore, we conclude that the shruti passages setting forth the origin etc. of the universe must be for establishing the identity of the individual self and supreme self. Vedas in this respect say, 'A certain prince was discarded by his parents as soon as he was born and brought up in a fowlers' home. Not knowing his princely descent, he thought himself to be a fowler and pursued the fowlers' duties, not those of a king, as he would, if he knew himself to be such. When, however, a very compassionate man, who knew the prince's fitness for attaining a kingdom, told him who he was — that he was not a fowler but the son of such and such king, and had by some chance come to live in the fowlers' home — he, thus informed, gave up the notion and the duties of a fowler and knowing that he was a king, took to the ways of his ancestors.' Similarly, this individual self, which is of the same category, being separated from it like a spark of fire and so on, has penetrated this wilderness of the body, organs etc. and although really transcends, takes as the attributes of the latters which are relative and thinks that it is this aggregate of the body and organs that it is lean or stout, happy or miserable — for it does not know that it is the Supreme self but when the teacher enlightens it that it is not the body etc., but transcendent Supreme Brahma, then it gives up the pursuit of the three kinds of desires (for a son, wealth and heaven) and is convinced that it is Brahma. Gita too says, 'All beings are in me' etc. Therefore, there is no other entity called the relative self but the supreme Brahma. Hence it is well said in hundreds of shrutis' passages, 'This was indeed Brahma in the beginning, It knew only itself as "I am Brahma" 'There is no other witness but this, no other hearer but this' etc. Therefore, the highest secret name of the "Truth of truth" belongs only to Supreme Brahma. It is said that he who knows the calf with its abode, its special resort, its post and its tether, gets this result. He kills his seven kinsmen. Kinsmen are of two kinds — those who envy and those who do not envy ; here the former are meant. The seven organs (eyes, ears, nostrils and mouth), instruments for perceiving objects, that are in the head, that is to say, the attachment to the sense-objects, which they cause, are called kinsmen since they are born with a person and since they turn his vision from the self to the sense objects, they are envious kinsmen, since they thus hinder him from perceiving the inner self.

Mention has been made of the calf with its abode. Now what is the abode of that calf, that instrument of the self, the vital force, which is here likened to a calf. This body, which is an effect, is its abode. When the organs are withdrawn, the individual self is not noticed, it is only when they occupy their respective seats in the body that the individual self is noticed as perceiving things. This is proved by the sleeping man being roused by pushing with hand. Food is connecting link between the vital force and the body like a calf's tether with a loop at each end. Certain secret names with reference to the eye regarding the calf, living in its special resort, are being mentioned. These seven gods, that prevent decay, worship it. Through these pink lines in the eye, Rudra attends on it, through the water that is in the eye, 'Pranjanya'; through the pupil, the seen; through the dark portion, fire ; through the white portion, Indra; through the lower eye lid, the earth attends on it and through the upper eye lid, heaven. He, who knows it as such never has any decrease of food. Further, regarding this there is a verse. There is a bowl that have its opening below and bulges at the top. Various kinds of knowledge have been put in it. Seven sages sit by its side and the organ of speech, which has communication with the vedas, is the eighth. The bowl that has its opening below and bulges at the top is this head of yours, for it is like the bowl that has its opening below and bulges at the top. Various kinds of knowledge put in it, refer to the organs ; these indeed represent various kinds of knowledge. 'Seven sages sit by its side, refers to the organs ; they indeed are the sages. The organ of speech, which has communication with the vedas, is the eighth, because the organ of speech is the eight and communicate with the vedas. The two ears are Gautama and Bhardavaja there two eye are Viswamitra and Jamadagni. The two nostrils are Vasistha and Kashyapa. The tongue is Atri, for through tongue food is eaten. Atri is but this name 'Atti'. He, who knows it as such, becomes the eater of all and everything becomes his food.

Brahma has two forms — gross and subtle, mortal and immortal ; limited and unlimited ; defined and undefined. The gross form is that which is other than air and the ether. It is mortal, it is limited and it is defined. The essence of that which is gross, mortal, limited and defined is the sun that shines, for it is the essence of the defined. Now the subtle — it is air and the ether. It is immortal, unlimited and undefined. The essence of that which is subtle, immortal, unlimited and undefined is the being that is in the sun, as that is the essence of the undefined. This is with reference to gods. Now with reference to the body, this is the gross form, which is other than the corporeal air and the ether that is in the body. It is mortal, limited and defined. The essence of that, which is gross, mortal, limited, and defined is the eye, for it is the essence of the defined. The subtle, on the contrary, is the corporeal air and the ether that is in the body. It is immortal, unlimited and undefined. Its essence is this being that is in the right eye, for this is the essence of the undefined. The form of that being is like a cloth dyed with turmeric, or like grey sheep's wool; or like the scarlet insect called indragopa; or like tongue of fire; or like a white lotus ; or like a flash of lightening. He, who knows it as such, attains splendour like a flash of lightening. Now, therefore, the description of Brahma, 'Not this, not this', because there is no other and more appropriate description than this "Not this". Its name is "The truth of truth". The vital force is truth and it is the truth of that.

In order to describe the nature of the Supreme self, which is the truth of truth, the latter must be described in its entirety, and impressions being the particular forms of that truth, these forms of the impressions are being mentioned. These are the forms of this being i.e. of the subtle body that is being discussed. As in life we have a cloth dyed with turmeric, so in the presence of objects of enjoyment, the mind gets a similar colouring of impressions, whence a man under such circumstances, is said to be attached, as cloth, for instance, is dyed. Also as sheep's wool is grey, so are some other forms of impressions. The colouring varies according to the objects presented to the mind, and sometimes according to the tendencies of the mind itself. As again a tongue of fire is bright, so are some people's impressions at times. Like a white lotus too, are the impressions of some. As in nature a single flash of lightening illumines everything, so according to the intensity of the manifestation of knowledge do the impressions of some people. It is impossible to ascertain the beginning, middle or end or number, place, time and circumstances of these impressions for they are innumerable and infinite are their causes. Then how through the two terms 'Not this, not this,' is it sought to describe the truth of truth, is by the elimination of all differences due to limiting adjuncts, something that has no distinguishing mark such as name, form, or action or heterogeneity, or species or qualities. Words denote things through one or the other of these. But Brahma has none of these distinguishing marks. Hence it cannot be described as; 'It is such and such' as we can describe a cow by saying, 'There moves a white cow with horns'. Brahma is described by means of name, form and action, super-imposed on it, in such terms as knowledge bliss, Brahma and pure intelligence, and Atma. When, however, we wish to describe its true nature, free from all differences, due to limiting adjuncts, then it is an utter impossibility. Then there is only one way left viz to describe it as "Not this, not this", by eliminating all possible specifications of it that have been known. Since there is no other and more appropriate description of Brahma than this : "Not this, not this". Therefore, this is the one description of Brahma. Its secret name is the 'Truth of truth'. So the Supreme Brahma is the 'Truth of truth'. Therefore, the name of Brahma that has been mentioned is appropriate viz the 'Truth of truth'. The vital force is truth and it is the truth of that truth.

Then the self alone is to be meditated upon. Of all these, the self alone should be realised for it is dearer than a son etc. In the course of explanation of above passages, the aim of knowledge and its relation of that aim have been stated in the sentence 'It knows only itself' as 'I am Brahma.' Therefore, it became all. Thus it has been mentioned that the innerself is the domain of knowledge. While that of ignorance is relative existence, which consists of ends and means of rites with five factors, which again depend on the division of men in four castes, it is by nature alternatively manifest and unmanifest like the tree and the seed and is made up of name, form and action. Regarding relative existence of various gods, he who worships another god thinking 'He is one and I am another,' does not know. This indeed consists of three things : name, form and action, as already stated. One aspect of it is in accordance with the scriptures and makes for progress leading upto the world of Hirnyagarbha, while the other aspect is not in accordance with the scriptures and causes degration down to the level of stationary objects. This has already been dealt with. In order, however, to show how a man disgusted with this domain of ignorance, can qualify himself for the knowledge of Brahma, which deals with the innerself, the entire domain of ignorance has been concluded already. Rites with factors, such as the wife, son and wealth constitute the domain of ignorance, because they do not lead to the attainment of the self. If a thing calculated to produce a particular result is applied to bring about a different result it frustrates its purpose. Running and walking is not the means to appease, one's hunger or thirst. The son and the rest have been prescribed in the shruti as a means to the attainment of the world of men, of the manes and of the gods, not as means to the attainment of the self. They have been mentioned as producing those specific results and they have not been enjoined on the knower of Brahma, being classed by the shruti as rites with material ends, in the passage, 'This much indeed is desire', and the knower of Brahma has already attained all desires; he cannot for that very reason, have any more desires. The shruti too says, 'We, who have attained this self, This world'. On being asked there are two vedic injunctions, 'Perform rites and give up rites, what is the goal of knowledge and what of rites, as these two seemed mutually contradictory and been counter to each other,' Vyasa replied, thereby showing the contradiction, 'Men are bound by rites and freed by knowledge. Hence sages, who have known the truth, never perform rites and so on'. Therefore, the knowledge of Brahma leads to the highest goal for man not with but without the help of any auxiliary means as otherwise there would be contradiction all around. It is to show this that renunciation of the world, which consists in giving up all means, is sought to be enjoined as a subsidiary step. So it has been asserted, 'This much indeed is the means of immortality and we have also a reason for inference about this in the fact that Yajnavalakya, who was a ritualist, renounced the world'. Moreover, the knowledge of Brahma as a means to immortality has been imparted to Meitreyi, who was without the means to perform rites. Also wealth has been deprecated. If rites were means to immortality, the derogatory remarks on wealth would be out of place, since on it, rites with five factors depend. If, however, the rites are desired to be shunned, then it is proper to decry the means to them. Besides, in the state of knowledge, there is an absence of the consciousness about caste, order of life, etc. which are the qualifications for the performance of rites as, 'The Brahmin ousts one', 'the Kshtriya ousts one', etc. For a man, who does not identify himself as Brahmin, Kshatriya or the like, rites and their accessories, which are the effects of that consciousness, are automatically dropped because of the giving up of that consciousness. Therefore, the narration is with a view to enjoining renunciation of the world as part of the knowledge of self.

The sage Yajnavalkya told his wife Maitreyi, that he was going to renounce this house — holder's life and intended to take up the life of renunciation, which is the next higher life. Hence he asked for her permission. He further said that he wished to finish her's and his second wife Katyayani's relations i.e. put an end to the relationship that existed between them through him, the common husband, by dividing his property between them. He desired to separate them through wealth and go. Thereupon Maitreyi said, 'Sir if indeed this whole earth, full of wealth, be mine, shall I be immortal through that ?' 'No' replied Yajnavalkya, 'Your life will be just like that of people, who have plenty of things but there is no hope of immortality through wealth'.

Then Maitreyi asked as to what shall she do with that which would not make her immortal. She asked for that alone which he knew to be only means of immortality. Yajnavalkya told that, she had been his beloved even before, and she asked what was in her heart and told her to take her seat and listen to him and as he explained, she should meditate on its meaning. With a view to teaching renunciation as a means to immortality, Yajnavalkya creates a distaste for the wife, husband, sons etc. so that, they may be given up. He said, 'It is not for the sake of or necessity of the husband that he is loved by the wife but it is for her own sake that he is loved by her. Similarly, it is not for the sake of wife, etc., that she is loved by husband but for his own sake. Likewise it is not for the sake of the sons, wealth, the Brahmin, the Kshatriya, worlds, the gods, beings etc. that they are loved for their sake but for one's own sake. Hence it is a well-known fact that the self alone is dear and nothing else. Self is dearer than a son etc. too. Therefore, our love for other objects is secondary since they contribute to the pleasures of the self and our love for the self alone is primary. Therefore, the self should be realised, it is worthy of realisation and should be made the object of realisation. It should first be heard of from a teacher, and from the scriptures, then reflected on through reasoning and then steadfastly meditated upon'. Thus only is it realised — when these means viz. hearing, reflection and meditation, have been gone through ; when these three are combined, then only true realisation of the unity of Brahma is accomplished, not otherwise — by hearing alone. The different castes, various orders of life and so on upon which rites depend and which consist of actions and their factors and results are objects of notions superimposed on the self by ignorance. This can be known through hearing, reflection and meditation.

The Brahmin ousts slights, one who knows him as different from the self. The Kshatriya ousts one, who knows him different from the self. Worlds oust one, who knows them as different from the self. The gods oust one, who knows them as different from self. Being oust, one, who knows them as different from the self, all oust one, who knows it as different from the self. Infact, Brahmin, Kshatriya, these worlds, gods, beings and these all are this self as when drum is beaten, one cannot distinguish its various particular notes, but they are included in the general note of the drum or in the general sound, produced by different kinds of strokes. Similar is the position of blowing conch, playing vina, and kindling fire gives various kinds of smokes. As ocean is one goal of all sorts of water, as the skin is the one goal of all kinds of touch ; as the nostrils are goal of all odours ; tongue is goal of all savours ; eye is goal of all colours ; ear is goal of all sounds ; manas is the goal of all deliberations; intellect is one goal of all kinds of knowledge; hands are one goal of all sorts of work ; as the organ of generation is goal of all kinds of enjoyments ; anus is goal of all excretion; as the feet is goal of all kinds of walking; organ of speech is goal of all vedas — these are all general functions and nothing but vital force. Upanisada says, 'That which is the vital force is intelligence and that which is intelligence is the vital force. As a lump of salt dropped into water dissolves with its components in water and no one is able to pick it up, but from wherever one takes it, it tastes salt, even so, this great, endless, infinite reality is but pure intelligence. The self comes out as a separate entity from these elements and this separateness is destroyed with them. After attaining this oneness, the self freed from body and organs has no more particular consciousness as 'I so and so am the son of so and so ; this is my land and wealth; I am happy or miserable'. For it is due to ignorance, and since ignorance is absolutely destroyed by the realisation of Brahma, the knower of Brahma, who is established in his nature as pure intelligence, cannot possibly have any such particular consciousness. Even when a man is in the body, particular consciousness is sometimes impossible, therefore, it can never exist in a man, who has been absolutely freed from the body and organs. This is the philosophy of highest truth. Maitriyi told that she has been put to confusion by knowing that after attaining oneness, the self has no more consciousness. Yajnavalkya said he was not saying any thing confusing and that it was quite sufficient for knowledge. He did not also attribute pure intelligence and absence of consciousness to the same entity. What he said was when that individual existence of the self, which is superimposed by ignorance and is connected with the body and organs, is destroyed by knowledge, the particular consciousness, connected with the body etc., consisting of a false notion, is destroyed on the destruction of the limiting adjuncts, the body and organs, for they are deprived of their cause, just as the reflections of the moon etc. and their effects, the light and so forth, vanish when the water and the like, which form their support are gone. But just as the sun, moon, etc., which are the realities behind the reflections, remain as they are, so that pure intelligence, which is the transcendent Brahma, remains unchanged. So it has been referred to as 'Pure Intelligence'. It is the self or the whole universe and does not really pass out with the destruction of the elements. But the individual existence, which is due to ignorance, is destroyed. This self is indestructible. Therefore, this great endless, infinite reality is quite sufficient for knowledge,. He said that the knower's function of knowing can never be lost because it is immortality. Because when there is duality, as it were, then one smells something, one sees something, one hears something, one speaks something, one thinks something, and one knows something. But when to the knower of Brahma, everything has become the self, then what should one smell and through what ; what should one see and through what ; what should one hear and through what ; what should one speak and through what ; what should one think and through what ; what should one know and through what ? Through what should one know that owing to which all this is known, through what should one know the knower ? Even in the state of ignorance, when one sees something, through what instrument should one know that owing to which all this is known? For that instrument of knowledge itself falls under the category of objects. The knower may desire to know, not about itself but about objects. As fire does not burn itself, so the self does not know itself and the knower can have no knowledge of a thing that is not its object. Therefore, through what instrument should one know the knower owing to which this universe is known, and who else should know it ? And when to the knower of Brahma, who has discriminated the real from the unreal, there remains only the subject, absolute and one without a second, through what instrument should one know that knower.

This well-known earth is the honey or effect — being like money — of all beings from Hirnyagarbha down to a clump of grass. Just as a beehive is made by a great many bees, so is this earth made by all beings. Likewise, all beings are the honey or effect of this earth. Also the shining i.e. possessed of the light of intelligence and immortal being, who is in this earth, and the shining, immortal as above — corporeal being in the body i.e. the self as identified with the subtle body ; are like honey — being helpful — to all beings, and all beings are like honey to them. This self knowledge is the means of immortality; this underlying unity is Brahma, this knowledge of Brahma is the means of becoming all in the universe. Similarly, the water, fire, air, sun, quarters (directions), moon, lightening, cloud, ether, righteousness, truth, human species, and cosmic body are identified respectively with seed, organ of speech, vital force, eye, ear, mind, light, sound, ether in the heart, righteousness in the body, truth in the body, human species in the body, individual self, are all self. This self knowledge is the means of the immortality; this underlying unity is Brahma ; This knowledge of the Brahma is the means of becoming all. So this self, as already mentioned, is the ruler of all beings and the king of all beings. Just as all the spokes are fixed in the nave and the felloe of a chariot wheel, so are all beings, all gods, all worlds, all organs and all these individual-selves are fixed in the self. Thus the import of the scripture, that was briefly indicated, has been completely dealt with. Now illustrations are being given to show that in the knower of Brahma, who is the self of all and has realised himself as such, the whole universe is fixed. Just as all the spokes are fixed in the nave and the felloe of a chariot wheel, so are all beings from Hiranyagarbha, down to a clump of grass, all gods, such as fire, all worlds such as this earth, all organs as the organ of speech, and all selves, which penetrate every body like a reflection of the moon in water and are conjured up by ignorance. In short, the whole universe is fixed in the self, i.e. in the knower of Brahma, who has realised his identity with the Supreme self. Considering the scriptural texts, they, with a view to arriving at their true meaning on the strength of their own intellect, put forward fanciful interpretations, as for instance, that the self exists or does not exist, that it is or is not the agent, is free or bound, momentary, mere consciousness, or nothing — and never go beyond the domain of ignorance, because everywhere they see only contradictions. Therefore, those alone, who tread the path shown by shrutis and spiritual teachers, transcend ignorance. They alone will succeed in crossing this unfathomable ocean of delusion, and not those others, who follow the lead of their own clever intellect.

The knowledge of Brahma leading to immortality has been completely dealt with as asked by Maitreyi. In order to extend this knowledge of Brahma, a story is narrated in brief. As the rising sun dispel the gloom of night, so does the knowledge of Brahma, remove ignorance. Being in the custody of Indra, it was difficult even for gods to attain it and was attained after great pains even by the Asvinis, who are doctors to gods. The knowledge of Brahma is further extolled thus. It is well known in the world that rites are the means to attain all our life's ends, and their performance depends on wealth, which cannot possibly confer immortality. This can be attained only through self - knowledge independently of rites. Though it could easily be treated of in the ritualistic position under the 'Pravargya' rites, yet because of its contradiction to rites this self-knowledge, coupled only with renunciation of the world, is discussed as the means of immortality after the portion is passed. This shows that there is no other better means of attaining our life's ends than this. Yajnavalkya, though just like any other man, gave up, through his self-knowledge, his attachment to worldly objects, such as the wife, children and wealth, because satisfied with knowledge, he took delight only in the self. Further, since Yajnavalkya, on the eve of his departure from the worldly life, instructed his beloved wife about it just to please her saying 'You say what is after my heart.' 'Come take your seat', etc. Dadhyac, well-versed in Atharva Veda, dealing with meditation, came to teach. He said that Indra had told him that he would behead him the moment he taught it to anybody, therefore, he was afraid of him. He could, therefore, teach only if assured that Indra shall not behead him. The disciples assured of protection from Indra. On asking how they shall protect, they told, when they are accepted as disciples, they shall cut off his head, remove it elsewhere and preserve it and shall fix a horse's head on him. He shall then teach through that head and during that time Indra shall cut off that head. Then they shall fix his own head. The Brahmin accepted Asvinis' proposal when he started teaching, the Asvinis cut off his head and preserved it and fixed a horse's head. Indra cut off that head and then the Asvinis brought his own head and replaced it on him. On that occasion, however, only that portion of meditation, on things mutually helpful, was taught which formed part of the rite called 'Pravargya', but not the secret portion known as self-knowledge. So this is that meditation on things mutually helpful which Dadhyac, versed in the Atharva Veda taught the Asvinis through this device.

This is that meditation on things mutually helpful which Dadhyac taught the Asvinis. Perceiving this, the Rishi said 'O, Asvinis, you set a horse's head on the shoulders of Dadhyac and to keep his word, he taught you, the ritualistic meditation on things mutually helpful connected with the sun, as also the secret (spiritual) meditation on them'. He made bodies with two feet and bodies with four feet. That Supreme being first entered the bodies as a bird. On account of his dwelling in all bodies, he is called 'Purusa'. There is nothing that is not covered by him and nothing that is not pervaded by him. Then he transformed himself in accordance with each form; that form of his, was for the sake of making him known. The Lord on account of 'Maya' (notions superimposed by ignorance) is perceived as manifold, for to him are yoked ten organs, nay, hundreds of them. He is the organs. He is ten and thousands — many and infinite. That Brahma is without prior or posterior, without interior or exterior. This self, the perceiver of everything, is Brahma. This is the teaching. Therefore, self is known not in its true nature as homogenou's pure intelligence, but merely as the sense-object.

Another story is that there was a ruler of Videha, named Janaka. He performed a sacrifice in which gifts were freely distributed. Or the sacrifice itself may have had that name, Bahu-Dakshina, referred to else - where in vedas. Or the horse sacrifice may here be so called because of the abundance of gifts in it. Vedic scholars from Puru and Panchala — which are famous for their large number of scholars — were assembled in that sacrifice, either on invitation or as spectators. Seeing that large assembly of scholars, Emperor Janaka, the sacrificer, had a desire to know who was the greatest vedic scholar among them. He thought like this : 'Which is the most-erudite of these vedic scholars ? They are all versed in vedas, but which is the greatest of them' ? Being desirous of knowing this, he, as a means to finding it out, had a thousand young cows confined in a pen. On the horns of each cow were fixed ten padas — a pada being a quarter of a 'pala' of gold — five on each horn. He then told them that they were all vedic scholars but let him, who is specially so among them, drive those cows home. None of the Brahmins, so addressed, dared to announce his surpassing vedic scholarship. When they were thus silenced, Yajnavalkya said to a pupil of his to drive those cows home. He drove the cows towards his teacher's home. Yajnavalkya, by accepting the prize meant for the best vedic scholar, indirectly declared himself as such, so the Brahmins were enraged. The reason for their anger was how he dared to call himself the best vedic scholar among them, who are each a great scholar. Among the Brahmins, thus enraged, there was a Hotra of Janaka, the sacrificer named Asvala. He prided himself upon being the greatest vedic scholar and was insolent owing to royal patronage. So he challenged Yajnavalkya as follows : 'Yajnavalkya are you indeed the best vedic scholar among us' ? Yajnavalkya replied, 'I bow to the best vedic scholar, now I just want the cows'. When he accepted the prize meant for the best vedic scholar, the Hotra Asvala determined to interrogate him. He asked, 'When everything is overtaken by death, and swayed by it, by what means does the sacrificer go beyond the clutches of death' ? Yajnavalkya said it was through the organ of speech — through fire, which is the real priest called 'Hotra'. The sacrificer's organ of speech is the 'Hotra'. This organ of speech is fire and this fire is the Hotra ; this fire is liberation and this liberation is emancipation. The emancipation from death here dealt with is the same as that which has been described as a result in the section on the 'Udgitha' in the words, 'That fire having transcended death, shines' etc. He further asked that since all had been overtaken by day and night and swayed by them, by what means the sacrificer go beyond the clutches of day and night. Yajnavalkya replied that it was through the eye— through the sun, which is the real priest called Adhvaryu. The eye of the sacrificer is Adhvaryu. This eye is the sun, and sun is Adhvaryu liberation and liberation is emancipation. Then Hotra asked that since all is overtaken by bright and dark fortnights and swayed by them, by what means does the sacrificer go beyond the bright and dark fortnights ? Yajnavalkya replied, it is through the vital force through air, which is the real priest called 'Udgatra'. The vital force of sacrificer is 'Udgatra'. This vital force is air and 'Udgatra', this air is liberation and liberation is emancipation. Hotra then asked that since sky is, as it were, without a support, through what support does the sacrificer go to heaven. Yajnavalkya replied it is through mind — through the moon, which is the real priest, called Brahmin. The mind of the sacrificer is Brahmin, and this mind is the moon, the moon is Brahmin, the moon is liberation and liberation is emancipation.

So far the narration is about the ways of emancipation, now about the meditation based on resemblance are narrated. By this is meant a meditation, by virtue of some point of resemblance, on rites with inferior results like the Agnihotra, as rites with superior results, in order to obtain these results, or it is a meditation on some part of the lessor rite as those very results. So a man, who regularly tends the sacrificial fire, takes up any rites, such as the Agnihotra, that suits him and if he happens to know the results of particular rites, achieves the results he seeks through meditation. Otherwise it would be impossible even for the people of upper three castes, who are qualified for them to perform the Rajsuya, Aswamedha, Naramedha, or Sarvamedha sacrifices. Hotra then asked as to how many kinds of Rig, will the Hotra do his part in this sacrifice today ? Yajnavalkya replied that it is with three kinds ; which are preliminary, the sacrificial and the eulogistic hymns, and through these he wins all this that is living. Preliminary are the class of hymns, used before a sacrifice; the sacrificial are those hymns that are used in performing sacrifice, and the eulogistic hymns are used in praise to the deities. Every kind of Rig, whether used in praise or otherwise, is included in these three classes. Then Hotra asked how many kinds of oblations will the Adhvaryu offer in the sacrifice today. Yajnavalkya replied these are of three kinds — first those that blaze up on being offered such as oblation of wood; second are those that make of great noise such as flesh; and third are those that sink on being offered, like milk. Through those that blaze up on being offered, he wins the world of gods, as this world shines, as it were. Through those which made noise, when offered, one wins the world of manes; as this world is full of uproar ; and through those that sink, one wins the human world as this world is lower. Hotra asked through how many gods, does this Brahma, from the rites, protect the sacrifice today ? Yajnavalkya said through one, the mind. The mind is indeed infinite, and infinite are the Visvadevas. Therefore, through this meditation, he wins the infinite world. Hotra then asked how many classes of hymns will the 'Udgatra' chant in the sacrifice today. Yajnavlkya replied, three classes — preliminary, sacrificial and eulogistic hymns. 'Prana' is the preliminary hymn, 'Apan' is sacrificial hymn, and the 'Vyana' is the eulogistic hymn. Through preliminary hymns, he wins the earth, through the sacrificial hymns, he wins the sky and through the eulogistic hymns, he wins heaven. Thereupon, the Hotra kept silent.

The emancipation from Death in the form of time as well as rites has thus been explained. Now we have to see as to what is this death, the emancipation from which has been explained. It consists of 'Grahas' (Organs) and 'Atigrahas' (Objects), which are centered in the attachment due to our natural ignorance, and are limited by the objects relating to the body and the elements. Forms, such as fire and the sun, pertaining to one, who has been free from that death consisting in limitation have been explained and some details about them have been given in reply to Hotra. All that is the result of rites, coupled with meditation. Although the nature of an emancipated man has been described, yet such a man is not free from death in the form of the organs and objects. So it has been said with reference to the being, who is in the sun, for hunger is death, and this indeed is death and death through one has many forms. In other words, he alone, who has attained identity with the sun, is spoken of as escaping from the clutches of death, and the organs and objects, which are but forms of death, are not absent in the sun. Heaven is the body of mind and the mind is 'Graha' (organ) ; it is controlled by 'Atigrahas' (objects), desire, 'Prana' is 'Graha' (nose), it is controlled by 'Atigrah' (odour). Speech is 'Grah', controlled by 'Atigrah' name, and so on. He, who resorts to the succeeding forms of death (bodies), is freed from the preceding forms of it, he resorts to the former not to cling to them, but to turn away from them ; so everything is a form of death until duality is at an end and when this takes place, he really transcends death. Hence the intermediate liberation is but a relative and secondary one. Therefore, we conclude that death in the form of the organs and objects is bondage. We do not know the trick of taking up an intermediate position as between waking and sleeping states, it would be as absurd as the same person being one half old and one half young. So the whole range of ends and means constitute bondage, because it is not free from the organs and objects. Only when the fetters are known, can the fettered man try to get rid of them.

Artabhaga asked how many are the 'Grahas' and how many 'Atigrahas'. Yajnavalkya told there are eight-'Grahas' and eight 'Atigrahas'. 'Pran' (nose) is 'Graha' and it is controlled by Atigraha, 'Apana' (odour) for one smells odour with nose presented by air and breathed in 'Apana'.

The order of speech is the 'Graha'. It deals with things to which people are attached and makes utterances that are untrue, pernicious, rude, offensive and so on. It controls people, hence it is 'Graha'. Organ of speech is controlled by

'Atigraha' name, that is by whatever is uttered. As the organ of speech is meant to express something, it is used by that for just that purpose; hence it is controlled by that and there is no deliverance for it, until it has done this function. Therefore, the organ of speech is said to be controlled by 'Atigraha' name as it is a fact that people, impelled by this attachment to something to be expressed, get into all sorts of troubles. Then the tongue is 'Graha' and it is controlled by 'Atigraha' taste as one knows taste through tongue. Eye is 'Graha' and controlled by 'Atigraha', colour, as one sees colours through eye. Ear is 'Graha' and controlled by 'Atigraha' sound, as one hears sound through the ear. Mind is 'Graha', controlled by 'Atigraha', desire as one wishes desires through the mind only. Hands are 'Graha', controlled by 'Atigraha', work as one does work with hands only. The skin is 'Graha', controlled by 'Atigraha', touch as one feels touch through the skin. These are the eight 'Grahas' and 'Atigrahas'. He then asked that since all these are the food of death, who is that god, whose food is death, Yajnavalkya told that 'Fire' is death, it is the food of water and one who knows these, conquers further death. The intention of the question is that if Yajnavalkya mentions the death of death, it will lead to an infinite regress. If, on the other hand, he does not mention it, liberation from this death in the form of 'Grahas' and 'Atigrahas' will be impossible as liberation can take place only when this form of death is destroyed, and this world be possible if there be the death of death even. Hence considering the question unanswerable, he asked, who is that god. Fire is the death of all, being a destroyer, but it is swallowed by water, hence it is the food of water. Therefore, there is death of death and it swallows all the 'Grahas' and 'Atigrahas'. Therefore, one, who knows thus conquers further death. He further asked when, after death has been swallowed by another death viz the realisation of Supreme self, this liberated man of liberation dies, then do his organs such as speech called the 'Graha' and 'Atigraha' such as name, which in the form of impressions, are in him and impel him to action, go up from him, the dying knower of Bŗahma or do they not ? Yajnavalkya replied, 'No, they do not'. The organs and objects, becoming one with the Supreme self, attain identity with or merge in him only, their cause, the man of realisation, who is the reality of the Supreme Brahmin — like waves in the ocean.

The gist of the passage is that, the liberated man, after his bondage has been destroyed, does not go anywhere. Then he asked when this man dies, what is it that does not leave him? Yajnavalkya said, it is 'Name' that is everything is merged only in the name that he is the liberated man, is left because of its relation to the type, for the name is eternal. The name is infinite — the infinity of the name is its eternity — and infinite are the Visvadevas, because they possess the infinity of the name. He, who knows thus wins thereby a really infinite world. Then having identified himself with the Visvadevas, who possess the infinity of the name, he wins through this realisation, nothing less than an infinite world. He then asked when the vocal organ of a man, who dies, is merged in fire, the nose in air, the eye in the sun, the mind in the moon, ear in the quarters (directions) ; the body in the earth ; the ether of the heart in the external ether, the hair on the body in herbs ; that on the head in trees, and the blood and the seed are deposited in water, where is then the man ? Yajnavalkya asked for his hand and they shall decide within themselves as it could not be done in a crowded place. They went out and talked it over. What they mentioned there was only work, and what they praised there was also work alone. Therefore, one becomes 'good' through good work, and 'evil' through evil work. Thereupon the questioner kept silent. In this connection exponents of different schools have put forward different things viz nature, chance, time, work, destiny, mere consciousness, and void, as the support in question. Therefore, being open to various disputes, the truth cannot be ascertained by the usual method of defeating the opponent. If one wants to know the truth in this matter, therefore, he first talked about 'work' as the support, which caused the repeated talking up of the body and organs. Having accepted time, work, destiny and God as causes, what they praised then was work only. Now liberation is a cherished object with man, so, one may think that it too is attainable through work. Moreover the work is better and better, the result also is so, hence one may presume that a high degree of excellence in the work may lead to liberation. This idea has to be removed. The result of excellent work coupled with meditation is this much only for work and its results are confined to the manifested universe of name and form. Work has no access to that liberation, which is not an effect, which is eternal, unmanifested, beyond name and form and devoid of characteristics of action with its factors and results. And where it has access, it is just the relative world. The regular rites not being different from sacrifices, on account of their dependence on certain circumstances — the shrutis, for instance, enjoin them for life cannot have liberation as their result. Like light is an auxiliary to everyone's vision of colour, but owls etc. cannot see in light — their eyes differing in this respect from those of others. But because of this difference, we do not suppose that their eyes can also perceive taste etc. for we have no knowledge of any such power on their part. One speaks of regular rites producing a different effect like poison, curd and so forth in conjunction with special knowledge, charms, sugar etc. We accept this view and there is no dispute over this point. In other words if one maintains that disinterested work coupled with meditation, produces a different kind of effect, we do not contest this point, for between two persons, one sacrificing to the gods and the other sacrificing to the self, the shrutis state that the superiority of the latter in the passage, is 'One', who sacrifies to the self is better than one, who sacrifices to the gods' etc. and 'That alone which is performed with the help of meditation, is stronger' etc. Similarly, the samritis too, in the passage, 'Through the sacrifices relating to conception, etc., show that the regular rites purify the body and the organs and purified by those rites, the scarificer to the self, attains the sameness of vision, either in this or in some future life, he attains self realisation. Moreover, passage like, 'Sages are of the opinion that the attainment of oneness with Viraj, the world projectors, Yawa, Hiranyagarbha and the undifferentiated is the highest result produced by 'Sattva' or pure material (rites coupled with meditation) and they are merged in the five elements, show the mergence in the elements in addition to the attainment of the status of the gods. Further, none can think of any prescribed or forbidden acts, other than those mentioned in shrutis and samritis, the non-performance or performance respectively of which would cause one to become a spirit, a dog, a hog, a stationary object or the like — results, the existence of which we know from perception or inference, and none denies that, these states are the results of past actions. Therefore, just as these lower states — spirit, animal, or stationery existence — are the results of one's non-performance of the prescribed rites or commitment of the forbidden acts, similarly we must understand that the higher results culminating in oneness with Hiranyagarbha are as much the results of past actions.

Then another Brahmin asked him, that they travelled in Madra as students and came to the house of Patanchala of the line of Kapi. His daughter was possessed by a Gandharva. They asked him who he was. He said he was Sudhanvan, of the line of Angiras. When they asked him about the limits of the world, and where were the descendents of Parikshit. He asked the same thing from Yajnavalkya. Yajanavalkya said, 'The Gandharvas evidently told him that they went where the performers of the horse-sacrifice go and where do the performers of the horse sacrifice go ? The reply was thirty-two times the space covered by the sun's chariot in a day makes this world, around it, covering twice the area, is the earth, around the earth, covering twice the area is the ocean. Now, as is the edge of a razor, or the wing of a fly, so is there just that much opening at the junction of the two halves of the cosmic shell. Through that they go out. Fire in the form of a falcon, delivered them to the air; the air, putting them in itself, took them where the previous performers of the horse-sacrifice were'. Therefore, the air is the diversity of individuals and the air is the aggregate. He, who knows it as such conquers further death.

It has been stated that a man under the control of the organs and objects ('Grahas' and 'Atigrahas'), which are themselves directed by his merits and demerits, repeatedly takeup and discards the organs and objects and transmigrates. Now the question arises as to whether the entity that transmigrates under the control of the organs and objects exists or does not exist and if it exists, what is it like. So another Brahmin asked him to explain to him the Brahma that is Immediate and Direct — the self that is within all. Yajnavalkya replied that it was his self that is within all. That which is 'Immediate or unobstructed' and 'Direct' or used in its primary sense and which is Brahma or the vastest, the self of all and within all — all these specifications refer to the self. What is that 'this self of his that by which his body and organs are ensouled in himself, i.e., the self of the body and organs'? 'There is first the body within it is the subtle body consisting of the organs, and then is that whose existence is being doubted. Which of these did he mean as himself that is within all ?' Yajnavalkya further said, 'That which breaths through the 'Prana', which operates in the mouth and nose, in other words, 'which makes the 'Prana' breathe is yourself i.e. the individual self of the body and organs. That which moves downwards through the 'Apana', which pervades through the 'Vyana', by which the body and organs are made to breathe and do other functions like a wooden puppet. Unless they are operated by an intelligent principle, they cannot do any such function such as breathing, as is the case with the wooden puppet. Therefore, it is on account of being operated by the individual self, which is distinct from them, that they breathe and do other functions, as does the puppet. Hence that principle distinct from the body and organs exists which make them function.

Another Brahmin said that he (Yajnavalkya) had indicated it as one may say that a cow is such and such or a horse is such and such. He requested to be explained about the Brahma that is immediate and direct the self that is within all. Yajnavalkya said this is one's self that is within all but which is within all ? One cannot see that which is the witness of vision ; one cannot hear that which is the hearer of hearings ; one cannot think that which is the thinker of the thoughts ; one cannot know that which is knower of knowledge. This is one's self that is within all, everything else, but this, is perishable. But the way it has been explained viz that the self endowed with eternal vision as opposed to the ordinary vision, should be pointed out, accounts for the two words "Witness" and "Vision" as describing the subject and the object, with a view to defining the nature of the self. It will also agree with the passages, 'The vision of the witness can never be lost,' and 'Through which the eyes see'.

Then another Brahmin requested to be explained about the Brahma that is immediate and direct — the self that is within all and if this is one's self that is within all, then which is within all. Yajnavalkya told, that which transcends hunger and thirst, grief, delusion, decay and death, knowing this very self, the Brahmins renounce the desire for sons, for wealth and for the worlds and lead a medicants' life. That which is the desire for son is the desire for wealth, and that which is desire for wealth, is the desire for worlds, for both these are but desires. Therefore, the knower of Brahma, having known all about this strength and scholarship, he becomes meditative, having known all about both meditativeness and its opposite, he becomes a knower of Brahma. How does that knower of Brahma behave and howsoever he may behave, he is just such. Except this, everything is perishable. The discomfort that one feels as one reflects on some covetable thing is the seed of desire for one afflicted with a hankering, because it kindles desire while delusion is a mistake, a confusion, arising from a false notion, it is ignorance, the fruitful source of all troubles. Death is the fall of the body, the last modification to overtake it. These hunger and the rest, which centre in the vital force, mind and body and which are present in beings in an unbroken succession like day and night etc. and like the wave, of an ocean, are called the relative or transmigratory existence with regard to them. Knowing this very self, then own reality as 'I am this, the Supreme Brahma eternally devoid of relative attributes and even satisfied', the Brahmins renounce lit and rise up in an opposite direction to the desire for sons, as means to winning this world thinking 'We will win this world through sons,' in other words marriage. Hence the meaning is they do not marry. Further, every desire for means is a desire for results. Therefore, the text says that desire is one, that which is the desire for sons, is the desire for wealth, as both are equally means to tangible results. And that, which is the desire for worlds, for it is directed towards the results. People adopt different means actuated by the desire for results. Hence desire is one, because the desire for worlds cannot be attained without the requisite means for both these are but desires. One brings but the means to the other. Therefore, the knower of Brahma has nothing to do with rites or their accessories — the rites and their accessories here spoken of refer to the holy thread etc., which are means to the performance of rites pertaining to the gods, the means and the men, for through them these rites are performed. Moreover the knowledge and ignorance cannot co-exist in the same individual for they are contradictory like light and darkness. Therefore, the knower of self must not be supposed to have relations with the sphere of ignorance consisting of actions, their factors and their results, for it has been deprecated in such passages as 'goes from death to death' etc.

Since the ancient Brahmins, knowing this self as naturally different from the means and result of an action renounced all desires, which are such means and results, and led a medicants' life, giving up work, producing visible and invisible results, together with its means, therefore, to this day, the knower of Brahma having known all about scholarship or this knowledge of the self from the teacher and shrutis — having fully mastered it — should renounce desires. Further, since scholarship regarding the self cannot come without the elimination of desires, therefore, the renunciation of these is automatically enjoined by the knowledge of the self. Therefore, the knower of Brahma, after renouncing desires, should try to live upon that strength, which comes to knowledge. Those others, who are ignorant of the self, derive their strength from the means and results of actions. Having known all about this strength and scholarship, he becomes meditative or a yogin. What a knower of Brahma, should do is to eliminate all ideas of the non-self, doing this, he accomplishes his task and attains the conviction that all is Brahma.

Gargi, the daughter of Vacaknu, asked as under :

Gargi : If all this is pervaded by water by what is water pervaded ?

Yajnavalkya : By air.

Gargi : By what is pervaded air ?

Yajnavalkya : By the Sky.

Gargi : By what is sky pervaded ?

Yajnavalkya : By the world of the Gandharvas.

Gargi : By what is the world of Gandharvas pervaded?

Yajnavalkya : By the sun.

Gargi : By what the sun is pervaded ?

Yajnavalkya : By the moon.

Gargi : By what the moon is pervaded ?

Yajnavalkya : By the stars.

Gargi : By what the stars are pervaded ?

Yajnavalkya : By the world of the gods.

Gargi : By what is the world of gods pervaded ?

Yajnavalkya : By the world of Indra.

Gargi : By what is the world of Indra pervaded ?

Yajnavalkya : By the world of 'Viraj'.

Gargi : By what is the world of 'Viraj' pervaded ?

Yajnavalkya : By the world of 'Hirayangarbha.

Gargi : By what is the world of 'Hirayangarbha' pervaded?

Yajnavalkya : He asked Gargi, not to push her enquiries too far, lest her head should fall off, as she had been questioning about the deity that should not be reasoned about. Thereupon Gargi kept silent.

This is how the nature of that which has been stated to be the immediate and direct Brahma — the self that is within all, the three sections up to that dealing with the story of Sakalya are being introduced. The elements from earth up to the ether are arranged one within the other. The idea is to show how an aspirant the subject or seer can realise his own self, which is immediate and direct, which is within all and beyond all relative attributes, by taking up each relatively external element and eliminating it.

The Brahmins then discussed the sutra, by which this life, the next life and all beings are held together and the internal ruler, who controls this and the next life and all beings from within; and concluded that he, who knows that sutra and that internal ruler as above, knows Brahma, knows the worlds, knows the gods, knows the vedas, knows beings, knows the self, and knows everything. On Yajnavalkya having told that he knew these all, he was asked to narrate the same. Yajnavalkya said 'Vayu' (air) is that sutra, and through 'Vayu' alone, this and the next life and all beings are held together. Therefore, when a man dies, it is said that his limbs have been loosened as these are held together by 'Vayu'. He further told that he, who inhabits the earth, but is within it, whom the earth does not know ; whose body is the earth ; and who controls the earth from within, is the Internal Ruler, one's own immortal self. Similarly, water, fire, sky, air, heaven, sun, quarters, moon and stars, ether, darkness, light etc. are within it, whom they do not know but who controls them from within, is the Internal Ruler, one's own immortal self. This much with reference to the god, i.e. the meditation of the Internal Ruler as pertaining to gods. With reference to the beings i.e. the meditation of the Internal Ruler as pertaining to the different grades of beings from Hiranyagarbha down to a clump of grass. He, who inhabits all beings; who inhabits the organs of speech, nose, eye, ear, mind, intellect, organ of generation, are all within it but the organs donot know it, whose body are those organs and who controls those organs from within are the Internal Rulers, one's own immortal self. He is never seen but is the witness; never heard, but is hearer ; never thought but is the thinker; never known but is the knower. There is no other witness but Him; no other hearer but Him, no other thinker but Him, no other knower but Him, He is the Internal Ruler, one's ownself. Everything else but Him is mortal. On this the Brahmin kept quiet. Then, in the end, Gargi said that she shall ask a question and if that is answered, then none can beat Yajnavalkya.

Question : By what is that pervaded which is above heaven and below the earth ; which is this heaven and earth as well as between them and which it was, is and will be ?

Answer : Which is above heaven and below the earth and which is this heaven and earth as well as between them and which they say was, is and will be, is pervaded by the unmanifested ether and is also called 'Sutra'. This manifested universe, consisting of the Sutra, exists in the unmanifested ether, like earth in water, in the past, present and future, in its origin, continuance and dissolution. Gargi was fully satisfied with the answer.

Then another Brahmin asked as to how many gods were there. Yajnavalkya told as many as are indicated in the Nivid of the Visvadevas — three hundred and three and three thousand and three. Then it was asked how many gods exactly are there. Yajnavalkya told thirty three. Then again he was asked to tell how many gods exactly were, he told six ; then on asking again, he told three and then two and then one and a half and then 'ONE'. Then he was asked to explain which were those three hundred and three and three thousand and three. Yajnavalkya told that these are but the manifestations of them but there are only thirty three gods — eight Vasus, eleven Rudras and twelve Adityas and Indra and Prajapati. The Vasus are fire, earth, air, sky, sun, heaven, the moon and stars are in these all. They help everybody to live and they themselves live too. Since they help others to live, they are called Vasus. The Rudras are the ten organs in the human body and the mind make eleven. When they depart from the mortal body, they make one's relatives weep. Because they then make them weep, therefore, they are called Rudras. The Adityas are twelve months of a year as they go taking all this with them, they are called Adityas. The cloud is Indra, and the sacrifice is Prajapati. Then cloud is the 'thunder' (Strength) and the sacrifice is 'animal', as they are the means of a sacrifice because a sacrifice has no form of its own and depends on its means, the animals, therefore, they are called sacrifice. The six gods are fire, earth, air, sky, sun and heaven. These are six because all gods are comprised in these six. The three gods are the three worlds alone because in these, all gods are comprised. The earth and the fire, taken together, make one god, the sky and air make another and heaven and sun the third. The two gods are matter and the vital force. The one and a half gods are the air that blows. It is one and a half because through its presence, all this attains surpassing glory. The one god is the vital force, which is 'Brahma' as it is vast, being the sum total of all the gods and this 'Brahma' is called 'That'. He, who knows that being, whose abode is the earth, whose instrument of vision is fire, whose light is the manas and who is the ultimate resort of the entire body and organs, knows truly. He, who knows being whose abode is lust, colours, ether, darkness, water, seed, etc. whose instrument of vision is the intellect, whose light is the manas and who is the ultimate resort of the entire body and organs, knows truly. That being of whom Yajnavalkya spoke, is the ultimate resort of the entire body and organs. It is the very being, who is identified with the son, and whose deity is Prajapati, the father. Then they asked.

Question : On what do the body and heart rest ?

Answer : On the Prana.

Question : On what does the Prana rest ?

Answer : On the Apana.

Question : On what does the Apana rest ?

Answer : On Vyana.

Question : On what does the Vyana rest ?

Answer : On Odana.

Question : On what does the Odana rest ?

Answer : On Samana.

This self is that which has been described as, 'Not this, not this'. It is imperceptible, for it is never perceived ; undecaying, for it never decays ; unattached, as it is not attached ; unfettered, as it never feels pain and never suffers injury. Then Yajnavalkya asked Sakalya to tell the being who is to be known only from the upanisadas, who definitely projects those beings and withdraws them into himself ; and who is at the same time transcendent and if he could not tell them, his head shall fall. Sakalya could not tell and so his head fell, and his bones were snatched by robbers mistaking them something else (treasurer). The moral of the incident is that one should not be disrespectful, but, rather submissive to a true knower of Brahma. Then Yajnavalkya told the

Brahmins that whosoever amongst them, or even all, might interrogate him or he shall ask them question. He asked them through the following verse :-

यथा वृक्षो बनस्पतिस्तथैव पुरुषोड मृषा,

तस्य लोमानि पर्णानि, त्वगस्योत्पारिका बहिः ।

As a large tree, so indeed is a man, this is true. His hair are its leaves ; his skin its outer bark. It is from his skin that blood flows and from the bark, sap. Therefore, when a man is wounded, blood flows, as sap from a tree, that is injured. His flesh is its inner bark, and his tendons, its innermost layer of bark ; both are tough. His bones lie under, as does its wood ; his marrow is comparable to its pith. If a tree, after it is felled, springs again from its root in a newer form, from what root indeed does man spring forth after he is cut off by death. He said it is not from the seed as it is produced in a living man. A tree springs also from the seed after it is dead. If some one pulls out a tree with its roots, it no more sprouts. From what root does a man spring forth after he is cut off by death. It cannot be that he is not born as he is certainly born. Now who should again bring him forth ? Knowledge, Bliss, Brahma, the supreme goal of the dispenser of wealth, as well as of him, who has realised Brahma and lives in it. In this way, Yajnavalkya defeated the Brahmins and took away the cows. The shruti in its own form tell us of the root of the universe, about which Yajnavalkya asked the Brahmins, and gives the words that directly describe Brahma ; knowledge or pure intelligence, which is also bliss, not smitten with pain like sense perception, but serene, beneficient, matchless, spontaneous, ever content and homogenous. That is Brahma, which has both the characteristics (knowledge and bliss). The supreme goal, being the bestower of the fruits of actions of the dispenser of wealth i.e. of the sacrificer, who engages in rites — the word 'Rati' (wealth) has a possessive force — as well as the supreme goal of him, who has realised Brahma and lives in it alone, having renounced all desires and doing no ritualistic work. Then the word 'bliss' is generally known to denote pleasure and here we find the word bliss used as an epithet of Brahma in the expression 'Bliss, Brahma'. Elsewhere in the srutis too we have, 'He knew bliss to be Brahma'. 'Knowing the bliss of

Brahma' etc. The word 'bliss' is also commonly known to refer to pleasure that is cognised. The use of the word 'bliss' would be justified if this bliss of Brahma be an object of cognition. It may be urged on the authority of shrutis that Brahma is bliss that is congnised. But it is not so as we notice that the shruti texts are contradictory too. It is true that the word 'bliss' refers to Brahma in shrutis, but there is also the negation of knowledge when there is oneness. For example. 'But when to the knower of Brahma, everything has become the self, then what should one see and through what; what should one know and through what ?' 'When one sees nothing else, hears nothing else, knows nothing else, that is the infinite'. 'Being fully embraced by the Supreme self, he does not know anything outside of himself' etc. Therefore, on account of the contradictory shruti texts, a discussion is necessary. The Sankhya and Vaisesika schools while believing in liberation, hold that there is no joy to be cognised in it, thus differing from others, who maintain that there is surpassing joy in it, known only to the person concerned. The prima facie view is that there is joy to be cognised in liberation, for the shrutis mention bliss etc. with regard to it, as in the following passages. 'Laughing (or eating), playing and enjoying', 'If he desires to attain the world of the manas, by his mere wish, they appear'. 'That which knows things in a general and a particular way'; 'Enjoy all desires' etc. Hence all passages containing the word 'bliss' should be interpreted like the sentence, 'This is its supreme bliss'.

Once Yajnavalkya came to Janaka's 'Darbar' and asked to tell what his teachers had told him. Janaka told that his one teacher had told that, the organ of speech i.e. its presiding deity (fire) is Brahma. Yajnavalkya told that, as one who has a mother adequately to instruct him in his childhood; a father to instruct him after that and a teacher to instruct him from his initiation with the holy thread up to the completion of studies, should say to his disciple so had he said this that the organ of speech is Brahma. Of course a person, who cannot speak, can do nothing or achieve nothing, but did he tell him about the abode and support of that Brahma. 'Abode' means the body and 'support' means permanent resort. Janaka said No, he did not.' Yajnavalkya said, 'Then such a Brahma is only one-footed and will produce no effect even if meditated upon'. He said, 'The organ of speech, is it abode or the body of the deity of the organ of speech (fire) which is a form of Brahma and the ether known as the undifferentiated is its support at its origin, doing its continuance and at its dissolution'. It should be meditated upon as intelligence and the secret name of intelligence is the fourth quarter of Brahma. Janaka asked what then intelligence is ? Yajnavalkya told it is organ of speech itself. It is not different from the organ of speech. Through the organ of speech, a friend is known, when somebody says,' He is our friend'. Likewise, sacrifices mean the spiritual effects produced by them; the same with offering oblation, as well as giving food and drink. This world, the present life, the next world, the life to come and all beings are known through the organ of speech alone. Therefore, the organ of speech is the supreme Brahma. The organ of speech never leaves the knower of Brahma. Who knowing thus meditates upon it, all beings eagerly come to him with offerings etc. and being a god in this very life, he attains the gods and is merged in them after death.

Then Janaka told that another teacher had told him that the vital force (Vayu) is Brahma. Yajnavalkya said it is correct that the vital force is Brahma, as a person who does not live cannot do anything but did that teacher tell him about its abode and support. He replied in the negative. Yajnavalkya then told that the vital force is its abode and the ether (the undifferentiated) its support, and it should be meditated upon as dear, which is the vital force. For the sake of vital force, a man performs sacrifices for one for whom they should not be performed and accepts gifts from one from whom they should not be accepted and it is for the sake of vital force that one runs the risk of one's life in any quarter one may go to. Thus the vital force is supreme Brahma. It never leaves him, who knowing thus meditates upon it. All beings eagerly come to him and being a god, attain the gods.

Then Janaka told that one teacher had told him that eye (sun) is Brahma. Yajnavalkya again said it was correct as a man without eyes cannot see anything but what is its abode and support and he then told that eye is its abode and ether its support. It should be meditated upon as truth, which is eye itself because if a person says to one, who has seen with his eyes, 'Have you seen' and the latter answers 'yes, I have', then it is true. Therefore, eye is supreme Brahma and should be meditated upon to attain gods. Then Janaka told that another teacher had told him that ear is Brahma. Yajnavalkya told that it was correct as a person, who cannot hear, cannot do anything and told that ear is its abode and the ether is its support. It should be meditated upon as infinite, the quarters, themselves. Therefore, to whatever direction one may go, one never reaches its end, hence the quarters are infinite. So ear is supreme Brahma and should be meditated upon to attain gods. Then Janaka told that another teacher had told him that 'Manas' (here the moon) is Brahma. Yajnavalkya said 'Yes, since one cannot think of anything without 'Manas' and 'Manas' is its abode and ether is its support and it should be meditated upon as 'bliss', which is 'Manas' itself. With the 'Manas' a man fancies and woos a woman, a son resembling him is born of her, and he is the cause of bliss. So 'Manas' is supreme Brahma and should be meditated upon to attain gods. Then Janaka told that another teacher had told him that the heart (here Prajapati) is Brahma. Yajnavalkya said it is correct that heart is Brahma as one cannot have anything without heart and his abode is heart and the ether is his support, which should be meditated upon as stability, which is the heart itself. The heart is the abode of all beings and the heart is the support of all beings ; on heart all beings rest and heart is supreme Brahma and should be meditated upon to attain gods.

Yajnavalkya then asked Janaka if he had equipped his mind with so many secret names of Brahma and even after having studied vedas, did he know where he shall go after he had been separated from the body. He told that the being, who is in the right eye is named 'Indha'. Tough he is Indha but indirectly called Indra for the gods have fondness for indirect names and hate to be called direct. The human form that is in the left eye is his wife, Viraj (matter). The space that is within the heart is their place of union. Their food is the lump of blood (the essence of what we eat) in the heart. Their wrap is the net like structure in the heart. Their road for moving is the nerve that goes upward from the heart; it is like a hair-split into a thousand parts. In this body, there are nerves called 'Hita', which are placed in the heart. Through these, the essence of the food passes as it moves on. Therefore, the subtle body had finer food than the gross body. Of the sage (who is identified with the vital force), the east is the eastern vital force, the south, the southern vital force, the west, the western vital force, the north, the northern vital force ; the direction above the vital force, the direction below the vital force and all the quarters are the different vital forces. This self is that which has been described as, 'Not this, not this', it is imperceptible, as it is never perceived, undecaying as it never decays, unattached, as it is never attached and unfettered as it never feels pain or injury. Janaka, Yajnavalkya told, had attained that which is free from fear but, Janaka, told that whatever is free from fear be 'his' as he has made that which is free from fear known to him and offered his kingdom to him with respects.

On another meeting, Janaka asked him as to what served as the light for a man. Yajnavalkya told it is the light of the śun. It is through the light of the sun that he sits, goes out, works and returns. When the sun is set, the moon serves as his light. It is then through the light of the moon that he sits, goes out, works and returns. Then Janaka asked when sun and moon, both are not there, and fire has also gone out then what exactly serves as the light for a man. Yajnavalkya said it is speech (sound) that serves as his light as then it is through the light of speech that he sits, goes out, works and returns. Therefore, even when one's own hand is not clearly visible, if a sound is uttered, one manages to go there. But when speech is also out then self serves as his light and it is through the light of the self that he sits, goes out, works and returns. This seeing through the light of the self is possible as in dream and remembrance, the seer is other than the material body organs. Therefore, there is a light, which is other than the body and within it and it is the self. Further, the self is the infinite entity (Purusa) that is identified with the intellect and is in the midst of the organs the (self-effulgent) light within the heart (intellect). Assuming the likeness (of the intellect), it moves between the two worlds ; it thinks, as it were and shakes, as it were. Being identified with dream, it transcends this world — the forms of death (ignorance) etc. The self is in the midst of the organs but is different from the organs as a rock in the midst of trees indicates only nearness, for there is a doubt about the identity of difference of the self from the organs. In the midst of the organs means also different from the organs for that which is in the midst of certain other things, is of course different from them as a tree amidst rocks. Intelligence, being transparent and next to self, easily catches the reflection of the intelligence of the self. Therefore, even wise men happen to identify themselves with it first. Next comes 'Manas', which catches the reflection of the self through intellect and then the organs. The intellect and 'Manas' are consciousness. During waking state, the light called the self, being beyond the organs and being particularly mixed up in the diversity of functions of the body and the organs, internal and external, such as intellect, cannot be shown extricated from them. Therefore, it cannot be taken apart from anything else like a stalk of grass from its sheath, and shown in its self — effulgent form. Having been identified with dream etc., the self seems to become whatever the intellect, which it resembles, becomes. Therefore, when the intellect turns into dream, i.e. takes on the modification, called dream, the self also assumes that form, and when the intellect wants to wake up, it too does that. However, all the assumptions are contrary to the vedic path of well-being that we are discussing since they deny the light of the self as distinct from the body and illumining the consciousness of the intellect. Objects such as a jar are not self-luminous. A jar in darkness never reveals itself but is noticed as being regularly revealed by coming in contact with the light of a lamp etc. Then we say that the jar is in contact with light. Even though the jar and the light are in contact, they are distinct from each other, as we see their difference as between a rope and a jar when they repeatedly come in contract and are disjoined. This means that the jar is revealed by something else, it certainly does not reveal itself.

The man, when he is born or attains a body, is connected with evils (the body and organs) ; and when he dies, or leaves the body; he discards those evils. That man has only two abodes, this and the next world. The dream state, which is the third, is at the junction of the two. Staying at that junction, he survey the two abodes, this and the next world. Whatever outfit he may have for the next world, providing himself with that, he sees both evils, sufferings and joys. When he dreams, he takes away a little of the impression of this all-embracing world, in the waking state himself puts the body aside and himself creates a dream body in its place, revealing his own lustre by his own light and dreams. In this state the man himself becomes the light. There are no chariots, nor animals to be yoked to there, nor roads there, but he creates the chariots, the animals and the roads. There are no pleasures, joys or delights but he creates the pleasures, joys and delights. There are no pools, tanks or rivers but he creates the pools, tanks and rivers as he is the agent. Shruti also says, 'It is through the light of the self that he sits, goes out, works and returns'. There too, the light of the self has no direct agency except that it is illuminer of everything. It thinks as it were, and shakes, as it were, as he is the agent in order to furnish reason for the creation of chariots in dream. The radiant infinite being (Purusa), who moves alone, puts the body aside in the dream state, and remaining awake himself and taking the shining functions of the organs with him, watches those, that are asleep. Again he comes to the waking state. The radiant infinite being, who is immortal, and moves alone, preserves the unclean nest, the body with the help of the vital force, and roams out of the nest. Himself immortal, he goes whereever he likes and for whatever objects his desire is aroused, he attains them in the form of impressions. In the dream world, the shining one, attaining higher and lower states, puts forth innumerable forms. He seems to be enjoying himself in the company of women, or laughing or even seeing frightful things. All see his sports, but none sees him. They say, 'Do not wake him suddenly'. If he does not find the right organ, the body becomes difficult to doctor. Others, however, say that the dream state of a man is nothing but the waking state because he sees in dream only those things that he sees in the waking state. This is wrong. In the dream state, the man himself becomes the light.

By the illustration of dream, it has been proved that there is the self-luminous 'Atman', and that it transcends the forms of death. Since it alternatively moves between this world and the next, and so on, it is distinct from them. Likewise, it is distinct from the nests of the waking and dream states. And Yajnavalkya has proved that since it moves alternatively from one to the other, it is eternal. Hence, to requite the knowledge received, Janaka offered one thousand cows and asked further about liberation. Yajnavalkya told that after enjoying himself and roaming, and merely seeing the result of good and evil, in dream, he stays in a state of profound sleep, and comes back in the inverse order to his former condition, the dream state. After enjoying himself and roaming in the dream state, and merely seeing the result of good and evil, he comes back in the inverse order to his former's condition, the waking state. He is untouched by whatever he sees in that state, for this infinite being is unattached. Similarly, after enjoying himself and roaming in the waking state and merely seeing the result of good and evil, he comes back in the inverse order to his former condition, the dream state or that of profound sleep.

Thus the idea that has been established by the above three positions, is that this self is itself the light and distinct from the body and organs and their stimulating causes, desire and work on account of its non-attachment for this infinite being is unattached. We know that the self is unattached because it moves by turn from the waking to the dream state, from this to the state of profound sleep, from that again to the dream state, then to the waking state, from that again to the dream state and so on, which proves that it is in distinct forms, the three states. This idea has also been introduced in the passage, 'Being identified with dream, it transcends this world — the form of death'. Having treated this, the shruti now gives illustration. As a great fish swims alternatively to both the banks of a river, eastern and western, so does this infinite being move to both these states, the dream and the waking state.

In the preceding paragraphs, the self-luminous 'Atman', which is different from body and organs, has been stated to be distinct from desire and work for, it moves alternately to the three states. Its relative existence is only due to its limiting adjuncts, and is super-imposed by ignorance. This has been stated to be the gist of the whole passage. Then, however, the three states of waking, dream and profound sleep, have been described separately—not shown together as a group. For instance, it has been shown that in the waking state, the self appears through ignorance as connected with attachment, death; and the body and organs; in the dream state, it is perceived as connected with desire but free from the forms of death, and in the state of profound sleep, it is perfectly serene and unattached, this non-attachment being the additional feature. If we consider all these passages together, the resulting sense is that the self is by nature eternal, free, enlightened and pure. It will be stated later on that the self becomes such only in the state of profound sleep, 'That is his form — beyond desire, free from evils, and fearless.' As a hawk or a falcon, flying in the sky, becomes tired, and stretching its wings, is bound for its nest, so does this infinite being run for this state, when falling asleep, he craves no desire and sees no dreams. In him, in this man with a head, hands etc., are those nerves called 'Hita', which are as fine as a hair, split into thousand parts, and they are filled with white, blue, brown, green and red serums. Many and various are the colours of serums, owing to the intermixture in various proportions, of nerve matter, bile and phlegm. The subtle body with its seventeen constituents has its seat in these nerves, which have the fineness of the thousandth part of the top of a hair are filled with serums, white and so on, and spread all over the body. All impressions due to the experience of high and low attributes of the relative universe are centred in this. This subtle body, in which the impressions are stored, is transparent like a crystal because of its fineness, but owing to its contact with foreign matter, viz. the serums in the nerves, it undergoes modifications under the influence of past merit and demerit, and manifest itself as impression in the forms of women, chariots, elephants etc. Now, such being the case, when a man has the false notion called ignorance, based on past impressions, that some people — enemies or robbers — have come and are going to kill him, 'As if he the dreamer, were being killed or overpowered.' Nobody is killing or overpowering him, it is simply his mistake due to the past impressions created by ignorance. On being pursued or chased by an elephant, or falling into a pit, a dilapidated well, for instance. He fancies himself in this position. Such are the false impressions that arise in him — extremely low ones, resting on the modifications of the mind brought about by his past inequity, as is evidenced, by their painful nature. In short, he conjures up at the time i.e. in dream, when there is no elephant or the like, through the impressions created by ignorance, which have falsely manifested themselves, whatever terrible things, such as an elephant, he has experienced in the waking state. Then when ignorance decreases and knowledge increases and when one himself becomes a god, as it were, when in the waking state, modification regarding the gods prevails, he considers himself as god, on account of the impressions generated by it. During dream too, he becomes a god or a king, as it were. Having been installed as the ruler of a waking state, he thinks in his dreams also that he is a king as he is imbued with the impressions of his kingly by state. Similarly, when in the waking state, his ignorance is extremely attenuated, and the knowledge that he comprises, all arises, he thinks under the influence of these impressions in the dream state also. This universe is myself, who am all. That, this identity, with all the universe is his highest state, the 'Atma's own natural, supreme state. When prior to this realisation of identity with all he views the latter as other than himself even by a hair's breadth, thinking, 'This is not myself', that is the state of ignorance, down to stationary existence, are all inferior states. Compared with these states with which the 'Jiva' the individual self, has relative dealings — the above state of identity with all, infinite and without interior or exterior, is his supreme state. Therefore, when ignorance is eliminated and knowledge reaches its perfection, the state of identity with all, which is another name for liberation, is attained. That is to say just as the self-effulgence of the 'Atman' is directly perceived in the dream state, so is this result of knowledge. Similarly, when ignorance increases and knowledge vanishes, the results of ignorance are also directly perceived in dream, 'Now when he feels as if he were being killed or overpowered' etc. Thus the results of knowledge and ignorance are identity with all and identity with finite things respectively. Through pure knowledge, a man is identified with all, and through ignorance, he is identified with finite things or separated from something else. He is in conflict with that from which he is separated and because of this conflict, he is killed, overpowered or pursued. All this takes place because the result of ignorance being finite, things are separated from him. Hence the nature of ignorance proves to be this, that it represents that which is infinite as finite presents things other than self that are non-existent and makes the self appear as limited. Hence arises the desire for that from which he is separated; desire prompts him to action, which produces results. Therefore, ignorance is not a natural characteristic of the self, for that which is natural to a thing can never be eliminated, as the heat and light of the sun. Therefore, liberation from ignorance is possible.

The 'Atman' is itself the light that is pure intelligence, and reveals everything by its own intelligence. It has been said that he is untouched by the roaming or by whatever he sees, or enjoys or knows in that dream state and it is also proved by reasoning that the eternal nature of the self is that it is the light of pure intelligence. Now, if the self remains in tact, in its own form, in the state of profound sleep, why does it not know itself as 'I am this', or know all those things that are outside as it does in the waking or dream stage. It is because as in the world, a man, fully embraced by his beloved wife, both desiring each other's company, does not know anything at all, either external to himself, as, 'This is something other than myself' or internal as, 'I am this or I am happy or miserable' — but he knows everything outside and inside when he is not embraced by her and is separated, and fails to know only during the embrace owing to the attainment of unity — so, like the example cited, does this infinite being, the individual self, who is separated from the Supreme self, like a lump of salt, through contact with a little of the elements (the body and organs) and enters this body and organs, like the reflection of the moon etc. in water and so forth, being fully embraced by or unified with the supreme self, his own real, natural, supremely effulgent self, and being identified with all, without the least break not know anything at all, either external, something outside or internal, within himself such as 'I am this, or I am happy or miserable'. So all objects of desire are but the self in waking state. In states other than that of profound sleep i.e. in the waking and dream states, things are separated, as it were, from the self and are desired as such. But to one, who is fast asleep, they become the self, since there is no ignorance to project the idea of difference. Hence also is this form free from desire, because there is nothing to be desired, and devoid of grief. Thus the form of the self is free from grief.

In this state, a father is no father, a mother no mother, worlds no worlds, the gods no gods,. vedas no vedas. In this state a thing is nothing, the killer of a noble Brahmin, no killer, a chandala, no chandala, a monk no monk etc. This form of his is untouched by good work and untouched by evil works, for he is then beyond all the woes of his heart, intellect and so he is beyond desire and since he transcends all desires, he is said to be untouched by good work etc.

It has been said that the self does not see in the state of profound sleep on account of unity, as in the case of the couple, fully embracing each other and that it is self-effulgent. Self-effulgence means being pure intelligence by nature. Now the question is, if this intelligence is the very nature of the self like the heat etc., or fire, how should it, inspite of the unity, give up its nature and fail to know ? And if it does not give up its nature, how is it that it does not see in the state of profound sleep ? It is self-contradictory to say that intelligence is the nature of the self and again that it does not know. The answer is it is not self-contradictory and these both are possible. That it does not see in that state is because, though seeing then, it does not see, for the vision of the witness can never be lost, because it is imperishable, but there is not that second thing separate from it, which it can see. Similarly, it does not smell in the state because, though smelling then, it does not smell for the smeller's function of smelling can never be lost as it is imperishable. But there is no second thing which it can smell. It does not taste in that state as the taster's function of tasting can never be lost as it is imperishable and there is nothing else, which it can taste. It does not speak in that state because, though speaking, it does not speak as the speaker's function of speaking can never be lost as it is imperishable and there is nothing else, which it can speak. It does not hear as the listener's function is never lost as it is imperishable and there is none separate from it, which it can hear. It does not think as thinker's function is never lost being imperishable and there being nothing else, which it can think. It does not touch as the toucher's function of touching can never be lost being imperishable and there being nothing else, which it can touch. It does not know in that state because though knowing then, it does not know for the knower's function of knowing can never be lost being imperishable and there being no second which it can know. But then it has been said that in the state of profound sleep, there is not, as in the waking and dream states, that second thing differentiated from the self, which it can know ; hence it knows no particulars in profound sleep. When in the waking or dream state, there is something else, besides the self, as it were, presented by ignorance, then one thinking of oneself as different from that something — though there is nothing different from the self, nor is there any self different from it — can see something. This has been shown by a reference to one's experience in the dream state in the passage, 'As if he were being killed or overpowered'. Similarly, one can smell, taste, speak, hear, think, touch and know something. When, however, that ignorance, which presents things, other than the self is at rest, in the state of deep sleep, there being nothing separated from the self by ignorance, what should one see, smell or know and through what. Therefore, being fully embraced by his own-self luminous Supreme self, the 'Jiva' (individual self), becomes infinite, perfectly serene, with all his desires attained and the self, the only object of his desire, transparent like water, because there is no second. It is ignorance, that separates a second entity, and that is at rest in the state of profound sleep ; hence one. The witness, because the vision that is identical with the light of the self, is never lost and without a second, for there is no second entity, different from the self, to be seen. This is immortal and fearless. This is the sphere of Brahma, the world that is Brahma, in profound sleep the self, bereft of its limiting adjuncts, the body and organs, remain in its own Supreme light the 'Atman', free from all relations. This is its supreme attainment ; this is its supreme glory. This is its highest world, this is its supreme bliss and on a particle of this very bliss, other beings live. He, who is perfect of physique and prosperous among men, the ruler of others, and most lavishly supplied with all human enjoyments, represents greatest joy among men. This human joy, multiplied a hundred times, makes one unit of joy for the manes, who have won that world of theirs. The joy of these manes, who have won that world multiplied a hundred times, makes one unit of joy in the world of the celestial minstrels. This joy in the world of celestial minstrels multiplied a hundred times, makes one unit of joy for the gods by action — those, who have attained their godhood by their actions. This joy of the gods by action multiplied a hundred times, makes one unit of joy for the gods by birth as also of one, who is versed in the vedas, sinless and free from desires. This joy of the gods by birth multiplied hundred times makes one unit of joy in the world of Prajapati (Viraj) as well as of one, who is versed in vedas, sinless and free from desires. This joy in the world of Prajapati multiplied a hundred times, makes one unit of joy in the world of Brahma (Hiranyagarbha) as well as of one, who is versed in vedas, sinless and free from desires. This indeed is the supreme bliss and this is the state of Brahma.

After enjoying himself and roaming in the dream state, and merely seeing the effects of merits and demerits, he comes back in the inverse order to his former condition, the waking state. From here onwards, transmigration of self is being described. To show that as the self came from the dream to the waking state, so it will pass from this body to the next, as an example, just as in life a cart, fully or heavily loaded with utensils and other such household effects as a mortar and pestle, a winnowing fan and cooking vessels, as also eatables, goes on rumbling under the load, driven by the carter, so does the self, that is in the body, i.e. the self that has the subtle body, as its limiting adjunct, which moves between this and the next world, as between the waking and dream states, through birth and death, consisting respectively in the association with and dissociation from the body and organs, called evils and the departure of which is immediately followed by that of the vital force etc., being presided over, or revealed, by the self-luminous, Supreme self, go making noises. As had been said, 'It is through the light of the self that he sits, goes out, etc. It should be noted here that when the subtle body, which has the vital force as its chief constituent and which is revealed by the self-luminous 'Atman', goes, the self, of which it is limiting adjunct, also seems to go. When this body becomes thin — is emaciated through old age or disease — then, as a mango, or a fig or a fruit of the peepal tree is detached from its stalk, so does this infinite being, completely detaching himself, from the parts of the body, again go, in the same way that he came, to particular bodies, for the unfoldment of his vital force. Now it may be objected when the 'Jiva' goes leaving this body he has no power to take up another for he is dissociated from his body and organs. Nor are there others, who, like servants, would wait for him with another body made ready, as a king's retinue waits for him with a horse kept ready. In the circumstances how he can take up another body, is because he has adopted the whole universe as his means to the realisation of the results of this work, and he is going from one body to another to fulfil this object. Therefore, the whole universe impelled by his work, waits for him with the requisite means for the realisation of the results of his work, made ready. Shruti says, 'A man is born into the body that has been made for him'. It is analogous to the case of a man about to return from the dream to the waking state. Like just as when a king is coming to some place within his kingdom, the Ugras, a particular caste, or so called from their fierce deeds, sit against particular offences, appointed to punish thieves etc., the Sutas, a hybrid caste and the leaders of the village, anticipating the king's visit, wait for him with varieties of food and mansions, ready saying, 'Here he comes, here he comes', so for the person, who knows about the results of his work i.e. transmigration of self — for the results of one's work are the topics under consideration and they are referred to by the word 'evam' (thus) — all the elements that make up his body, together with the presiding deities, Indra and the rest, who help the organs to function, wait with the means of enjoying the fruits of his work made ready — being impelled by his work saying, 'Here comes Brahma', our enjoyer and master, 'Here he comes'. Further, just as when the king wishes to depart, the Ugras set against particular offences, the Sutas and the leaders of the village approach him, so do all the organs approach the departing man at the time of death, when breathing becomes difficult.

When this self, which is under consideration, becomes weak; really it is the body that becomes weak but its weakness is figuratively spoken of as that of the self ; for being formless, it can never by itself become weak. Similarly, it becomes senseless, as it were, i.e., fails to discriminate. It cannot by itself be senseless or otherwise, as it is the eternal self-luminous intelligence, hence the expression 'As it were.' The state of helplessness noticeable at the time of death, which is caused by withdrawl of organs, is attributed by ordinary people to the self. So they say, 'Oh !, he has become senseless'. When the eyes become united with the subtle body, then people say 'He does not see'. When the nose becomes united they say, 'He does not smell'. When tongue becomes united, they say 'He does not speak/taste'. When ear becomes united, they say, 'He does not think'. When skin becomes united, they say, 'He does not touch'. When intellect becomes united, they say, 'He does not know'. The top of the heart brightens. Through that brightened top, the self departs, either through the eye, head, or through any other part of the body. When it departs, the vital force follows. Then the self has particular consciousness, and goes to the body, which is related to that consciousness. It is followed by knowledge, work and past experience.

Then the self has particular consciousness, as in dream, in consequence of its past work, not independently. If it had this consciousness independently, everybody would achieve the end of his life, but it never has that. Hence Vyasa says, 'A man attains whatever he thinks of at the moment of death, if he has always been inbred with that idea'. As a matter of fact, everybody has at that moment a consciousness which consists of impressions in the form of particular modifications of his mind, regarding the next life, that are induced by his past work and goes to the body which is related to that consciousness i.e., is revealed by that particular consciousness. Therefore, in order to have freedom of action at the time of death, those aspirants after the future life, who have faith, should be alert in the practice of system of yoga and right knowledge, and in the acquisition of particular merit, by doing good deeds. All sacred books seek to dissuade man from doing evil ; for nothing can be done at the dying moment, since there is no independence then for the man, who is carried away by his past work. It is said, 'One indeed becomes good through good work and bad through evil work'. There is no way to eradicate the evil completely except by following the course laid down by them. Therefore, all should try to practise the remedies prescribed by the upanisadas.

It has been stated that the departing self, loaded with

materials, goes making noises like a cart. Now, as it starts for the next world, what is its load on the way or for consumption on reaching that world, corresponding to the carter's load, and what are the materials for building its new body and organs. The answer is this self journey to the next world is followed by knowledge of all sorts, that which is enjoined or forbidden; also work, enjoined or forbidden, and neither enjoined or forbidden and past experience i.e. the impressions of experience regarding the results of past actions. These impressions take part in initiating fresh actions as also in bringing past actions to fruition; hence they too accompany. But when the organs are prompted to work by the impressions of past experience ; they can easily attain skill even without practice in this life. It is frequently observed that some are clever in certain kinds of work, such as painting, from their very birth, even without practice in this life, while others are unskilled even in some very easy tasks. Similarly, in the enjoyment of sense objects also, some are observed to be naturally skilful or dull. All this is due to the revival or non-revival of past experience. Therefore, without past experience, we cannot understand how anybody can proceed to do any work or to enjoy the results of past work. Hence these three — knowledge, work and past experience — are the food on the way to the next world, corresponding to the load of the carter, since these three are the means of attaining another body and enjoying the results of one's past work, therefore, one should cultivate only the good forms of them, so that one may have a desirable body and desirable enjoyment.

Now the question is, when the self loaded with knowledge etc. is about to go to another body, does it leave the old body and go to another like the bird going to another tree, or is it carried by another body serving as a vehicle to the place, where, according to its past work, it is to be born, or does it stay here, while its organs become all-pervading and function as such, or is it that so long as it remains in the body, its organs are contracted to the limits of that, but when it dies, they become all pervading — like the light of a lamp, when the enclosing jar is broken — and contract again when a new body is made or as in the Vaisesika system, does only the mind go to the place where the new body is to be made or is there any other theory in the system of vedanta. The answer is: we know from shruti, 'These are all equal, and all infinite,' that the organs are all-comprising. Another reason for this is their resting on the vital force, which is all comprising. Their limitation with reference to the body and the elements, as colour etc., is due to the work, knowledge and past impressions of men. Therefore, though the organs are naturally all-pervading and infinite, since the new body is made in accordance with the person's work, knowledge and past impressions, the functions of the organs also contract and expand accordingly. As it has been said, 'Equal to white ant, equal to a mosquito, equal to an elephant, equal to these three worlds, equal to this universe'. It is also supported by the following, 'He, who meditates upon these as infinite etc., and one becomes exactly as one meditates upon him, etc. Therefore, the impressions called past experience under the control of the person's knowledge and work stretch out, like a leach, from the body, retaining their seat in the heart, as with dream state, and build another body in accordance with his past work ; they leave their seat, the old body, when a new body is made. Just as a leech, supported on a straw, goes to the end of it, takes hold of another support and contracts itself, so does the self throw this body aside, makes it senseless, takes hold of another support and contracts itself. Further, just as a goldsmith takes apart a little quantity of gold and fashions another — a newer and better — form, so does the self throw this body away or make it senseless, and make another — a newer and better — form suited to the manes or the celestial minstrels or the gods or Viraj or Hiranyagarbha or other beings. That self is indeed Brahma, as also identified with the intellect, the 'Manas' and the vital force with the eyes, the ears, with earth, water air and the ether, with fire and what is other than fire, with desire and the absence of desire, with anger and the absence of anger with righteousness and unrighteousness with everything — identified, infact, with this (what is perceived) and with that (what is inferred). As it does and acts, so it becomes, by doing good, it becomes good, and by doing evil, it becomes evil, it becomes virtuous through good acts and vicious through evil acts. Others, however, say, 'The self is identified with desire alone. What it desires it resolves ; what it resolves it works out ; and what it works out, it attains'. Therefore, desire is the only cause of its identification with everything as also of undergoing transmigration. There is a verse in this regard, 'Being attached, he, together with the work, attains that result to which his subtle body or mind is attached. Exhausting the results of whatever work he did in his life, he returns from that world to this for fresh work. Thus does the man, who desires, never transmigrates and of him, who is without desires objects of whose desires have been attained, and to whom all objects of desire are but the self — the organs do not depart. Being but Brahma, he is merged with Brahma. Then since the man, who does not desire, has no work and, therefore, has no cause to go to the next world; his organs such as that of speech, do not depart or go up from the body. That man of realisation, who has attained all the objects of his desire, since they are but the self to him, becomes Brahma in this very life.

Transmigration, which was the thing that was sought to be explained by the example of going in to the waking and dream states has been described, so also its causes — knowledge, work and past experience. Those limiting adjuncts, the elements comprising the body and organs, surrounded by which the self experiences the transmigratory existence, have also been mentioned. After stating as a prima facie view that their immediate causes are good and bad deeds, the cause has finally been decided to be desire. Liberation consisting in the identity with all, which is the thing that was sought to be explained by the example of the state of profound sleep, has been described and the cause of liberation has been stated to be the attainment of all objects of desire, through their becoming the self. But since this state is unattainable without self- knowledge, the cause of liberation has huge implications, has been stated to be the knowledge of Brahma. Therefore, though desire has been said to be the root of bondage, it is ignorance, that being the opposite of what leads to liberation (knowledge), has virtually been stated to be the cause of bondage. Here also liberation and its means have been dealt with by the Brahmin. There is a verse, 'When all the desires that dwell in his heart (mind) are gone, then he, having been mortal, becomes immortal and attains Brahma in this very body. Just as the lifeless slough of a snake is cast off and lies in the ant hill, so does this body lie. Then the self becomes disembodied and immortal, becomes the 'Prana', Supreme self, Brahma, the Light'. Further, the liberation is attained by the knower of Brahma, all the objects of whose desire, are the self—a subject that has already been dealt with. The subtle being difficult to comprehend, extensive or on account of another reading, effectively leading to liberation; ancient primeval, being revealed by the external shrutis, not modern like the misleading paths emanating from the intellect of the logicians' way, the path of knowledge that conduces to liberation, touches the person i.e. has been reached by the person. That which is attained by somebody, is connected with him as if it touched him, hence the path of liberation, consisting in the knowledge of Brahma, having been attained, by him, is said to have touched him. He has not merely attained it but has realised it him-self. Realisation is that attainment which, as knowledge ripens, culminates in the ultimate results, as eating culminates in satisfaction. Through the path of knowledge of Brahma, sages, men of illumination, other knowers of Brahma, also go to the heavenly sphere or liberation, which is the result of the knowledge of Brahma — 'Heavenly sphere', generally means heaven, the abode of gods but here it means liberation—after the fall of this body, being freed even while living some speak of it as white, others as blue, grey, green or red. This path is realised by a Brahmin, knower of Brahma. Any other knower of Brahma, who has done good deeds and is identified with the Supreme light, also treads this path. On the other hand, those, who worship ignorance (rites), they enter into blinding darkness. Into greater darkness, as it were, than that enter, those, who are devoted to knowledge, the ceremonial portion of the vedas, the portion of vedas, which deals with things that are the outcome of ignorance i.e. the ritualistic portion. Those, who disregard the teachings of shrutis, say that, that portion alone which deals with the injunctions and prohibitions, is the vedas, and there is none other. But the worlds enveloped by that blinding darkness, i.e., ignorance, are miserable. To them, after death go those people, who are ignorant and unwise. If a man knows the self as, I am this, then desiring what and for whose sake will he suffer in the wake of the body.

He, who has realised and intimately known the self, that has entered this perilous and inaccessible place, the body, is the maker of the universe as he is the maker of all, all is his self, and he again is indeed the self of all. Being in this very body, we have somehow known that Brahma. If not, he should have been ignorant and great destruction would have taken place. Those, who know it, become immortal, while others attain misery alone. But, when a man, after receiving instructions from a teacher, directly realises this effulgent self, the Lord of all that has been and will be, he no longer wishes to hide himself from the Lord. Or, when he directly realises the effulgent Lord, as identical with his own self, he no longer blames any body, for he sees all as his self, and for that reason whom should he blame ? Further, it is by being revealed by the light of the 'Atman' that is 'Pure intelligence', its own self, that the vital force functions. Therefore, it is the vital force and those who have known the vital force of the vital force as also eye of the eye, the ear of the ear— the eye and the ear receive their powers of vision and so forth only by being inspired by the energy of Brahma, by themselves, diverted of the light of the 'Atman' that is 'Pure intelligence', they are like word or clods of earth, and the mind of the mind. In other words, those, who have known the self, not as a sense object, but as the innermost self, whose existence is inferred from the function of the eye etc., have realised, known with certainty, the ancient or eternal, and primordial Brahma, that which the knowers of the self realise. The means of the realisation of that Brahma, are through the mind alone, purified by the knowledge of the supreme truth, and in accordance with the instructions of the teacher, it is to be realised. There is no difference whatsoever in it, Brahma, the object of the realisation. Though there is no difference, one superimposes it through ignorance. He goes form death to death, who sees difference, as it were, in it. That is to say really there is no duality apart from the superimposition of ignorance. It should, therefore, be realised in one form only, for it is unknowable and eternal. The self is taintless, beyond the subtle ether, birthless, infinite and constant. The intelligent aspirant after Brahma, knowing about this alone, should attain intuitive knowledge. He should not think of too many words, for it is particularly fatiguing to the organ of speech.

That great, birthless self, which is identified with the intellect and is in the midst of the organs, lies in the ether, which is within the heart. It is the controller of all, the Lord of all and the ruler of all. It does not grow better through good work nor worsens through bad work. It is the Lord, the ruler and the protector of all beings. It is the bank that serves as the boundary to keep the different worlds apart. The Brahmins seek to know it through the study of the vedas, sacrifices, charity and austerity consisting in a dispassionate enjoyment of sense-objects. Knowing it alone, one becomes a sage. Desiring this world (the self) alone, monks renounce their homes. The ancient sages, did not desire children, thinking, 'What shall we achieve through children, we, who have attained this self, this world (results).' They renounce their desire for sons, for wealth and for the worlds and live in a mendicants' life. That which is the desire for sons is the desire for wealth and that which is the desire for wealth, is the desire for worlds, for both these are but desires. This self is that which has been described as 'Not this, not this'. It is imperceptible, for it is never perceived, undecaying for it never decays, unattached as it is never attached, unfettered as it never feels pain and never suffers injury. It is but proper that the sage is never overtaken by these two thoughts, 'I did an evil act for this', 'I did a good act for this'. He conquers both of them. Things done or not done do not trouble him. 'Just as a blazing fire burns the fuel to ashes', etc., the knower of Brahma burns all work to ashes with the fire of self-knowledge and as to those actions, that caused the present body, they are worked out through actual experience. Hence the knower of Brahma has no connection with work. This is also expressed in shrutis, 'This is the eternal glory of a knower of Brahma, it neither increases nor decreases through work. Therefore, one should know the nature of that alone. Knowing it, one is not touched by evil action. Therefore, he, who knows it as such, becomes self-controlled, calm, withdrawn into himself, enduring and concentrated, and sees the self in his own-self (body); he sees all as the self. Evil does not overtake him, but he transcends all evils. Evil does not trouble him, but he consumes all evils. He becomes sinless, taintless, free from doubts, and a Brahmin (knower of Brahma). This is the world of Brahma and Raja Janaka had attained it. The Raja gave away the entire empire and himself to serve on him. This finishes the topic of Brahma.

That great birthless self, which has been expounded in the story of Janaka and Yajnavalkya, is the eater of all food, by living in all beings and the giver of wealth i.e. the fruits of the actions of all, in other words, he connects all beings with the results of their respective actions. He who knows it, this birthless self, that is the eater of food and the giver of wealth, as such, as described above i.e. as endowed with these two attributes, eats food, as the self of all beings, and receives wealth, the entire fruits of everybody's actions, being their very self. Or the meaning may be, the self is to be meditated upon as endowed with these attributes even by a man who wants visible results. By that meditation, he becomes the eater of food and the receiver of wealth ; that is to say, he is thereby connected with visible results — with the power to eat plenty of food and with cows, horses etc.

Now the import of the whole upanisada is being summed up in this paragraph, as much as to say that this is the substance of the entire upanisada. That great birthless self is undecaying i.e. it does not wear off; immortal because it is undecaying. That which is born and decays, also dies, but because it is indestructible on account of its being birthless and undecaying, therefore, it is undying. That is to say since it is free from the other three changes of condition, birth and so on, it is also free from the other three changes of condition and their effects — desire, work, delusion etc., which are but forms of death, hence also it is fearless. Since it is possessed of the preceding attributes, it is devoid of fear. Besides, fear is one effect of ignorance; by the negation of that effect as well as of the six changes of condition, it is understood that ignorance too is negated. Brahma is the fearless self that is possessed of the above-mentioned attributes. It is vast or infinite and indeed fearless. It is a well- known fact. Therefore, it is but proper to say that the self endowed with the above attributes is Brahma. He, who knows it, the self described above, as such, as the fearless Brahma, certainly becomes the fearless Brahma. This is the purport of the whole upanisada, put in a nutshell. It is to bring home their purport that the ideas of projection, maintenance, dissolution etc. as well as those of action and its factors and results were superimposed on the self. Again, by that negation — by the elimination of the superimposed attributes through a process of 'Not this, not this,— the truth has been known. Just as, in order to explain the nature of numbers from one upto a hundred thousand billions, a man superimposes them on certain lines (digits), calling one of them one, another ten, another hundred, yet another thousand and so on, and in so doing, he only expounds the nature of numbers but he never says that the numbers are the lines, or just as in order to teach the alphabet, he has recourse to a combination of leaf, ink, lines etc. and through them explains the nature of the letters, but he never says that the letters are the leaf, ink, lines etc. Similarly, in this exposition, the only entity. Brahma, has been inculcated through various means, such as the projection of the universe. Again, to eliminate the differences created by those hypothetical means, the truth has been summed up as 'Not this, not this'. In the end that knowledge, further clarified so as to be undifferentiated, together with its results, has been concluded in this paragraph.

Now the present section relating to Maitreyi, the wife of Yajnavalkya, is being introduced as a conclusion of the proposition regarding the same topic. Yajnavalkya had two wives — Maitreyi and Katyayani. Of these, Maitreyi used to discuss Brahma while Katyayani had then only an essentially feminine outlook. One day Yajnavalkya, with a view to embracing another life said that he was going to renounce this life for monasticism and asked to finish between the two wives. Thereupon Maitreyi said if indeed this whole earth full of wealth be her's shall she be immortal through that or not. Yajnavalkya replied 'No', her life shall be just like that of people, who possessed plenty of wealth but there was no hope of immortality through wealth. Then Maitreyi said what shall she do with that which will not make her immortal. She wanted to be told that alone, which he knows to be the only means of immortality. Yajnavalkya said, she had been his beloved even before, and she had magnified what was after his heart. If she wished so he shall explain it to her and wanted that she should meditate on its meaning as he explained it.

YAJNAVALKYA further said, 'It is not for the sake of husband, that he is loved, but for one's own sake that he is loved. It is not for the sake of the wife, that she is loved, but for one's own sake that she is loved. It is not for the sake of sons, that they are loved but for one's own sake that they are loved. It is not for the sake of wealth, that it is loved but for one's own sake that it is loved. It is not for the sake of animals, that they are loved but for one's own sake. It is not for the sake of Brahma, that he is loved but for one's own sake. It is not for the sake of Kshatriya that he is loved but for one's own sake. It is not for the sake of worlds that they are loved but for one's own sake. Similarly, it is not for the sake of gods, vedas, beings and all that they are loved but are loved for one's own sake. The self should be realised — should be heard of, reflected on and meditated upon. When the self is realised by being heard of, reflected on and meditated upon, all this is known. The Brahmin ousts one, who knows him as different from the self. The Kshatriya ousts one, who knows him as different from the self. Worlds oust one, who knows them as different from the self. Similarly, gods, veda, beings and all others oust one, who knows it as different from the self. The Brahmin, Kshatriya, worlds, gods, vedas, the beings and these all are this self. As when a drum is beaten, one cannot distinguish its various particular notes, but they are included in the general note of the drum or in the general sound produced by different kinds of strokes. Also as when conch is blown, vina is played, one cannot distinguish its various particular notes. Further, as from the fire kindled with wet jaggot, diverse kinds of smoke issue, even so the Rig Veda, Yajurveda, Samaveda, Atharvangirasa, history, mythology, arts, upanisadas, pithy verses, aphorisms, elucidations, explanations, sacrifices, oblations in the fire, food, drink, this world, the next world and all beings are all like the breath of this infinite Reality. They are like the breath of this Supreme self. Also as ocean is the goal of all sorts of water, skin is the goal of all kinds of touch, nostrils are the goal of all odours, tongue is the goal of all savours, eye is the goal or all colours, ear is the goal of all sounds, manas is the goal of all deliberations, intellect is the goal of all knowledge, as the hands are the goal of all sorts of work, organ of generation is the goal of all kinds of enjoyments, anus is the goal of all excretions, feet are the goal of all kinds of motions, organ of speech is one goal of all vedas. As the lump of salt is without interior or exterior, entire and purely saline in taste, even so is the self, without interior or exterior, entire and pure intelligence alone. The self comes out as a separate entity from these elements and this separateness is destroyed with them. After attaining this oneness, it has no more particular consciousness. Maitreyi said that she had been led in the midst of confusion. Yajnavalkya told that the self is indeed immutable and indestructible. Because when there is duality, as it were, then one sees something, one smells something, one tastes something, one speaks something, one hears something, one thinks something, one touches something and one knows something. But when to the knower of Brahma, everything has become the self, then what should one see, smell, hear, speak, think, touch, know and through what. Through what should one know that owing to which all this is known ? This self is that which has been described as, 'Not this, not this'. It is imperceptible, for it is never perceived, undecaying, as it never decays, unattached as it is never attached, unfettered as it never feels pain and never suffers injury.

Now we shall discuss to get a clear conception of the meaning of scriptures as we find conflicting statements. For instance, the following texts indicate that there is only one order of life, the householder's : 'One should perform the 'agnihotra' for life'. 'One should wish to live a hundred years on earth only performing rites'. 'This Agnihotra is a sacrifice that must be continued till decay and death comes', and so on. There are also statements establishing another order of life, monasticism, 'Knowing the self, they give up desires, and renounce their homes'. 'After finishing the student life, he should be a householder, from that he should pass on to the life of a hermit in the forest, and then become a monk, or he may do otherwise — he should renounce the world from the student life itself or from the householder's life or from the hermit's life'. 'There are but two paths — first the path of rites and the next monasticism ; of these, the latter excels and neither through rites nor through progeny nor through wealth, but through renunciation, some attained immortality. Similarly, as per smirits, 'One, who leads the student life renounces' ; 'One who leads a perfectly celibate life, may enter into any order of life.' Some say, one has to choose, either after studying the vedas as a student, he should seek to have sons and grandsons to purify his ancestors. Lighting the sacred fires and making sacrifices according to the injunctions, he should retire into the forest and then seek to become a monk. Thus, hundreds of contradictory passages from the shrutis and samritis are found, inculcating an option with regard to renunciation, or a succession among the orders of life or the adoption of anyone of them at will. The prima facie view, therefore, is that the the vedas inculcate only rites, from such shruti passage as 'One should perform agnihotra for life', admit of no other meaning. The shrutis speak of the last rite of a man in these terms, 'They burn him with the sacrificial verses'. There is also the statement about the rites being continued till decay and death comes. Further, all rites are for the unenlightened man with desire. Is it not absolutely that rites are enjoined for life ? For men are generally full of desires, which concern various objects and require the help of many rites and their means. The vedic rites are the means of various results and are to be performed by a man related to a wife and the fire, they produce many results, being performed again and again, like agriculture etc. and take a hundred years to finish either in the householders' life or in the forest life. Hence shruti enjoins life-long rites saying 'One should wish to live a hundred years on earth only performing rites. Or it may be that the injunctions of the shrutis about the life-long performance of rites concern the other two castes except the Brahmin, as the Kshatriya and Vaishyas are not entitled to the monastic life. The teachers speaking of only one order of life, would refer to Kshatriyas and Vaishyas. Therefore, in accordance with a person's capacity, knowledge, non-attachment, desire etc. the various methods of an option with regard to renunciation or a succession among the order of life, or the embracing of the monastic life, are not contradictory. And since monasticism has been separately enjoined on those, who are unfit for rites, in the passage, 'Whether he has completed his course of study or not, whether he has discarded the fire or been released from it' etc. Therefore, it is proved that the three orders of life (besides the householder's life) are surely meant for those, who are qualified for rites.

'OM' is the ether, Brahma, is a Mantra. No direction for its use has been given elsewhere; the Brahmin here directs that it is to be used in meditation. Brahma in this mantra is the entity specified and 'Ether' is its description. In the terms 'ether Brahma', the entity specified and the description are coordinate, as in the expression 'A blue lotus'. The word 'Brahma', without any qualifying word would mean any vast object, hence it is specified as 'Ether Brahma'. The 'Ether Brahma' is either the import of the word 'OM' or identical with it. In either case, the coordinate relation holds good. Here the word 'OM' is used to serve as a means to the meditation on Brahma. As other shrutis say, 'This is the best help to the realisation of Brahma and the highest, one should concentrate on the self, uttering 'OM'. One should meditate upon the supreme being only through the syllable 'OM'. Meditate upon the self with the help of 'OM' and so on. The instruction of the word 'OM' here is for the purpose of presenting it as a means to meditation only. Although the words 'Brahma'. 'Atman' etc. are names of Brahma, yet on the authority of shruti, we know that 'OM' is its most intimate appellation. Therefore, it is the best means for the realisation of Brahma. It is so as a symbol and as a name. As a symbol, just as the image of Vishnu or any other God is regarded as identical with that god (for purposes of worship), so is 'OM' to be treated as Brahma, because Brahma is pleased with one, who uses 'OM' as an aid for the shruti says, 'This is the best help and the highest, knowing this help one is glorified in the world of Brahma'. Now last 'Ether' should mean the material ether, the text says, 'The eternal ether, i.e., the ether which is the supreme self.' Because the latter, being beyond the reach of the eye and other organs, cannot be perceived without some help, therefore, the aspirant super imposes it with faith, devotion and great rapture on the syllable 'OM' as people superimpose Vishnu on images of stone etc. with carvings of His features. The ether containing air, just the ordinary ether, not the eternal ether, says 'The word ether is primarily used in the sense of the ether containing air, so he thinks that should be taken, now whether it is the 'eternal ether', meaning the unconditioned Brahma, or it is the 'ether containing air' meaning the conditioned Brahma, in either case, the syllable 'OM' as a symbol becomes a means of realising it like an image. Another shruti says, 'The syllable 'OM' is the higher and lower Brahma. The one difference is over the meaning of the word 'ether'.

This 'OM' is the veda as through it, one knows what is to be known. Therefore, 'OM' is the veda or name of Brahma. Through that name, the aspirant knows or realises what is to be known, viz Brahma, which is the object signified or designated by the name. Therefore, the Brahmins know that it is the veda. They mean that as a name it is intended as a means to the realisation of Brahma. Or the passage, 'It is the veda' etc., may be a eulogy because 'OM' is enjoined as a symbol of Brahma, for it is coordinated with the word 'Brahma' in the sentence, 'OM is the Ether Brahma'. Now it is being praised as the veda, for the entire vedas are but 'OM'. They all issue out of it and consist of it, this 'OM' is differentiated into divisions of Rig, Yajur, Sama etc., for another shruti says, 'As by a stick all leaves are pierced, so all speech is pierced by 'OM'. Here is another reason why 'OM' is the veda — through it, this OM 'OM knows whatever is to be known', hence this 'OM' is the veda. The other vedas owe their vedahood to this. Therefore, 'OM' being so important, should be used as a means to self - realisation. Or the passage in question may be thus interpreted. It is the veda that 'OM', 'Which the Brahmins know' as it should be known by the Brahmins in various forms such as 'Pranava' and 'Udgitha'. If it is used as a means of realisation, the entire vedas are particularly used.

5

Svetasvatara Upanisada

Discussion on what is the nature of Brahma, the source; from what have we been born; by what do we live; where do we exist; and controlled by whom, we follow the rule regarding joy and its opposite.

The basic principle is that the intelligent self is neither born nor does it die. This surely dies when separated from the individual soul but the soul does not die; the decrepitude and death are of the body only and the self is immutable and indestructible. However, the birthless one is said to be born on account of its becoming embodied. The time, inherent nature, fate, chance, the elements, the individual soul, as the source, need consideration. But their combination is not the source because they exist for the soul. The soul too is not independent on account of joy and sorrow. The time and inherent nature are to be connected with source. Time is that which is the cause of transformation of all entities and inherent nature means the power of things as ordained respectively, for instance, the heat of fire. Fate means dissimilar actions in the form of virtue or vice. Chance means unforeseen acquisition. The elements are like space etc. The individual soul is identified with intelligence. It is, however, not possible for time etc. to be the source individually, because this contradicts experience as it is seen in the world that, only the combination of time, space and causation becomes the source of creation. As already indicated, the soul too is not independent on account of joy and sorrow. Therefore, the soul too, not being independent, is not the source. Then the non-independent soul cannot be the cause of the world, which is differentiated into such divisions as the physical etc. and which is the cause of happiness, sorrow etc. After having thus demolished the different views and not finding another means of determining the entity that defies all the other means of proof, they themselves realised the supreme primary source by practising the yoga of meditation.

By practising the yoga of meditation, they realised the power of Deity Himself, hidden by its own effects — the Lord who, alone rules all those sources associated with i.e. including time and the individual soul. Meditation means concentration of mind. That itself is the yoga — in the sense of that through which one becomes connected with the goal of meditation i.e. the means of making the object of meditation one's own. By practising that, they realised the power of the Deity, Himself. Now the question arises as to whether Brahma is the source or is it the time etc. or is Brahma the cause or is it distinct from cause and effect or is it the cause or is it not the cause. Even if it be the cause, is it the material or the efficient cause or what is the characteristic of Brahma, which is the cause in both the senses or which is not the cause ? The answer is it is neither the 'cause' nor the 'not cause' neither is it both, nor is it different from both, neither is it the efficient cause nor the material cause, nor both. After deliberation, they realised as the source, the power, identical with Himself, not independent, not free and separate like the 'Pradhan' nature, imagined by the Sankhyas — of the deity endowed with effulgence etc. the Lord of Maya, the Supreme Lord, the Supreme self. One should, therefore, know that the nature is surely 'Maya' and the Supreme Lord is the Ruler of Maya. This 'Maya', the highest nature, diversified into twenty four categories, has sprung from this. So also, under him, as the supervisor, the nature produces the world with all the moving and the non-moving things. In the power of the Deity Himself and the Lord, who alone, rules all those sources associated with time and the individual soul, it has been mentioned that the same non-dual Supreme self becomes the efficient cause and the material cause from the points of view of its nature in reality and its appearance as the power. As the ruler of 'Maya', it appears as

God and as constituted by the three gods and as omniscient. When bereft of 'Maya', it has the non-dual nature of truth, knowledge and bliss. Now by establishing that a cause and an effect are non-different, the upanisada shows that very entity as the self of all. With the purpose of revealing the real nature of Brahma as non-dual, without cause and effect, possessed of a nature described as, 'Not this, not this' beyond speech, untouched by hunger etc., devoid of differences, and as consciousness, existence and bliss — as stated that 'All transformation has speech as the basis and it is name only.' The upanisada presents the meditation on that Supreme Brahma — which, because of nature itself, has assumed the delusive form of the phenomenal world — as God, who is omniscient and free from sins etc., as the Deity manifested in the form of Brahma and others as the effects viz space etc., and as Vaisvanara (Virat) etc., for the sake of acquiring purity of mind that is a pre-requisite for emancipation and for the sake of attaining all the glories as they are stated in, 'Should he become desirous of the manas' and for the sake of becoming unified with the deity, as it is stated in, 'Invariably, he attains Me or Sankara, and for the sake of attaining Vaisvanara etc., and it also presents the tradition of numerous conventional and vedic rites.

Should it not be present as cause and effect, and in its true nature, as Brahma which is consciousness, existence and bliss, then, due to the absence of things to be enjoyed, the enjoyer and the controller, there will surely be no worldly existence and liberation as due to the absence of any eligible person, there will be no world as a means to spiritual disciplines, and God also, who is the giver of fruit of those disciplines, will have no existence. Accordingly, God is shown as the cause of worldly existence etc., 'He is the cause of the worldly state, liberation, existence and bondage.' In that case there will indeed be an absence of transmigration and liberation. They saw Him as having one rim, three tiers, sixteen ends, fifty spokes, twenty fasters, six sets of eight, one bondage of numerous forms, three different paths, and a single delusion that is the cause of the two. Here one rim means He alone rules all the sources, called by such names as source, nature, maya, power, cause, space ignorance, unreality but is like a rim, the support of all. Three tier means — Sattava, Rajas and Tamas — constituents of nature. Sixteen ends are sixteen transformations, five elements (earth, water, fire, air and space), eleven organs (mind, five sense organs and five motor organs), for its ends. Fifty spokes are fifty different notions classed as misconceptions, disabilities, satisfaction and successes etc. Five misconceptions are obscurity, delusion, extreme delusion, gloom and utter darkness. Disability is of twenty eight kinds, satisfactions of nine kinds and success is of eight kinds. These are fifty kinds of motions. Twenty fastners are the ten organs and their objects viz sound, touch, form, taste, smell, speaking, grasping, walking, excretion and enjoyment. Six sets of eight—His nature is divided eight fold as earth, water, fire, air, space, mind, intellect and egoism. The octad of bodily substances are internal skin, external skin, flesh, blood, fat, bone, marrow and semen. The octad of yogic power are those of becoming minute etc.. The eight states of mind are virtue, knowledge, detachment, majesty, vice, ignorance, attachment and poverty. Eight supernumeral beings are Brahma, Prajapati, gods, Gandharva, Yaksas, demons, manes and ghouls. The eight qualities of mind are kindness to all beings, forbearance, absence of jealousy, purity, ease, goodness, generosity and contentment. One bondage is desire, which is of numerous forms due to diversity in the form of heaven, son, edible food, etc. Three different paths are righteousness, unrighteousness and knowledge. Single delusion is the idea identifying oneself with the body, senses, mind, intellect, caste etc., that are not the self — which is the cause of the two, virtue and vice.

Similar is the case with river, which has five whirlpools — the objects viz sound etc. the rush of water is constituted by the five sorrows — of being in the womb, of birth, of decrepitude, of disease and of death and five stages, which are ignorance, egoism, attachment, aversion, and clinging to life. In this way Brahma has been shown here with the analogies of the river and the wheel of Brahma. Now with a view to pointing out the cause of transmigration and liberation i.e. why one revolves in this wheel of Brahma consisting of cause and effect, and how one becomes liberated, the upanisada says, 'The individual soul, considering itself and the controller as different, revolves in this great wheel of Brahma that is the sustenance of all and the place of dissolution of all. One's self is adored as identified with the God, then thereby one attains immortality. One is liberated, when one's self is adored with Him, with God, with the non-dual Brahma i.e. by nature, consciousness, existence and bliss i.e. becoming absorbed in the realisation, 'I am Brahma'. Then one attains immortality. He, who realises his self as identical with Brahma, becomes liberated. Also whoever in the like manner knows it as 'I am Brahma', becomes all this universe. Even the gods cannot prevail against him. But it has to be kept in mind that it is not that Brahma together with creation, that has been presented by the text, 'They saw him as having one rim' etc. That being so, even when one realises one's identity with Brahma as 'I am Brahma', Brahma together indeed with creation will be realised as one's self. Hence in accordance with 'One becomes just what one thinks of Him in his meditation', then will verily accrue to him the attainment of Brahma together with the universe. And, therefore, owing to the non-elimination of the phenomenal world, there will be no liberation. From this, it follows that the instruction about liberation when one's self is adored, as identified with Him (God), then thereby one attains immortality, is surely illogical. Having this apprehension, the upanisada says that. Brahma, which is verily the best, has been proclaimed to be distinct. On it exist the three. It is the excellent substraction and it is certainly immutable. The knowers of Brahma, having realised the distinction here and remaining absorbed in it, get merged in Brahma and become freed from birth.

If Brahma is inalienable from creation, then there will really be an absence of liberation. But that is not so since it has been proclaimed to be distinct, taught by the upanisada, by distinguishing it from the manifested world consisting of cause and effect. The purport is that Brahma is known to be verily untouched by the world from such texts as:

'That Brahma is surely different from the known'

and again 'He is above the unknown'.

'You know that alone to be Brahma, and not what people worship as one object.'

'That which is soundless, touchless'.

'This self is that which has been described as 'Not this, not this'.

Further, if the supreme self is admitted to be non-dual then since the difference also between the individual soul and God, ceases to exist, therefore, the upanisidic text, 'Get merged in Brahma' declaiming merger — which means the identity of the individual soul with Brahma becomes illogical. Having this apprehension in mind, the upanisada first shows the distinction between the individual soul and God due to the limiting adjuncts in the empirical state, and then reveals immortality as a consequence of the realisation of that Supreme Self.

The Lord nourishes this universe consisting of the mutually associated manifested and the unmanifested which are respectively the mutable and the immutable. The individual soul, which is not independent, becomes bound due to its sense of being the enjoyer, realising the effulgent being, it becomes freed from all bondages. So there are two persons in the world — the mutable and the immutable. The mutable consists of all things; the one existing as 'Maya' is called the immutable. They are also the material and the Godly.

Then the two (i.e. God and the individual soul) are both birthless and respectively are all-knowing and ignorant, and almighty and powerless, since the birthless one viz. 'Maya' is employed for bringing into being the enjoyer, the enjoyable and the enjoyment. The self is infinite since it has the universe as its appearance; and hence it is not an agent. One becomes liberated when one knows the three as this Brahma. He made bodies with two feet and bodies with four feet. That supreme being first entered the bodies as a bird (the subtle body). Similarly, the self inside all beings, though one, assumes a form in respect of each shape, and it is outside. Upanisada says, 'Since the birthless one viz 'Maya', is employed for bringing into being the enjoyer, the enjoyable and the enjoyment, if the universe be totally inadmissible, then there will be no such difference as God etc.' However, the universe certainty is admissible.

Even when it is admitted that the Supreme self is one

and homogenous, all usages, both conventional and vedic, indicative of such distinctions as 'soul' 'God' etc., become justifiable. And there does not arise the possibility of duality on account of the existence of either of them as a separate entity, for 'Maya', being indefinable, it has no possibility, of being a substance. Thus has it been said, 'This, indeed, is the 'Maya' of God, which defies being expressed as existence or non-existence'. Since the birthless one (Maya) alone has assumed the form of the enjoyer etc., therefore, everything that is comprised in it, is unreal and unsubstantial. Hence 'Atma', the self, is verily the particle, is infinite. This self is verily infinite in the sense that it has no limitation, caused by space, time and matter. Again, when does the soul — which in reality is thus infinite and has the universe as its appearance, and is devoid of all mundane attributes like agentship etc. and free — remain established as the non-dual Brahma, that is absolute bliss. In answer to this, the upanisada says 'When it realises the three as this Brahma, when it realises that the three viz those in the form of enjoyer, the enjoyment and the enjoyable, do not exist apart from Brahma, since they are inherently, different forms cf 'Maya', but they are Brahma itself, then it continues in the state of being freed from all doubts, identified with Brahma that is absolute bliss and non-dual, devoid of all mundane attributes like agentship etc., free from sorrow and self-fulfilled. Or, when one realises as Brahma the three in the form of the individual soul, God and nature, which are characterised, as all-knowing, ignorant and birthless, then one becomes free. Thus after stating the distinction between God and the soul, it has been shown that immortality comes from the knowledge of Brahma. Further, nature is mutable and the Supreme God is immortal and immutable. The one deity rules the mutable and the soul. And from the repeated meditation on Him, union with and contemplation on reality, there comes about, at the end, the cessation of 'Maya' in the form of universe. By knowing the deity, comes the snapping of all bondages, on the attenuation of the pain-bearing obstructions, comes the eradication of birth and death. From meditation on Him, there accrues, on the fall of the body, the third, the full divine power. And he becomes absolute — and self- fulfilled. On the other hand, intelligence produced from meditation cannot, all of a sudden, proceed, to the formless entity. Hence, since meditation is concerned with the conditioned Brahma, therefore, in accordance with the maxim of getting a result just as one meditates on Him, after enjoying full glory by attaining the conditioned Brahma, characterised as full glory, one realises as one's self the unconditioned Brahma, is that absolute bliss. From meditation comes in comparable divine power ; from divine power follows great happiness. Rejecting them through enlightenment, one should become detached from the body and attain liberation. After that, in 'The enlightened man attains that three-fold world through 'OM' only and through 'OM' as an aid, he reaches that also which is the Supreme reality that is quiet and beyond old age, death and fear. Instruction is given about liberation, as a result of full enlightenment, and, 'One who knows it thus, becomes immortal here', reveals that immortality is achieved here itself by the enlightened person, without going along the part of light etc. commencing with, but the man who does not desire, never transmigrates. Of him, the organs do not depart. Being but Brahma, he is merged with Brahma and that for the enlightened person ensues liberation even before departing from the body.

Therefore, the meditator, after departing from the body, having reached Brahma, that is possessed of all divine powers by proceeding along the path of the gods through light etc. and having enjoyed the divine powers and becoming desirous solely of the self, attains liberation by realising there itself the absolute self, Brahma, which is free from differences and is full bliss and non-dual and by seeing equally God, who is present alike everywhere, he does not injure the self by the self, therefore, he attains the supreme goal. Now since the supreme goal is attained after enlightenment, therefore, after knowing all these three kinds — the enjoyer (the individual soul), the things of enjoyment and the internal ruler — that have been spoken of as Brahma — this is to be invariably known as existing in one's own heart, since there is nothing to be known beyond this. The yogis realise Shiva in their hearts, and not in image. One, who, leaving aside Shiva, existing within the heart, worships Him as existing externally, is like one, who, rejecting a morsel of food on his palm, licks his own elbow. As a blind man does not see the sun that is risen, similarly they do not see here Shiva, who exists everywhere and is of serene appearance, because they are devoid of the eye of knowledge. He, who, realises the all-pervasive Shiva has Him seated in his heart and those, who do not see Shiva within the heart, seek him in places of pilgrimage. He, who, ignoring the holy place in the heart, goes to external holy places etc. is like one who, throwing away a great gem in his own hand, searches for the glass. Also, according to the upanisada text, 'Any one, who meditates on the Supreme 'Purusa' with the help of this very syllable 'OM', one should fix one's mind on the self with the help of 'OM' and one should meditate on the self with the help of 'OM', it is enjoined that 'OM' should be meditated upon when one engages in meditation on the supreme reality with a view to realising the self, therefore, the text presents 'OM' as a part of meditation. As the form of fire is not seen when it lies in its sources, and yet its latent form is not destroyed, and that fire, is perceptible after repeated rubbing of its source, the fuel — as in the case of those two, viz fire and its subtle form, similarly the self is realised in the body with the help of 'OM'. This is possible by making one's own body the lower 'Arani' (piece of wood used for kindling fire by attrition) and 'OM', the upper 'Arani', one should through the practice of meditation, that is analogous to rubbing, realise the deity, which is hidden, as it were. Similarly, as oil is found in sesamum, clarified butter (ghee) in curd, water in rivers (underground) and fire in the 'aranis', so this self is realised in oneself by him, who sees this 'OM' through truth and concentration. One sees the self — which, like clarified butter inherent in milk, is all pervasive and which is the source of self- knowledge and concentration — as that Brahma on which is establishing the highest God. For them is that taintless world of Brahma, in whom there is no crookedness, no falsehood and no dissimulation.

Here meditation has been spoken of as a means to the realisation of the Supreme self. Now is narrated the view to enjoining the disciplines on which it depends. As to that, 'Sun' is first implored for the acquisition of those disciplines. At first there is prayer to the Sun for withdrawing mind engaged in the pursuit of knowledge from the perception of external objects for the sake of fixing it on the Supreme self, may the Sun, i.e. the Deity, through whose grace one attains Yoga, establish on our organs such a speech etc. all the powers that the presiding deities, fire and others, have, of revealing all objects. Then, with the mind fixed on the Supreme self, we having the approval of the deity, the Sun, strive according to ability in the act of meditation, which is the cause of attainment of the Supreme self. The Brahmins, who, with their mind and organs with the self, are expected to praise the Deity. In this way of prayer to the sun and other has been presented in while first engaging the mind. etc. He, who engages in yoga without prayer and without being given consent by them, engages merely in works that bring enjoyment. Where fire is kindled by rubbing, where the air is made expressive, where soma becomes abundant, there in that sacrifice the mind gets engrossed. Since one whose heart is purified by 'Pranayama', realises that Supreme self, therefore, the shruti says that there is nothing greater than the 'Pranayama'. When those sins accumulated during many lives of transmigration, become dissipated, then there grows in people the inclination towards Govinda. Devotion to Krishna is born in people, whose sins have become attenuated through austerity, knowledge and concentration practised in thousands of past births.

Therefore, performance of sacrifices, etc., comes first, then comes 'Pranayama' etc. and after that comes self-absorption, then is acquired the knowledge of the meaning of the great upanisadic sayings and thereafter comes self-fulfilment. After being permitted by the sun, the producer of grains, one should adore the eternal Brahma. One should generate steadfastness in that. Action sanctioned by the samritis will certainty not bind him. But what shall happen to him from that while he is engaged thus ? The answer as per upanisada is, 'Action sanctioned by samritis as also the sacrifices etc. again bind him for the purpose of enjoyment, because it has been burnt away, together with its seed, by the fire of knowledge. It has been said, 'You should have general steadfastness in that'. Then how to generate steadfastness is by the process of keeping steady the body that has its three parts erect, and withdrawing the organs into the heart with the help of the mind, the enlightened person should cross over all the terrible currents by means of the float that Brahma is. That body in which the three viz chest, neck and head, are erect, remains steady by withdrawing into the heart, the organs — mind, eyes etc. with the help of the mind by means of the float that Brahma is. Brahma itself is the float that is the means of crossing, by means of that float of Brahma or 'OM'. 'Pranayama' is presented because the heart of a person, whose mental defects have been removed by 'Pranayama' becomes fixed in Brahma. The nerves have to be purified first, then one acquires the fitness for 'Pranayama'. Closing the right nostril with the thumb, one should inhale air through the left nostril according to capacity. Immediately after that, releasing the right nostril, one should exhale through the right nostril. In the same way ; one should also close the left nostril again inhaling through the right and should exhale through the left according to capacity. To one, who practises thus either three times or five times during the four periods of the day viz. at the close of the night, at noon, at dusk and at midnight, comes purity in a fortnight or a month. Therefore, 'Pranayama' consists of three parts - exhaling, inhaling and with-holding. Similarly, one should purify the nerves by sitting comfortably on a seat, placing on the left hand the other hand, holding the neck and head straight, closing the mouth completely, becoming totally motionless, facing either east or north, fixing the eyes on the tip of the nose and avoiding with adequate effort either eating too much or too little, one should diligently purify the nerves according to the process prescribed. Then fixing the two eyes on the tip of the nose and visualising the world — pervading mantra of Moon, associated with moonlight and the mantra 'Vam', — one should fill in with the external air through the 'Ida' for twelve moments. Then one should meditate on 'Ram' existing in the hall of fire and should again slowly exhale the air through the 'Pingla'. Once more, filling up the right nostril through the 'Pingla' should likewise exhale the air slowly through the Ida. For three or four years, one should practise in this way in a solitary place, according to the instructions of the teacher and exercise six 'Pranayama' in a day. Thus shall one attain purification of the nerves. Lightness of the body, brightness, increase in power of digestion and audibility of the 'Nada', these are the signs of the purification. The three exhaling, with-holding and inhaling, are also equated with creation, preservation and destruction respectively. This 'Pranayama' is the cause of success of the yogis in this world.

By 'Pranayama', one gets what is mentally desired and becomes victorious over all the vital forces. One should burn away the bodily impurities through 'Pranayama', the sins through concentration, attachment, through restraint of senses and through meditation the idea of one's non-divinity.

One, who is duly restrained in his actions, should, having fully controlled the vital forces in this body, exhale through the nose when the vital force has become powerless. The unerring wise man should hold the mind under control like keeping under control a chariot to which is yoked an unruly horse. Having fully controlled the vital force, in this body, one, who is duly restrained in his actions, he, whose actions are adequately restrained, in the manner, stated in the verse, 'Yoga is not for one, who eats excessively. One should slowly exhale through the openings of the nose — not through the mouth — when the vital force has become powerless, when the mind has become fine, that is holding the air in, he should slowly release it through the nose, the unerring man, fully concentrated in mind, should hold the mind, in contemplation like keeping in place a charioteer, who has to control a chariot to which is yoked an unruly horse. One should fix the mind on the Supreme self while dwelling in a shelter, such as a cave free from wind, that is even, free from pebbles, fire and sand, and free from sound and water, and that is not a public shelter, and that is pleasing to the mind but not painful to the eyes. The modification of the mind emerges in that form together with the vital force — after that it appears like smoke, then it appears like the sun, and after that like the wind. Thereafter blows a wind, very hot like fire in its brightness and power of burning, it blows like the powerful and agitated external wind. Sometimes it (mind) is seen like the sky studded with fireflies. It is visualised as resplendent like lightening, crystal or full moon. These forms become the fore-runners, when Brahma is being revealed in Yoga undertaken for that purpose. Then follows the highest success in Yoga. Then, when earth, water, air and space come into being and when the five-fold attributes of Yoga have emerged, then for the man who has attained a body, made of the fire of yoga, there is no disease, nor decrepitude, nor death. It is said that the first signs of entering yoga are lightness, health, non-covetousness, clearness of complexion and a beautiful voice, an agreeable odour in the body and scantiness of urine and faeces. It has also been said that the manifestations are said to be of four kinds : Full of brightness, full of touch, and so also the other full of taste and good smell. Among these different manifestations of yoga, should even one emerge, then the yogis, who are adept in yoga, speak of him as having entered the path of yoga. Further, just as a disc, covered with earth shines as full of light when washed well, similarly the embodied being, visualising that very reality that is the self, becomes non-dual, self-fulfilled and free from sorrows. Further, the kind of knowledge through which one becomes free from sorrow is told. When the yogi realises here the reality of Brahma — which is birthless, unchanging and untouched by all the categories — as the very reality of his own self that is comparable to a lamp, then he becomes free of all bondages by knowing the deity. It is here also said that the Supreme self is to be known as one's own self. This is possible as this very deity is all the directions and all the intermediate directions. He was born as the first. He again, exists in the womb. He varily is the one born; he is also the one going to be born. He exists in all beings. He has his faces everywhere.

Now, with a view to showing that, like yoga, other practices such as salutations are necessary. The text says : 'Salutations again and again to that deity, who is in fire, who is in water, who has entered with the entire creation, who is in the herbs and who is in the trees.

Now, how can the non-dual Supreme self have such states as 'rulership' and 'the ruled'? The text says, 'The non-dual one' who, being the possessor of the net (Maya), rules through His (divine) powers, rules over all the worlds through his powers of rulership, who is verily alone when in association with the divine powers and when manifested — those who know this become immortal. Then why should he be possessed by 'Maya' is, because since Rudra — who rules these worlds through his divine powers, who resides within every being, who after projecting all the worlds and becoming the protector, withdraws them during dissolution — is one, therefore, they did not wait in anticipation of a second. It has its eyes everywhere, its face everywhere, its arms everywhere, and also its feet everywhere. The one deity, while creating heaven and earth, conjoins the human beings with hands, and the birds with wings. While explaining the projection of 'Hiranyagarbha' by that very self, the text prays for what the seers of mantras cherish. Rudra, who is the origin and the source of the divine powers of the gods, who is the protector of the universe and the great seer, projected 'Hiranyagarbha' in the beginning. May he endow us with good understanding and once again, while revealing His true nature, the text for the cherished objective. 'O Rudra! through that holy form, which you have, which is not terrifying, and which reveals virtue through that most joyous form of yours, O Girisanta, pleas look at us'.

The Supreme self, which is the Lord of the entire world, consisting of the unmoving and the moving, moves outward by becoming embodied in the city of nine gates. So far Brahma has been propounded as all pervasive. Now in order to reveal the Supreme self as changeless and bliss and nature, and as existing in its state of knowledge that has no beginning and no end, the text says : 'He is without hands and feet and yet moves and grasps ; He sees though without eyes ; He hears though without ears ; He knows whatever is to be known, and of him there is no knower. They speak of him as the first, the 'Purusa' and the great. The self that is subtler than the subtle and greater than the great, is lodged in the heart of every creature. Through the grace of the Lord, one, who sees that self as desireless, sees its glory as God becomes sorrowless. The ancient one is known as one, who is free from decrepitude, who is the self of all, and who is omnipresent by virtue of pervasiveness, regarding whom, the deliberators on Brahma speak of birthlessness and whom they speak of as eternal. That deity, who is one and casteless, and has an inscrutable purpose, who by virtue of His possessing multifarious powers bring into being many castes in the beginning and in whom the world dissolves at the end, may he endow us with a pure intellect. It is further stated that since He is the creator, and dissolutions too, occur in Him, therefore, he alone is everything; there exists nothing differentiated from Him. That indeed is fire, sun, air, moon, pure, Brahma, water, Prajapati and one is the woman, the man, the boy, a girl, old man tottering with a stick or taking bath, one has his face everywhere. One is also the blue bee, the green parrot, possessed of lightening in his womb, the seasons of the seas, without beginning, existing as the omnipresent from whom have sprung all the worlds. One he-goat sleeping with she-goat enjoys, gives birth to offsprings and leaves her when she has been enjoyed. Similarly, two birds that are ever associated and have similar names, cling to the same tree. Of these two, one eats the fruit of divergent tastes and the other looks on without eating. On the same tree, the individual soul remains drowned, as it were, and so, being deluded, it moans because of its impotence. When it realises thus, the other, the adorable Lord, and his glory, then it becomes liberated from sorrow. The vedas are established on the imperishable supreme space where all the gods dwell. What will one achieve through the vedas, who does not know it ? Those who know it thus, they, who are such, remain self-fulfilled. We have now to see distinctly, how, by assuming 'Maya' as the limiting adjunct, that very immutable becomes the creator of the world and also its efficient cause. The vedas say that one should know that the nature is surely 'Maya' and the Supreme Lord is the ruler of 'Maya' to be sure. This whole universe is verily pervaded by what are His limbs. The unchanging entity, which is the source of 'Maya' and its effects, is the basis of everything through its own power ; that it is the cause of the origin of such effects as space etc. and that liberation follows from the knowledge of identity as 'I am Brahma' with that which in reality is existence knowledge - bliss and which is regarded as the substrtum of all. By realising that non-dual one, who exists as the ruler in every Prakriti, into whom this universe enters, and from whom it emerges diversely, and who is the controller, benevolent, effulgent and adorable, one attains this Peace absolutely.

As the cream floating on the surface of clarified butter is an object of great pleasure to its possessor, similarly, to the people desirous of liberation, the Supreme self is an object of infinite joy, on account of being the source of a joy that is the quintessence. By knowing Shiva, who is very subtle, is the form of bliss, which is like that, like the cream of clarified butter, as hidden in all beings viz. in those from Brahma to the clump of grass, hidden because, he is within the preview of direct perception as the witness of the enjoyment of the fruits of action, still his divinity is ignored by them. Now the text states that the self, which is for ever the same continuous bliss, is the Projector of the universe; that it permeats it and that by nature it is liberation attainable by monks. This effulgent one, whose work is this universe and who is all-pervasive, is ever present in the hearts of beings. He is revealed through the instruction, 'Not this, not this', through discriminating intelligence and through the knowledge of unity. Those who know this self, they become immortal. Now since it is well ascertained that the Supreme self remains unchanged even during the three periods (past, present and future) and also at the time of liberation, dissolution etc., therefore, it is through ignorance that it appears to possess duality in the waking and dream states as well. But in reality it is verily undivided at all times. Where there is no darkness, there is neither day nor night, neither superimposition of existence nor of non-existence. There remains only Shiva, the absolute that is immutable, that is worthy of adoration by the sun and the ancient enlightenment has spread verily from it. Nobody can grasp him from above, nor across, nor in the middle. There is no likeness of Him whose name is great fame or the God is not the object of organs etc. that He, by nature, exists within, and that liberation comes from the knowledge of one's identity with Him.

His form does not exist within the range of vision, nobody sees this one with the eye. Those, who know this one thus as existing in heart, through a pure intellect and mind, they become immortal. Since Rudra is birthless, therefore, some terror-stricken persons take refuge in Him. 'O Rudra ! protect such persons for ever through that face of His which is benign and please do not bring destruction to their sons and grandsons; do not bring destruction to their lives; do not bring destruction to their horses'. 'O Rudra! being angry do not kill their courageous servants. They shall always invoke Him thus with oblation and invoke for protection'.

He, who is immutable, infinite and higher than Brahma, and in whom lie hidden the two, knowledge and ignorance, and who controls knowledge and ignorance, is different from them. Ignorance is mutable, but knowledge is verily immutable. He is the one who rules all the places and is all the colours and all the sources ; who filled with multifarious knowledge the sage Kapila, when he was born in the beginning, and whom He saw as he was being born as the birth of this very one is heard of in projected 'Hiranyagarbha' in the beginning and the birth of anyone else is not heard of. Later on also it will be said, 'He who created Brahma in the beginning and who, indeed delivered the vedas to him; from the Pauranic sentence, 'Kapila' was the first born', it follows that 'Hiranyagarbha' indeed, is indicated by the word 'Kapila'. The sage 'Kapila', a part of Lord Vishnu, who is all pervasive, has come for the destruction of delusion in the world. In the Golden age, the all-pervasive one, taking the form of Kapila and others bestows the highest knowledge that is conducive to the good of the whole world. He is Indra among all the gods, Brahma among the knowers of Brahma, the deity 'Air', among the mighty ones and among the yogis, he is Sanat Kumara. This is the great sage well known. It is met within the Mundaka Upaisada. Then at that time this world existed in this one, 'Hiranyagarbha'. After that Kapila among the sages, who exists beyond darkness, came out of all pervasive Vishnu. He is the person possessing sixteen weapons. He himself became well-known as Kapila in the beginning of the creation and whom He saw as he was being born. This deity making each individual net diverse on this field, withdraws it. And the Lord, the great self, after creating again the rulers as before, presides over them all. Further, he shines illuminating all the directions above, below and others as does the sun. In this way, that God, the effulgent and adorable one, rules alone over all those that stand as the source. That Brahma, who rules alone this whole universe, lies hidden in the upanisadas that are the mystical parts of the vedas. Brahma knows that which has the vedas as its valid source of knowledge. Those ancient gods and seers, who knew it, they being full of its thought, became immortal indeed. That individual soul is to be known as the size of the tip of a hair imagined to be divided into a hundredth of its hundredth part and yet it happens to be infinite. This one is surely not a woman, nor is that a man and this one is certainly not a eunuch.

It is protected by those very bodies whichever it takes up. Just as by the pouring in of food and drink comes about the growth of the body, so the embodied one assumes in succession different forms in different places, in accordance with actions through thought, touch, vision and delusion. The embodied one adopts gross and subtle bodies as also many others through its own tendencies. It is seen as though different from Brahma and as the cause of their contact with objects owing to the results of actions and tendencies of mind. One becomes free from all the fetters by realising the effulgent one, who is beginningless and infinite, who exists in the midst of the inscrutable world as its witness, who is the projector of the universe, who has multifarious forms, and who is the one entity, encompassing the universe. They give up the body who know the pure, effulgent one, who is realised through the pure heart, who is called the bodiless, who is the creator and the destroyer, and who is the projector of the sixteen parts. He creates 'Prana' etc.

Some intelligent persons speak of inherent nature as the cause; similarly, others speak of time. The mention of time and inherent nature is suggestive of even those others referred to previously, being under delusion, the non-discriminating persons, who are enamoured of objects, do not know fully. This glory belongs to the effulgent one because of whom this wheel of Brahma revolves. Also it is to be thought that, He, by whom is pervaded all this in an orderly way and who is enlightened, the maker of time, possessed of qualities and all knowing being ordained by Him this well-known work viz. earth, water, fire, air and space, remain super-imposed. He is to be thought of who having finished that work and witnessing it, and having again brought about the combination of the self with the principles of nature—with one, two, three or eight and with time as well, exists in association with the subtle qualities of the internal organ. Now the primary purpose of work after having performed actions that are associated with the three qualities, he, who surrenders them as also all his inclinations of mind — then, in the absence of these, there follows the dissipation of the results of work done before. When the results of works became dissipated, he becomes different from Prakriti and the elements. In Gita too it is said, 'O Son of Kunti ! whatever you do, whatever you eat, whatever you offer as sacrifice, whatever you give and whatever austerities you undertake, all that is offered to me. Thus you will become free from bondages in the form of actions that are productive of good and bad results'. One, who acts by dedicating actions to Brahma and by renouncing attachment, he does not become polluted by sins, just as a lotus leaf is not affected by water or mud. By giving up attachments, the yogis undertake work merely through the body, mind, intellect and even the organs, for the purification of themselves. He is the source, and the cause that brings about association, He is seen as beyond the three times and even as without the parts. After meditating first on the effulgent one, who is possessed of all the forms, who is the origin and truth by nature, who is worshipful and who exists in one's heart, one becomes different from the 'Prakriti' and the elements. He, because of whom this phenomenal world revolves, is above all that takes the form of the tree of the world and time and he is different knowing the source of virtue, the destroyer of sin, the Lord of divine powers etc., as existing in the intellect and as the immortal support of the universe, one becomes different from 'Prakriti' and the elements. We know Him, the effulgent one, who is the Supreme, great Lord of the Lords, Him, who is the Supreme God of gods, the Ruler of the rulers, who is higher than the highest i.e. 'Maya', who is the Lord of the worlds and who is worshipful. He is great Lord having neither a body nor any organs, none is seen to be either equal or superior to Him. His supreme power is heard of as diverse, indeed, and it consists of the spontaneous act of knowing and the act of control. Therefore, there is no ruler of Him in this world, nor any controller, nor indeed is there any ground of inference with regard to Him. He is the cause, the overlord of the lords of the organs. And there is none, who is His procreator, nor even an overlord. The one deity, who covered Himself naturally with the effects of 'Pradhana', as a spider covers itself with its thread, may He grant me unification with Brahma. The same deity remains hidden in all beings, and is all-pervasive and the indwelling self of all beings. He is the supervisor of actions, lives in all beings, He is the witness, the bestower of intelligence, the absolute and devoid of the three qualities (gunas). Then the everlasting happiness is for those — and not for others — who are wise and who realise as seated in their intellect, Him, who is one and independent and who makes diverse the single seed of the many, which are actionless. While the actions are being done, in every way by the qualities of nature, one, who is deluded by egoism, thinks that he is the doer. But, the one, who is knower of the facts about the varieties of the gunas and actions, does not become attached, thinking that the organs act on the objects of the organs. One becomes freed from all the bondages by knowing that deity, who is the cause and who can be known through sankhya and yoga, who—being the eternal among the eternal, the consciousness among the conscious — alone dispenses the desired objects to the many. It has been said that one becomes free by knowing the deity. Why, again, is it that one becomes liberated by knowing Him alone and not through any other means (deity)? The answer is that there is one Supreme self in the midst of this universe. He himself is the fire, that is fully established in the water (body). By knowing Him alone, one goes beyond death, there is no other path to go by. For the attainment of the supreme goal, He Himself is once again specially presented by the upanisada. He is the creator of the Universe, the knower of the Universe, the self and the source, the knower, the maker of time, the possessor of attributes, omniscient, the protector of the unmanifested and the individual soul, the Lord of the three qualities, and the cause of transmigration, liberation, existence and bondage. He is the self of the universe, immortal, fully established as the Lord, the knower, omnipresent and the protector of this universe, who eternally rules this universe. There is no other agent for ruling the world. Therefore, a seeker of liberation should take refuge in Him with his whole being. Upanisada also says, 'He, who created Brahma in the beginning and who indeed, delivered the vedas to him — is that very deity, who is the revealer of the knowledge regarding the self, I being verily desirous of liberation seek refuge in Him, who is partless, actionless, tranquil, faultless, taintless, the supreme bridge to immortality and like a fire with burning fuel'. So long as one does not know the Supreme self as one's own self, for that long does one, though verily birthless, assumes the form of an individual soul among ghouls, animals, human beings, and others, and being under delusion, transmigrates, dragged hither and thither by attachment etc. as though by crocodiles etc., and overwhelmed by the three kinds of sorrows where again, he realises the Supreme self, which is without cause and effect, characterised, as 'Not this, not this', 'untouched by hunger' etc., and which exists as knowledge by nature, having no beginning or end, and which is absolute bliss, then, becoming free from nescience and its effect, he becomes, absolute bliss. This is the purport. It has also been said, 'Knowledge remains covered by ignorance'. Thereby the creatures become deluded. But in the case of those of whom that ignorance of their's becomes destroyed by the knowledge of the self, their knowledge like the sun, reveals that supreme reality. Those, who have their intellect absorbed in that, whose self is that, who are steadfast in that, who have that as their supreme goal — they attain the state of non-returning, their dirt having been removed by knowledge.

If there be not abundant detachment, then the indirect knowledge of Brahma remains infructuous. Therefore, a wise man should for ever diligently maintain detachment, and in another samriti too it is said, 'When there arises in the mind, dispassion towards all objects, then only should a man of knowledge take to monasticism'. Otherwise he will become degraded. Thus the sanyasins verily belong to the most adorable state of life. The knowledge of upanisada is not to be given to one who has no self-control, nor to one, who is not a son, nor again to one, who is not a disciple. He, wo has supreme devotion to deity and as much of it to the guru as to the deity, to him indeed, to the great souled one these subject-matters that have been spoken, become revealed.

6

Kenopnisada

This Kenopnishada deals with the power, who controls, directs and puts into action all the senses in the human beings. On the pupil having asked who that power is, the guru told that it is the self or soul only, who is responsible for listening, speaking, seeing and the senses are only the tools in that soul. Even one gets life because of soul only. Soul only is the knowledge, the conscience and the all-in-all in the body. The soul only creates feelings in the senses and those who are able to realise this self or the soul, are able to attain salvation. God is not the worldly instinct and cannot therefore, be known by the instincts—speech, hearing, seeing etc. He cannot be explained by any one as one is not able to talk to Him, see Him and feel Him closely although he is in ears, tongue, eyes and all senses and the soul. He is everywhere but cannot be seen or assumed. He does not see but because of Him, the human beings are able to see. He does not hear but because of him, the human beings are able to hear. He does not breathe but the breathing is because of Him. He is not life but the life in human beings is because of Him (God). This is possible after the knowledge of God and the actions are co-incided as only knowledge without commensurate actions and only actions without knowledge of God lead one to no-where. As a person reaches the destination with the help of eyes and legs, so the persons could reach God by his knowledge and commensurate actions. Those, who sit idle and do not perform at all, suffer most ; those, who believe in enjoying the natural instincts in satisfying the same, also suffer and those, who are above the feeling of satisfaction of worldly instincts and get into devotion for Him, reach the God and get absorbed in Him. Apart from the satisfaction of instincts and pleasures, those who are involved in greed, affection and attachment in this universe, are rather in the dark and unless they come out of these desires, they cannot attain salvation. It is, therefore, necessary to realise self and then involve oneself in the nature to enable him to reach the almighty. One, who, taking God as available anywhere and everywhere, devotes himself fully to Him selflessly and takes His refuge only, reaches Him and this infact is the Para-Bhakti of God.

There are various kinds of meditations and these meditations are recited by different kinds of songs (samas). Then there is the meditation on the Gayastra sama, which ends with a succession of teachers and pupils and which relates to effects of action. If all these rites and meditations are properly observed, they become the cause of purification of the mind of one, who is free from desires and longs for emancipation but one who cherishes desires and has no enlightenment (knowledge of gods), the rites by themselves, as enjoined in the vedas and samritis, become the cause of attainment of the Southern Path and for return to this world in one specie or the other. The longing for the knowledge of the indwelling self arises only in that desireless man of pure mind, who has renounced all transitory, external means and ends by virtue of the emergence of a special kind of tendency, created by works done in this life or in the previous ones. In order to know the Reality fully, one must go, with sacrificial faggots in hand, only to a teacher well-versed in the vedas and is established in Brahma. In this way alone, does a man of detachment, acquire the competence of hearing, meditating and realising the knowledge of the indwelling self, and not otherwise. Besides, as a result of this realisation of the indwelling self as Brahma, there comes the total cessation of ignorance, which is the seed of bondage and the cause of the emergence of desire and activity, in accordance with the verse, 'What sorrow and what delusion can there be for that seer of oneness'? Also the knower of the self transcends sorrow. When both the cause and effect are realised, the knot of the heart gets untied and all doubts are resolved. Therefore, one's duty is to renounce all desires after the realisation of the unity of the indwelling self and Brahma. The desire to know the indwelling self in the case of a man, who has renounced all seen and unseen results, attainable by external means, is being shown in this upanisada. Knowledge, therefore, is essential to digest all this and knowledge can be acquired from a teacher. If it is learnt through obeisance, it can be imagined that someone, having found no refuge in anything, other than the indwelling self, and having a longing for the fearless, eternal, auspicious and unshakable Brahma, approached a teacher, who is established in Brahma and asked, 'Willed by whom does the directed mind go towards its object ; being directed by whom, does the vital force that precedes all, proceed towards its duty, by whom is this speech willed that people utter and who is the effulgent being, who directs the eyes and the ears' ?

Such an enquiry can be made by a man, who has become disgusted with the ephemeral works and their results such as the assemblage of the body, senses etc., and seeks to know some things which are unchangeable and eternal, through the directorship of the group of body through will, word and act, which is a familiar fact. But since it is not a well-known fact that the mind is free and goes independently to its own object, it may be said that if the mind were independent in engaging and disengaging itself, then the body would have contemplated any evil and yet the mind, though conscious of consequences, wills, evils, and though discussed, it does go in deeds of intensely sorrowful results. The teacher only tells about who that effulgent being is, who directs the mind and other organs towards their own objects and how does he direct. Here one has to dwell on the main parts of the body—the ear, the mind, the speech, the life and the eye. The intelligent man gives up the self-identification with these senses and renouncing the world, sees Brahma in all the above parts of the body, as all these parts are directed to function by self, who, after renouncement, becomes one with God, hence all the parts of the body too become Brahma. If the director of ears etc. could be known as possessed of his own activity, independently of the activities of ears etc, then there would be incongruity. So, no director of ears etc., possessed of his own activity, is apprehended here but God can be known as existing unmixed with the ears etc., from the logical necessity that such activities as deliberations, volition, determination of those very composite things viz the ears etc., must be meant for some one's benefit. Thus from the fact that composite things exist for the need of some one else, a director of the ears etc. can be known and, therefore, the God is the ear of ear etc. The question then arises as to why should there be an ear for ear (God as ear). As light does not need another light, why ear should need another ear. The fact, however, lies in the matter that the ability of the ear is to reveal its own object, which is possible only if the eternal non-composite, all pervading light of the self is there and not otherwise. Hence the expression ear for ear is justifiable. In Gita too Krishna has told the light to be His, which is in the sun and which illumines the whole universe. Further, it is a commonly accepted belief that the ears etc. constitute the self of all, and that these are conscious. Then, there is something which is known to the intellect of the men of realisation, which dwells in the inmost recess of all, which is changeless, undecaying, immortal, fearless and unborn, and which is the ears etc. of even the ears, i.e. the source of their capacity to act. Also the mind, being an internal organ, is not able to perform its own functions — thinking, determination etc. — unless it is illumined by the light of consciousness. Therefore, there is some mind of the mind too.

This other mind is the life. A thing asked about should properly be denoted in the first instance. the life has ensured the capacity of the vital force to discharge its functions of sustaining life and this is because there can be no sustaining of life by anything that is not presided over by self, 'Who will inhale and who will exhale if Brahma be not there within the heart, in which someone pushes the 'prana' upward and impels the 'apana' inward'. Like ears of life, he is the eye of the eye, speech of the speech and so on. Those, who give up self-identification with the ears etc., are the intelligent, because the self-identification with the ear etc. cannot be given up unless one is endowed with uncommon intellect. From this world of empirical dealings involving ideas of, 'I and mine', 'with regard to sons, friends, wealth, having renounced all desires, they become immortal and immune from death. This is as per vadas as 'Not by work, not by progeny, not by wealth, but by renunciation some one attains immortality.' The self-existent Lord destroys the outgoing senses, hence one perceives the external things and not the self within, when all desires that cling to one's heart fall off, then one attains Brahma.

Since Brahma, as the ear of the ear etc. is the self of those organs, therefore, then to that Brahma, eyes do not go as it is not possible to go to oneself. Similarly, speech does not go. When a word, as expressed by the organ of speech, reveals its own ideas, speech is said to be doing its object. But Brahma is the self of that world as also of the organ that utters it, therefore, speech does not do. Similarly, though the mind thinks and determines other things, it does not think or determine itself, for of it too Brahma is the self. As Brahma is not an object of perception to these, therefore, we do not know. Further, Brahma is not possessed of class etc., hence it is very difficult to convince the disciples about it through instructions. In this way, the upanisada shows the necessity of putting forth great effort in the matter of imparting instructions and comprehending its meaning. Since we do not know Brahma, we are not aware of any process of instructing about it except as explained below. True, it is that one cannot impart knowledge about the Highest with the help of such means of valid knowledge as the evidence of senses, but the knowledge can be produced with the help of traditional authority. Traditional authority can, therefore, only be quoted for the sake of imparting instructions about it.

That Brahma is surely different from the known and again it is above the unknown—such was the utterance, we heard from the ancient teachers, who explained it to us. All that is manifested is certainly known. But Brahma is different from that as whatever is known is limited, mortal and full of misery and hence it is to be rejected. So when it is said that Brahma is different from the unknown, it amounts to saying that it is not a thing to be obtained. Thus, the statement that Brahma is different from the known and the unknown having amounted to Brahma, being denied as an object to be acquired or rejected, the desire of the disciple to know Brahma objectively comes to an end, as Brahma is non-different from the self. As nothing other than one's own self can possibly be different from the known and the unknown, therefore, self is Brahma. Now the idea that the self is Brahma having been established through the sentence, 'That is surely different from the known and again that is above the unknown', one can doubt how can the self be Brahma as self is familiarly known to be that which is entitled to undertake rites and meditation and which, being subject to birth and death, seeks to attain either the gods headed by Brahma or heaven by undertaking the practice of rites or meditation. Therefore, some adorable being other than the self e.g. Vishnu, Indra, Iswara or Prana may well be Brahma, but not so the self, for this is opposed to common sense. Therefore, it is reasonable that, that should be Brahma, which is known and adorable and the worshipper should be one, who is different from this. That Brahma is not the one worshipped by people as an object but the one which can not be uttered by speech and by which speech is revealed or that is the speech of speech. Similarly, he cannot be comprehended by the mind but by which the mind is encompassed. Here mind means the internal organs comprising of mind and intellect and Brahma enlightens the mind as mind enlightens all other senses to act. Also Brahma cannot be seen by eyes but by Him only, as man perceives the activities of eye and He cannot be heard by ear but by virtue of the force of Brahma only man knows his ears. Man does not also smell Him but by which the organ of smell is impelled, know that Brahma.

If one thinks that he has known Brahma well enough, then he has known very little of Him that is to the extent to which it is in the human mind and the little of Him which is in the gods. Therefore, Brahma is still to be deliberated by him. If one is told that he is the self, which is opposed to the acceptable and the unacceptable and which is Brahma, one may conclude that he knows himself well enough and he infact is Brahma. A firm conviction for this is required but at the same time one cannot claim that he knows Him well enough. The well-established purport of all the upanisadas is that the personal self of each knower is Brahma. In ordinary life it is seen that of the disciples hearing from the same teacher, some one understands accurately, some one inaccurately, some one contrarily and some one nothing at all. Therefore, though the statement, 'Brahma has been realised', is made with firm conviction, still the teacher's apprehensive remark, 'If you think' etc., is quite appropriate in view of the comprehension being difficult. So the purport is that the Brahma, that is free from all distinctions, that is one without a second and that is known as great and eternal, cannot be known as a fully comprehended object. Therefore, Brahma has still to be deliberated upon for such persons.

Then how is Brahma known :-

नाहं मन्ये सुवेदेति नो न वेदेति वेद च,

यो नस्तद्वेद नो न वेदेति वेद च ।

(I donot think I know well enough. I consider, I know and I do not know as well, knows that Brahma.) It seems contradictory to say that the very same thing which is known by a man is not known well enough by him. Nor can a restrictive rule be laid down to the effect that Brahma is to be known as an object of doubt or false knowledge as doubt and false knowledge are everywhere known to be the causes of harm. So Brahma is known to those, who do not know, to those who have not got full realisation — that is to say, to those who identify the self merely with the senses, the mind, and the intellect but not to those, whose intelligence is extremely primitive, for the latter do not have the consciousness, 'Brahma is known to us, is possible for those, who, by reason of non-discrimination between Brahma and the limiting adjuncts, and because of their familiarity with the limiting adjuncts such as the intellect, consider the sense, the mind and the intellect as the self. Hence the incomplete knowledge is presented as a view to be refuted in the text 'Known to those who do not know'. It has been ascertained that Brahma is unknown to those who know. If Brahma be wholly unknown then there remains no distinction between the ordinary people and the knowers of Brahma. Besides, the statement 'Unknown to those who know', is self contradictory. How then can Brahma be known adequately. To explain this, the upanisad tells that Brahma is really known when it is known with each state of consciousness, because thereby one gets immortality. Since through one's own self is acquired strength, therefore, through knowledge is attained immortality. The immortality is, therefore, attained through one's own self by attaining strength and capacity. Now strength got from wealth, friend, incantation, medicine, austerity or yoga, cannot conquer death, for it is produced by impermanent things. But the strength, consequent on the knowledge of the self, is acquired through the self alone and not through anything else. Thus, since the strength resulting from the knowledge of the self is independent of any means of acquisition, that strength alone is able to conquer death. Since the strength produced by the knowledge of the self is thus attained through the self, therefore, through knowledge about the self, attains immortality. This self is not attained by one, who has no strength.

If one has realised here that through ignorance, birth, old age, death etc. among multitudes of beings such as gods, men, animals etc., in whom, there is an abundance of misery, natural to transmigratory existence, then there is truth, if he has not realised here, then there is great destruction.

The wise men having realised Brahma in all beings and having turned away from this world, become immortal. If a man, having scriptural sanction and ability, has known the self as defined and in the manner already explained, then there is truth, there subsists in this human birth, the values consisting in long life, wealth and holiness or supreme reality. Therefore, the wise, who are thus familiar with merits and demerits, having known, realised, the one reality on the self in all beings — moving and unmoving — turning away desisting from this world of ignorance — the world consisting of 'My and mine' — i.e. having attained the non-dual state consisting in becoming identified with the self of all, become immortal, become Brahma indeed — this is the idea as it has been said in vedas, 'He, who knows that supreme Brahma, becomes Brahma indeed.'

It was Brahma indeed, that achieved victory for the sake of the gods. In that victory which was infact Brahma's, the gods became elated. Some people may still have delusion, 'It is seen that whatever exists is known through the valid means of cognition, and whatever does not exist remains unknown, and absolutely non-existent'. Similarly, this Brahma, being unknown is certainly non-existent. Lest there be this delusion, this story is begun. Since that Brahma is the ruler in every way, the supreme deity of even the deities, the supreme Lord over the lordly beings, inscrutable, the cause of the victory of gods, and the cause of the defeat of devils, therefore, how can it be non-existent. The Supreme Brahma, already spoken of verily for the sake of gods, achieved victory in the fight between gods and the devils. Brahma, after conquering the devils, the enemies of the world and transgressors of divine rules, gave to the gods, the victory and its results for ensuring the stability of the world. But in the victory, which was Brahma's, the gods, fire etc., became elated and thought that it was their victory and Brahma knew this pretension of theirs. Then, not knowing that this victory and the glory belonged to God, who sits in the hearts as the indwelling self—omniscient, dispenser of the fruits of all works of all creatures, omnipotent, and desirous of encompassing the stability of the world. God, however, said, 'In order that the gods may not be defeated like the devils, as a consequence of their vain glory. I shall, out of grace for them, favour the gods by removing their presumptuousness'. With this idea, for their sake, He appeared as an object of perception to the gods, through an unprecidentedly wonderful an astonishing form created by Brahma's own power of 'Maya'. It appeared as an object of perception to the senses of the gods. Gods, however, did not comprehend that the Brahma, which had become manifest as to what this venerable, great being might be. They said to fire to find out as to what Yaksha (Brahma) is. Fire approached the Yaksha. Having been asked by Yaksha, who he was, fire introduced himself showing his self importance. Yaksha asked what power he had, and fire advised she could burn everything on the earth. Yaksha offered a straw to be burnt, but fire could not burn it. Fire returned saying he could not ascertain who this Yaksha was. Yaksha, however, told that if he could not burn the straw then he should give up his vanity as a consumer everywhere. Then gods sent Air to find out who the Yaksha was. Yaksha was approached, who gave him a straw to be blown away. But Air could not. So Yaksha asked him too to give up the vanity of being the blower of everything. Then gods approached Indra to find out, who the Yaksha was, Indra approached Yaksha but Yaksha (Brahma) disappeared from the sight and in this way Indra's pride was totally eradicated. Then Indra approached Uma in the space and asked her about Yaksha. She said it was Brahma and in Brahma's victory only the gods became elated. From her, Indra learnt that it was Brahma, who had conquered devils. Then Indra came back and narrated all that he had seen to other gods. Therefore, indeed these gods viz Fire, Air and Indra did excel other gods for they indeed touched and had conversation with Brahma most proximately and they knew him first as Brahma and out of these three too, since Indra had first known him as Brahma and told fire and Air, he excelled there too and thereby became supreme in all gods.

There is also instruction through analogy in the context of the self. The fact that the mind goes to Brahma and the fact that Brahma is repeatedly remembered through the mind, as also the thought that the mind has with regard to Brahma is being told the analogical instruction in the context of the soul with regard to the indwelling self. There, Brahma is well-known as the one adorable to all creatures, hence it is to be meditated upon with the help of the name. After all, all creatures pray to anyone, who meditate on Brahma in this way. Therefore, Brahma is well known as the one to be adored by all beings and anyone, who meditates on this name, becomes possessed of all qualities of Brahma. Therefore, upanisada is nothing but the upanisada of the Supreme self. Further, it is not reasonable that the knowledge of Brahma, which repels all ideas of distinction of deeds, doers and results, should have dependence on any attributive constituent, or any relation with any helpful accessory and because the knowledge of Brahma and its result, freedom are concerned only with the self, which is un-associated with any object, he, who wants emancipation, should for ever give up all works together with their instruments because it is known only by the man of renunciation. This knowledge is adequate for the attainment of knowledge without depending on anything else.

Concentration, cessation from sense objects, rites etc. are its legs, the vedas are all limbs and truth is its abode. The concentration of the body, the senses and the mind (तप, दम), cessation from sense objects, rites, yagyas etc. are the means, for it is found that the knowledge of Brahma arises in a man, who has attained the requisite holiness by means of purification of the heart through these. The vedas are the legs because they reveal the rites and knowledge, and all the subsidiaries are so because they are meant for the protection of the vedas. As on the legs rests the entire body so in the vedas, 'Satya' is the dwelling place, where the secret teachings, reside. 'Satya' also means freedom from deceit and crookedness in speech, mind and body, for knowledge abides in those, who are free from deceit, and who are holy and not in those, who are devilish by nature and are deceitful as per vedas. 'Those in whom there are no crookedness, falsehood and deceit'. Although the truth can also be indicated as legs, cessation, concentration, still its allusion again as the abode is for indicating that as a means for the acquisition of knowledge, it excels others as the samriti says, 'One truth outweighs a thousand horse sacrifice'. So anyone, who knows this thus, he having dispelled sin, remains firmly seated in the boundless, blissful and highest Brahma, He remains firmly seated there and he does not again return to this world.

7

Katha Upanisada

As already indicated, the word 'Upanisad' is derived by adding Upa (Near) and ni (with certainty) as prefixes and keep as a suffix to the root 'sad' meaning to split up (destroy), go or loosen i.e. the knowledge of the knowable entity presented in the book that is going to be explained. It splits up, injures, or destroys the seeds of worldly existence such as ignorance etc. in the case of those seekers of emancipation, who, after becoming detached, approach the knowledge that is called 'Upanisad' and that bears the characteristics to be presented hereafter and who then deliberate on it with steadiness and Certainty. Through the very derivation of the word 'Upanisad', the person particularly qualified for knowledge has been pointed out and the subject matter of the knowledge is the Supreme Brahma that is the indwelling self, and the purpose of this upanisada is the absolute cessation of the transmigratory state, which consists in the attainment of Brahma. Thus these cantos themselves are meant for special persons competent for their study, and have a special subject matter, a special purpose and a special connection in as much as they reveal like an apple, placed in the hand, the knowledge that is meant for a man of special competence.

In a historical story, it is narrated that once upon a time, the son of Vajasrava, being desirous of fruit of his doings, gave away everything. He had a son Nichiketa. As the presents (cows) were being carried to the Brahamanas, faith took possession of him, who was still a boy. He thought, he too shall be handed over to someone like the cows being offered to

Brahmins. He, therefore, asked his father, to whom he shall hand him over to. He repeated his question several times, until the father told him that he shall be offered to death. The son sorrowfully cogitated in a solitary place how his father had said so since he ranked highest amongst some of his kind and in the middle amongst others. He was thinking as to what purpose his father would achieve by handing him over to death. He thought his father would have spoken in anger, without any consideration of purpose. But still he thought that utterance of his father should not be falsified. On the other side, the father too remorsefully thought what he had uttered. The son, on the contrary, asked the father to protect his own truth and send him to death. Father accordingly sent him to death. He lived there for three nights as Yama (Death) was out. On return of Yama his people told him about the arrival of a Brahmin guest. Yama asked his people to offer propitiation (feet washing and providing seat etc.) to the guest, as if in anyone's house, a Brahmin guest abides without food, that Brahmin destroys hope and expectation, the results of holy association, and sweet discourse, sacrifices and charities of that man of little intelligence, where a Brahmin lives without food and water. The idea is that a guest should not be neglected under any condition. Then Yama approached Nichiketa with adoration and said "O Brahmin ! since you have lived in my house for three nights without food; a guest and an adorable person as you are, let my salutations be to you, and let good accrue to me by averting the fault arising from that lapse. Ask for three boons one in respect of each night". Nicheketa asked the first of the three boons that his father be free from anxiety. He should be calm of mind, freed from anger towards him and he be recognised by him and talked to him when freed by Yama. Yama told him that 'He shall be recognised by his father, when he goes back as before'. He shall also get over his anger and will sleep happily for many a night. Nichiketa further said that there was no fear in Heaven ; Yama was not there; nobody had any fear of old age and one enjoys living in heavenly world having been absolved of hunger and thirst, mental unhappiness and sorrows. Then Nichiketa asked about the 'Fire', that is the means for the attainment of heaven with above qualities. Nichiketa asked for the knowledge about fire being told to him. Yama asked him to listen to him attentively about that fire which is the means for the attainment of heaven and which is the support of the world being established in the intellect of the enlightened ones. Yama told him that fire is the source of the world. The fire is the first embodied being created by Brahma. Further, fire for the yagya is required at first, then bricks are required to be placed for bedi, their number has to be known and then how the fire has to be arranged is to be known. By understanding this, Nichiketa repeated verbatim in confirmation. Then being satisfied with his repetition, Yama told him to ask for the third boon. Yama also told that the yagya fire shall be known by his name. He also offered to him a multiformed necklace set with jewels of various hues or meaning that it consisted of rites and was not ignoble and Yama asked him to have this additional knowledge as it leads to various results. Yama then praised the 'Karma' too. Yama told that piling up the Nichiketa fire thrice or undertaking connection with the three — the mother, the father and the guru — as clarity follows from the knowledge gained by these three or the 'thrice' means the possessing of the knowledge; studying it and then performing it and who undertakes three kinds of 'Karma' sacrifice, study of vedas, and charity, crosses over birth and death. Also the three means, born from Brahma, becomes Brahma and illumined with Brahma.

Yama further told that one, who performed the above mentioned Nicheketa sacrifice thrice as also having known the fire thus as identified with oneself, accomplishes the fire, performs the sacrifice casts of the snares of death — consisting in vice, ignorant, desire, hatred etc., off even earlier to death, crosses over sorrows i.e. frees himself from mental sorrows, rejoices in heaven and in the world by having identified with Him. Then Nicheketa was asked to ask for the third boon. The two boons did not grant him the true knowledge of the reality called the self, which was not attainable through earlier mantras. Therefore, for the elimination of the natural ignorance, which is the seed of mundane existence, which consists of superimposing activity, agentship and enjoyment of the self and which has for its contents, those objects of prohibition and injunction, it is necessary to speak of the knowledge of the unity of self and Brahma, which knowledge is opposed to the ignorance is devoid of any tinge of super imposition of activity and enjoyment and has for its object absolete emancipation.

Nichiketa told that a doubt arises consequent on the death of a man — some say, 'It exists' and others say, 'It does not exist'. So he wanted to know this clearly and may be treated as the third boon. Then with a view to testing whether this one is abolutely fit for the knowledge of the self, which knowledge is the means for the highest consummation. Yama told that even the gods entertained doubts in the days of yore, for being subtle, this substance, the self, is not truly comprehended. He, therefore, persuaded Nicheketa to ask for some other boon and should not press for it. Then Nichiketa said that since gods entertained doubts with regard to this thing and since he too said that it was not truly comprehended and since any other instructor like him could not be had, therefore, there was no other boon comparable to what had been asked. Yama then asked him to ask for sons and grandsons that will be centenarians, or ask for more animals, elephants and gold and horses and a vast expanse of earth or he himself could live for as many years as he liked or ask for wealth, become a ruler over large area, or be fit for the enjoyment of all delectable things — divine as well as human — as he, being a deity, could ordain anything. He also said that whatever things there be that are desirable but difficult to get could be his — the women, chariots, musical instruments as are not had by mortals, but give up asking about death. Although Yama tempted him by offering all these things yet Nichiketa could not be moved and said that those things were all emphermeral and waste away the vigour of all the organs that a man has; even life is short, so he might keep all these things and he be granted whatever he had asked for. Nicheketa further told that a man is not satisfied with wealth and he being at his backing, he could easily get wealth, also he could live as long as desired as he himself was the death. So the boon actually fit for being asked is as asked by him that is the doubt entertained by people in the context of next world and whose knowledge leads to a great result.

Now having tested Nicheketa and finding him fit for the desired knowledge, Yama said that preferable, the supreme goal of freedom is certainly different from mere pleasantries. Therefore, all men are bound by these two through their sense of duty with regard to what leads to the pleasurable or the preferable. He, who is short-sighted, the ignorant man gets alienated from the object through God's 'Maya' and falls from the eternal supreme purpose. Such a man opts for the pleasures and even if both are offered, people shall opt for the pleasures mostly. However, the intelligent one selects the electable in preference to the detectable, the non-intelligent select the detectable for the sake of growth and protection of the body etc. Yama told him that he had not accepted the path of wealth in which many a man comes to grief and good befalls him, who accepts the preferable amongst the two, and he, who selects pleasurable, falls from the true end. It is so because that which is known as knowledge and that which is known as ignorance, are widely contradictory, and they follow divergent courses. Yama told that he considered him aspirant for knowledge because the enjoyable things did not tempt him, like a blind man led by another blind does not reach the destination, men living in ignorance and considering themselves intelligent and enlightened go round and round following crooked courses. The means for the attainment of the other world do not become revealed to the non-discriminating man, who blunders, being befooled by the lure of wealth. One, who constantly thinks that there is only this world, and none hereafter, comes under his sway again and again.

The self is not adequately known when spoken of by an inferior person for it is thought of variously, when taught by one, who has become identified with it, there is no further cogitation with regard to it as it is beyond argumentation, being subtler even than the atomic quantity. Or when self that is one's very self, is adequately told, there is no other comprehension of the self because nothing remains to be known as realisation of the unity of the self is the culmination of all knowledge. Therefore, as there is no knowable, there remains nothing to be known here. Or when the non-different self is spoken of, there remains no transmigration, for emancipation, which is the result of that realisation, follows immediately. Or, when the self is spoken of by a teacher, who has become identified with Brahma that he speaks of, there is no non-comprehension or non-realisation. To the hearer, the realisation about that self does come as, 'I am that self', just as it did in the case of that teacher. Thus the self is well understood when it is taught to be non-different from the taught by a teacher, who is well-versed in the scriptures, else the self becomes more subtle even than an atomic thing.

Yama told that since he knew that the worldly treasure is impermanent — for that permanent entity cannot be attained through impermanent things — therefore, knowingly did he pile up the Nichiketa fire with impermanent things and have thereby attained relative permanence, the acquisition of heavenly bliss as accomplished with impermanent things and Nichiketa having been enlightened, rejected them all by examining patiently the highest reach of desire, the support of the universe, the infinite results of meditation, the other shore of fearlessness, the extensive course of 'Hiranyagarbha' that is praise-worthy and great as also his own state. But he having seen the end of desire because of his all pervasiveness of the world comprising all that is personal, elemental, heavenly etc. the intelligent man gives up happiness and sorrow by developing concentration of mind on the self and thereby meditating on the old deity, who is inscrutable, lodged inaccessibly, located in the intellect and seated in the midst of misery. Yama further told that after hearing this, grasping it fully, separating this righteous thing from the body and attaining this subtly thing, that mortal rejoices, for he has obtained that which is the cause of delight, he considered that Brahma was quite widely open to Nichiketa.

Nichiketa then said that in case he was fit and he too was pleased with him then he may be advised of the thing which is considered different from virtue, different from vice, different from this cause and effect and different from the past and the future. Then Yama started narrating to him about the goal, which all vedas, with one voice, propound, which all the austerities speak of and wishing for which people practise Brahmcharya. It is 'OM' and symbol of Brahma. Anybody, who, while meditating on this letter, wants any of the two, to him comes that. One should meditate thus: 'I am Brahma, as signified by 'OM' and as conditioned by 'Maya' in which the 'Sattva quality' preponderates'. If, however, one is not able to do so, one would superimpose the idea of Brahma on the symbol 'OM'. However, the best minds can think of Brahma without 'OM' and the inferior ones can worship Brahma in the symbol 'OM', therefore, the letter 'OM' is inferior as well as superior to Brahma, depending upon who meditates. Nevertheless, this method is the best, this medium is the supreme. Meditating on this medium, one becomes adorable in the world of Brahma. For the aspirants of medium and inferior quality, 'OM' has been indicated both as a medium for meditation on and a symbol for worship of, the self which is devoid of all attritbutes and which was inquired about in 'Tell me of that thing which you see as different from virtue etc.' and it has also been presented similarly for similar aspirants, who wish to know the inferior Brahma.

न जायते म्रियते व विपश्चि-
न्नायं कुतश्चिन्न बभूव कश्चित्।
अजो नित्यः शाश्वतोऽयं पुराणो,
न हन्यते हन्यमाने शरीरे। (18)

(The intelligent self is neither born nor does it die. It did not orinigate from anyting nor did anything originate from it. It is birthless, eternal, undecaying and ancient. It is not injured even when the body is killed).

If the killer thinks in terms of killing and if the killed thinks of it as killed, both of them do not know. It does not kill nor is it killed as in the case of space. Therefore, the worldly existence, consisting of virtue and vice, relates merely to the ignorant man, it does not belong to the knower of Brahma, because for him virtue and vice are inappropriate according to both the vedic authority and logic. Then how again does one know the self. The self, that is subtler than the sutble and greater than the great, is lodged in the heart of every creature. A desireless man sees that glory of the self through the serenity of the organs and thereby he becomes free from sorrows, as he directly realises the self as, 'I am the self', otherwise the self is difficult to be known by ordinary people, who are possessed of desire, because, while sitting, it travels far away, while sleeping it goes everywhere. He can only know that deity, who is both joyful and joyless. Sleep is the cessation of the activities of the senses. The delimitation of consciousness, caused by the senses, ceases for a sleeping man. Where the self is in such a state of sleep, its consciousness being of a general character, it seems to go to be present everywhere. In reality it continues here in the body only.

Now we have to see how from the knowledge of self comes the elimination of grief as well. Having meditated on the self, as bodiless in the midst of the impermanent, and as great and pervasive, the wise man does not grieve. Since self is like space, it is bodyless but as it is in the body, it is amidst the body too. Here the word 'Self' is used to show the non-distinction of Brahma from one's self. The word primarily means the indwelling self. On this self that is of this kind, the wise man does not grieve, as grief cannot reasonably belong to a man of this kind, who has known the self. Though this self is difficult to be known, it can be known well through proper means. Also this self cannot be known through much study, nor through the intellect, nor through much hearing. It can be known through the self alone that the aspirant prays to this self and that seeker reveals its true nature. Meaning thereby that to a desireless man, who seeks for the self alone, the self becomes known of its own accord. It is being said that this self of that seeker of the self reveals its own — its real body i.e. its own nature. One who has not desisted from bad conduct, whose senses are not under control, whose mind is not concentrated, whose mind is not free from anxiety (about the result of concentration) cannot attain this self through such knowledge. But the man, who has desisted from bad conduct as also from the lure of the senses, whose mind has become concentrated and who is also free from anxiety about the results of concentration, attains the aforesaid self through knowledge. Then how can one know thus as to where it (the self) is for which both the Brahmin and the Kshatriya become food, and for which death takes the place of a curry.

The knowers of Brahma, the worshippers of the five fires (Garhapatya, Ahavaniya, Dakshinagni, Sabhya and Avasathya or heaven, cloud, earth, man and woman) and those who perform the Nicheketa sacrifice thrice, compare to shade and light, the two enjoyers of the inevitable results of work, who have entered within the body, into the cavity of the heart, which is the supreme abode of the most high (Brahma). There are two drinkers of truth i.e. the results of work (which is called truth) because of its inevitability. Of these two, one drinks, enjoys the fruit of work and not the other. Still both are called enjoyers because of association with the enjoyer, on the analogy of the expression the possessor of the umbrella. We have since known that Nichiketa fire, which is the bridge for the sacrificers, as also that which is the undecaying Supreme Brahma beyond fear for those who want to cross over the world. For the sake of that one among these (two selves), which has through limiting adjuncts become the transmigrating soul and is fit for knowledge and ignorance, a chariot to attain either emancipation or the worldly state, is being imagined as a means to its reaching either. One, therefore, has to know the self as a master of the chariot, and the body as the chariot and to know the intellect as the charioteer, and the mind as verily the bridle. Then just as the horses act when held in by the reins, similarly the organs such as ears etc. act when held in by the mind. So the organs are called the horses, the organs as horses know the objects as the roads. The discriminating people call that self the enjoyer when it is associated with the body, organs and mind. But the organs of that intellect, which being ever associated with an uncontrolled mind, becomes devoid of discrimination, are unruly like the vicious horses of the charioteer. Then of the intellect which, being ever associated with a restrained mind, is endowed with discrimination, the organs are controllable like the good horses of the charioteer. This is the result that is being foretold for the aforesaid rider, who has a non-discriminating intellect as his charioteer. But the master of the chariot, does not attain that goal through that intellect, who, being associated with a non-discriminating intellect and an uncontrollable mind, is ever impure, and he attains worldly existence. That master of chariot, however, who is associated with a discriminating intellect, and being endowed with a controlled mind, is ever pure, attains that goal from which he is not born again. Then one desires to know what that goal is. The man who has as his charioteer a discriminating intellect, and who has under control the reins of the mind, attains the end of the road and that is the highest place of Vishnu, or the goal of life, of the all pervading Brahma of the Supreme self, who is called Vasudeva (He who provides dwelling place (vasa) for all in himself is 'Vasu' and 'Deva' is effulgent i.e. self-luminous), which this man of knowldge attains. Now we have to see how the goal (i.e. the Brahma), is to be reached, is to be realised as the indwelling self through an ascending gradation, from grossness to subtleness, commencing from the gross senses. The sense-objects are higher than the senses, and the mind is higher than the sense-object, but the intellect is higher than the mind, and the great soul is higher than the intellect. Now the senses are gross. The sense-objects, by which those senses were created for their (sense-objects) own revelation are certainly higher—subtler, more pervasive, and are their inner selves, than those senses—which are their own effects (the sense-organs having been created from sense-objects for perceiving them). The principle called 'Hiranyagarbha', which was born before all from the unmanifested (Maya), and which consists of both intelligence and activity, is called the great soul that is higher than the intellect. So the unmanifested is higher than the Mahat, the 'Purusa' is higher than the unmanifested. There is nothing higher than the 'Purusa'. He is the culmination. He is the highest goal or 'Paramgati' or supreme goal of all travellers, all individual souls that transmigrate, because the samriti says, 'Going from where they do not return.'

Brahma is hidden in all beings, and hence he does not appear as the self (of all). But by the seers of subtle things, he is seen through a pointed and fine intellect. Since he is not known to a man, whose intellect has not been purified, it is said, he does not appear. He is seen through purified intellect through the pointed intellect, that intellect, which is like a point is through that intellect, which is associated with concentration through the subtle intellect that is engaged in ascertaining subtle things. Then comes the means of his attainment. The discriminating man should merge the organ of speech into the mind; he should merge that mind into the intelligent self; he should merge the intelligent self into the great soul; he should merge the great soul into the peaceful self. The idea is that one should make the intelligence as clear in its nature as is the first born or the great soul again should sink into peaceful. Just as the water in a mirage, the snake in a rope, and dirt in the sky, are eliminated through the perception of the real nature of mirage, rope and the sky, similarly He, dissolving the 'Purusa' the self - through the knowledge of the true nature of one's own self, all that is projected by unreal ignorance, which is characterised by action, instrument and result, which is but constituted by the three—name, form and action — one becomes established in the self and peaceful in mind and he has his goal achieved. Since this is so, therefore, for the sake of realising this, one should arise, awake and learn by approaching the excellent ones. The wise ones describe that path to be as impassable as a razor's edge, which, when sharpened, is difficult to tread on. The idea is that since the object to be known is very subtle, they speak of the path of knowledge leading to it as impassable. Then question is how is the thing to be known very subtle. Now since this earth is gross, developed as it is, by the principles of sound, touch, colour, taste, and smell and it is an object of perception to all the senses, so also is the body. Here a gradation of subtleness, pervasiveness, purity, permanence etc. is noticed in water etc., through the elimination of the attributes of smell etc., one by one, till one reaches space. Therefore, what need is there to speak of the unsurpassable subtleness etc. of that in which do not exist those attributes—beginning with smell and ending with sound — those are the causes of grossness. That is what upanisada shows. One becomes freed from the jaws of death by knowing that which is soundless, touchless, colourless, undiminishing, and also tasteless, eternal, odourless, without beginning and without end, distinct from Mahat, and ever constant. Relating and hearing this eternal anecdote — as received by Nichiketa and as told by death — the intelligent man becomes glorified in the region that is Brahma. So should anyone, after purification, get this highest secret recited before an assembly of Brahmins, or at the time of ceremonies for the dead, then that ceremony becomes conducive to eternal result. Brahma is thus hidden in all beings and hence he does not appear as the self of all, but is seen through a pointed and fine intellect. Then what this obstacle is to the pointed intellect, because of which there is an absence of that intellect and the self is not seen. So first we have to find out the cause of that bar and then make effort to remove that bar.

The self-existing Lord destroys the outgoing senses. Therefore, one sees the outer things (ears etc.) and not the inner self. A rare discriminating man, desiring immortality, turns his eyes away and then sees the indwelling self as it is not possible for the same person to be engaged in the thought of sense-objects and to have the vision of the self as well. The un-intelligent people follow the external desires they get entangled in the snares of the wide-spread death. Therefore, the discriminating people having known what true immortality is in the midst of impermanent things, do not pray for anything here. Now then the natural tendencey to perceive only the outwardly things that are not the self, if the cause of obstruction of the vision of the self and it is ignorance since it is opposed to that vision. And there is that thirst for the enjoyment of those very outer things — whether seen or unseen — which are presented by ignorance. Those whose vision of the self is obstructed by those two — ignorance and thirst — those men of little intelligence follow only the external desirable things. They, because of that reason, get entangled in the snares, by which one is bound, consisting in the association with or dissociation from the body-senses etc. Having known the constant and unshakable immortality, which is of this kind, having ascertained it from amidst all impermanent things, the knowers of Brahma do not pray for anything in this world, which is full of evils, because all this is opposed to the vision of the innermost self. The idea is that they inevitably rise above the desires for progeny, wealth and worldly enjoyments. What remains here unknowlable to the self, through which the very self people perceive colour, taste, smell, sound, touch, and sexual pleasures ? This indeed is that self asked for by Nichiketa. Now, having realised the great and all-pervading self, through which a man perceives the objects in both the sleep and the waking states, a wise man does not grieve. Anyone, who knows proximately this self — the enjoyer of the fruits of work, the supporter of life etc. — as the Lord of the past and the future, does not want to save the self just because of that knowledge. This indeed is that. Here it is being shown that the indwelling self, which has been indentified with God, is the self of all. He sees this very aforesaid Brahma, who sees the just Born — born before the five elements from consciousness Brahma — as existing in the cavity of the heart; in the midst of the body and senses, after having entered there, perceiving sound etc., i.e., anyone who sees thus, he sees this very one Brahma, that is under discussion. Furthermore, is that Aditi, who comprises all deities, who takes birth as 'Hiranyagarbha' from the Supreme Brahma. That very Aditi is being distinguished, which as associated with the elements took birth i.e. was created. The sacrificial fire, lodged in two fires — producing pieces of wood, as also the fire lodged in the wants of yogis, that is well protected — just as much as the foetus by pregnant woman — and the fire that is adorable every day by vigilant men with oblation and contemplation— that fire too is but this Brahma. There, all the deities are fixed on that from which the sun rises and in which it sets. None ever transcends that. This indeed is Brahma.

A doubt then arises in mind about the entity, which exists in all beings from Brahma down to the immovable and appears as non-Brahma owing to those particular limiting adjuncts is an individual soul different from the supreme Brahma and is subject to birth and death. It may be explained that what indeed is here, is there and likewise what is there is here. He, who sees as though there is difference here, goes from death to death. This being so, anyone, who being deluded by ignorance that consists in seeing differences that are natural to the limiting adjuncts, sees, perceives here in Brahma, which is not a plurality as though there is difference — feels such differences as, 'I am different from the Supreme self, and the Supreme Brahma is different from me', he gets death after death; he becomes subject to repeated birth and after death he becomes subject to repeated birth and death, Therefore, one should not perceive like that and should perceive like this 'I am indeed Brahma', which is homogeneous consciousness and which pervades everything through and through like space, and this is to be attained through the mind indeed. There is no diversity here whatsoever. He who sees as though there is difference here, goes from death to death and birth to birth even by superimposing the slightest difference. The 'Purusha' of the size of a thumb resides in the body. One does not want to save the self by virtue of the knowledge that he is the ruler of the past and the future. The 'Purusha' is like a light without smoke. He exists today and will exist tomorrow. As water rained on an inaccessible height gets dispersed on lower hilly region, similarly, one, who perceives the selves differently, runs after them only.

Now it is stated as to how the nature of the self is attained by one, who is a man of realisation, for whom has been destroyed the perception of difference that is created by limiting adjuncts, who sees the non-dual self, which a homogenous mass of pure consciousness and who is possessed of knowledge and is engaged in meditation. Further, as pure water poured on pure water becomes verily the same, so also does become the self of the man of knowledge, who is given to deliberation on the self. Therefore, giving up the perception of duality that bad logicians have and the erroneous notions that the non-believers entertain, the people, whose pride has been quelled, should eagerly seek after the realisation of the unity of the self, which is inculcated by vedas that are more beneficient than thousands of fathers and mothers.

As Brahma is difficult to know, we have to find out another way for ascertaining the reality. Of the unborn one, whose consciousness is unflickering, there is a city with eleven gates. Meditating on him one does not grieve and becoming freed, one becomes emancipated. This indeed is that way. As the moving sun, he dwells in heaven; as air, he pervades all and dwells in the interspace; as fire, he resides on the earth; as soma, he stays in the jar; he lives amongst men; he lives among gods ; he dwells in truth; he dwells in space ; he is born in water ; he takes birth from the earth; he is born in the sacrifice; he emerges from the mountains; he is changing and he is great. The meaning, therefore, is that the world has but one self which is all pervasive, and that there is no plurality of selves. All deities worship that adorable one. Sitting in the middle, he leads higher up from the heart; the air functioning as exhalation; similarly thrusts inward, downward, the air functioning as inhalation that adorable sitting in the middle—sitting in the space inside the lotus of the heart, shining in the intellect as revealed knowledge; all deities—the organs such as eye etc. worship — by carrying to him presents in the form of perception of colour etc. just as the subjects do to the king. The idea is that they never cease from the activity meant for him, and he, for whom, and under whose direction, exists all the activities of the organs, and the vital force, is proved to be different from them, and when this dweller in the body, becomes detached, when he is freed from the body, what else remains here in this body is that. No mortal lives by 'prana' (exhale) or 'apana' (inhale) but all live by something else due to which these two find asylum, and for the benefit of which uncombined self, prana, apana, etc. exist as a combination, performing their own functions — that self is established to be distinct from them.

Now comes eternal Brahma and also how the self fares after death. Some souls enter the womb for acquiring bodies and others follow the motionless in accordance with their work and in conformity with their knowledge. The 'Purusha', who keeps awake and goes on creating desirable things even when the senses fall asleep, is pure, and he is Brahma, and he is called the immortal. All the worlds are fixed on him and none can transcend him. Since the knowledge of the unity of the self, though validated by proof and reitrated more than once, does not find a lodging in the hearts of those Brahmins of insincere intellect, whose minds are swayed by the perverted intellect of numerous logicians, therefore, the upanisada, being eager to inculcate it, says again and again that just as fire, through one, having entered the world, assumes separate forms in respect of different shapes, similarly, the self inside all beings, though one, assumes a form in respect of each shape and yet it is outside. Similarly, air, though one, assumes a form in respect of each shape and yet is outside. Now the contingency arises that if a single entity is the self of all, then the sorrowfulness of the world will belong to the Supreme Brahma itself. Similar is the case of sun. So the external peace is for those — and not for others who are discriminating and who realise in their hearts, Him, who being one — the controller, and the inner self of all — makes a single form multifarious. Also, same is the case when one realises in his heart, Him, who being the eternal among the ephemeral, the consciousness among the conscious — alone dispenses the desired objects to many.

Then how shall one know that Supreme, unspeakable bliss

which they realise directly as this ? Is it self effulgent — does it shine distinctly, or does it not ? The answer to this is that it is both self - effulgent and shines distinctly or multifariously. There the sun does not shine, neither do the moon and the stars, nor do these flashes of lightening shine. Then how can this fire, that is seen by us, shine. These all, therefore, shine as he, the supreme Lord, shines. Just as hot water, fire brand etc. owing to their contact with fire, burn according as the fire does, but not independently, similarly it is verily by his effulgence that all this — the sun etc. shine varioulsy. This being so, it is that Brahma itself, that is effulgent and shines varioulsy. Through the various kinds of effulgence in the effects, it is known that the characteristic of luminosity is intrinsic to that Brahma. Indeed, that which does not have intrinsic luminosity, cannot impart it to others for a pot etc. are not seen to illuminate others, whereas luminous things like the sun etc. are seen to do so.

In order now to ascertain the real nature of Brahma through the determination of the tree which is the effect that the world is, of which Brahma is the root, let us take the peepal tree that has its roots above and branches down. That which is its root, is pure, that is Brahma and that is called immortal. On that are fixed all the worlds ; none transcends that. It consists of many evils, such as birth, old age, death, sorrow etc., it changes itself every moment, in as much as no sooner is it seen than its nature is destroyed like magic, water in a mirage, a city in the sky etc. and it ceases to exist ultimately like a tree; it is without any heart — wood like the stem of a plantain tree; it is subject to hundreds of doubts in the minds of sceptics; its reality is determined in its true colour by the seekers of truth; its essence lies in its root, the supreme Brahma ascertained in vedanta; it grows from out of the seed of ignorance, desire, action and the unmanifested; it has for its sprout 'Hiranyagarbha', the inferior Brahma, comprising the two powers of knowledge and action ; it has from its trunk, the diverse subtle bodies of all creatures ; its vigour of growth results from the sprinkling of the water of desire; it has for its tender sprouts, the objects of sense of knowldge; its leaves are the vedas, the samritis, logic, learning and instructions; its lovely flowers are the many deeds such as sacrifice, charity, austerity etc.; its various tastes are the experience of happiness and sorrow; its fruits are the means of subsistence of beings; it has its secondary roots too well developed, entwined and firmly fixed through the sprinkling of water of desire for those fruits; it has for its nests the seven worlds beginning from the one called 'Satya', built by birds, which are the living beings from Brahma downwards; it has its uproar, rendered tumultuous through the various sounds arising from dancing, singing, instrumental music, clapping on the arms, laughing, crying etc. induced by mirth and grief arising from the enjoyment and pain of living being; and it is felled by the weapon of detachment consisting of the realisation of the identity of Brahma and the self as inculcated by vedanta, shaker as it is by the wind of desire and deeds. The root of the world is the light of the self, which is consciouness, that indeed is Brahma, being the greatest of all and indestructible by nature being steady because of truth and the jugglery of the universal vanishes on the realisation of this Supreme truth. It may in the end be said that the very root of the world, Brahma, by realising which it is stated that people become immortal, does not exist and that this universe has emerged out of nothing. But this is wrong as all this universe that is there, emerges and moves because there is the Supreme Brahma, which is a great terror like an uplift thunderbolt and those who know this, become immortal. It is because of the fear from him that fire burns, from fear sun shines and from fear Indra and Air and death run. If one realises this before the falling of the body as it is here alone, that it is possible for the vision of the self to be as clear as that of a face in a mirror, whereas this is not possible. In other worlds, apart from that of Brahma, which, however, is difficult to attain because as one sees in a mirror, so in one's intellect; as in a dream so in the world of manes; as it is seen in water so in the world of Gandharvas; as it is in the case of shade and light, so in the world of Brahma, but that world is difficult to attain being the result of many special kinds of work and knowledge i.e. of rites and meditation. Therefore, efforts should be made for the realisation of the self here itself.

Now having known the dissimilarity of the senses that originate separately, as also their rising and setting, the intelligent man does not grieve. 'The knower of the self crosses over sorrow'. So the self, in relation to which dissimilarity of the senses has been pointed, is not to be realised outside, for it is the innermost self of all as the mind is superior to the organs ; the intellect is superior to the mind; the great soul is superior to the intellect; the unmanifested is superior to the soul. The sense-objects, belonging to the same class as the senses, are understood to be enumerated by the mention of the senses. But the 'Purusha', who is pervasive and is, indeed, without worldly attributes, knowing whom a man becomes freed and attains immortality, is superior to the unmanifested. Then we have to see how can there be any possibility of the vision of the incomprehensible. This is because his form does not exist within the range of vision, and nobody sees him with eyes. When this self is revealed through deliberation, it is realised by the intellect, the ruler of the mind that resides in the heart and those who know this fact that the self is Brahma, they become immortal. The ruler of the heart can be attained by inculcating yoga i.e. when the five senses of knowledge come to rest together with the mind and the intellect too does not function in its own activities, that state is called the highest state. This is also the yoga. One becomes vigilant at that time for yoga is subject to growth and decay. If Brahma be an object of the activities of the intellect etc., then it should be specifically apprehended as 'This is such and such' and since it cannot be perceived on the cessation of the intellect etc., there being then no instrument for cognition, Brahma should surely have no existence then. It is a well-known fact in the world that a thing exists so long as it is within the range of an instrument of recognition, and the contrary one is non-existent. Hence yoga is useless or Brahma is to be perceived as non-existing in as much as it cannot be cognized. Further, it cannot be attained through speech, nor through mind nor through eye. How can it then be known to anyone apart from him, who speaks of it as existing. Therefore, eschewing the devilish company of those who advance the theory of non-existence, the self should be realised as existing as productive of effects in which existence inheres, and as having the intellect etc. as its limiting adjuncts. But when the self is devoid of all that and is not subject to changes — and effects do not exist apart from their cause, because of the vedic text, 'All transformation has speech as its basis and it is name only.' Earth as such is the reality — then of that unconditioned, attributeless self that is free from becoming an object of such concepts as existence and non-existence, the true nature is revealed and in that form too is the self to be realised.

When all desires clinging to one's heart fall off, then a mortal becomes immortal, and he attains Brahma and becomes Brahma here itself and this is the supreme reality. When all the knots of the heart are destroyed even while a man is alive, then also a mortal becomes immortal. This much alone is the instruction of all upanisadas by asserting, 'He attains Brahma here,' it has been declared that there is no going for an enlightened man of whom all the knots of ignorance become destroyed on the realisation of the identity of the self with the all pervading and absolutely attributeless Brahma and who becomes Brahma even while living as also supported by vedas, 'Of him the organs do not depart. Being but Brahma he is merged in Brahma.' But for those, who are not much advanced in the knowledge of Brahma, who are engaged in other kinds of knowledge i.e. in worship and meditation and who are fit for the world of Brahma, as also for those who are opposite of these and one fit for worldly existence, this particular kind of path is stated with a view to eulogizing the superior result of the knowledge of Brahma.

The nerves of the heart are a hundred and one in number. Of them, one passes through the crown of the head. Going up through that nerve, one gets immortality. The others that have different directions, become the cause of death or after having enjoyed incomparable pleasures abounding in the world of Brahma, one attains immortality in due course of time and the other nerves that branch out in different directions become the causes of death i.e. for the attainment of the worldly state alone. The 'Purusa', the indwelling self, of the size of a thumb, is ever seated in the hearts of men. One should unerringly separate him from one's body like a stalk from the 'munja' grass. One should know him as pure and immortal.

Nichiketa, having first become free from virtue and vice, as also desire and ignorance, by acquiring this knowledge imparted by death, as also the process of yoga in its totality, attained Brahma. Anyone else, too, who becomes a knower thus like Nichiketa, of the indwelling self, attains Brahma. In the end, a prayer is uttered with a view to removing all faults incurred by the disciple and the teacher through lapses resulting from inadvertence during the course of acquiring or imparting the knowledge.

May He protect us both (by revealing knowledge). May He protect us both by vouchsafing the result of knowledge. May we attain vigour together. Let what we study be invigorating. May we not cavil at each other. Om ! Peace ! Peace ! Peace ! (The repetition for three times is to avert all evils).

8

Taittriya Upanisada

This upanisada deals with the knowledge of Brahma with a view to eschewing the causes that lead to the performance of Karmas (Rites, duties etc. enjoined by scriptures), since it stimultes actions, for no impulsion to activity is possible in the case of those, whose desires have been fulfilled, they being then established in their own self as a result of the absence of desire and fulfilment of desires follows from the desire for the self in as much as the self, indeed, is Brahma, and for the knower of Brahma will be declared the attainment of the highest. Therefore, the continuance in one's own self, on the eradication of ignorance. tantamonts to the attainment of salvation. 'Karma' is multifarious, and as such, there is the possibility that there are actions — done in many previous births and bearing fruits in this life or remaining in abeyance — which have opposite results. Accordingly, since those of the actions that have not begun to bear fruits in this life, cannot possibely become exhausted through enjoyment in this one single birth, it is reasonable that a fresh body shall be created as a result of the residual fruits of action and the existence of residual fruits of work is also proved by hundreds of vedic and samriti texts such as, 'Among them, those, who were performers of meritorious deeds here, they will attain good births'. Now since desires, which are the springs of actions, cannot cease unless there is enlightenment, there is no possibility of the eradication of actions as a whole by the obligatory duties and since desire has for its objects, things other than the self, it belongs to one, who has not realised the self that there can be no desire in one's own self, it being ever realised; and that the self is the Supreme Brahma. Then emancipation is attainable through activity in as much as the unsurpassable happiness, called heaven, is a result of 'Karma' that too is wrong. For emancipation is a permanent entity, and nothing that is everlasting, can ever have a beginning. Whatever is produced in this world is impermanent. Therefore, emancipation is not a creation of 'Karma'. Emancipation consists in continuance in one's own self on the cessation of the material cause in the form of ignorance, desire, and activity. Self, as such, is Brahma, and from the knowledge of Brahma, follows liberation consisting in the eradication of ignorance.

To start, one has to pray and ask for the blessings of the gods. Therefore, the prayer is for the blessings of Mitra, Varuna, Indra, Brahaspati, Vishnu, Brahma, Vayu, Guru and utters OM, Shanti, Shanti, Shanti. Then comes the way of pronunciation. The things to be learnt are the alphabets, accent, measure, emphasis, uniformity, and juxtaposition. This is necessary so that there may not be any slackness in the effort involved in the recital of the text for the comprehension of meaning plays a prominent part in the upanisada. Signifying that through which something is learnt, is the science of pronunciation of letters etc. then the prayer is for attainment of fame to both the teacher and the taught and the spiritual pre-eminence, splendour, that results from it, may too occur simultaneoulsy to us both. There are five headings, through five means of subjects of knowledge. Those are meditation that refers to the worlds ; meditation concerning lights; meditation concerning knowledge; meditation concerning progeny and meditation concerning body. These five are great juxtapositions since they relate to great things like the world and the being as well. Then there is mention of persons, who want intelligence and wealth, a prayer and sacrifice which are the means for their acquisition and this conclusion is born out by the indications implied in, 'May he who is Indra gratify me with intelligence and then bring for me wealth'. 'Om' is, however, the object to be worshipped here, hence its eulogy through such words as 'bull' is rather appropriate. 'OM' appeared as the quintessence when Prajapati performed austerity with a view to extracting the first essence from the worlds, the gods and the vedas. For 'OM' is everlasting and for it no real origination can properly be imagined. Therefore, the prayer is directed towards one to grant strength and intelligence and knowledge of Brahma, the cause of immortality.

Then, there are mantras to be used for offering oblations by one who wants prosperity. Since prosperity to an unwise man is surely a cause of evil, therefore, after that after vouchsafing intelligence, bring the prosperity by giving clothes, cattle, food and drink. But in fact what kind of prosperity is this ? The prosperity which is endowed with animals etc. This however, is not the prosperity. Prosperity is in asking for Brahmcharya, control of body, control of senses and mind.

Then one wishes to have fame. For this, the prayer is to become famous among people, become praiseworthy among the wealthy and then the prayer is to bless entry into Him, such as he is in the self and then to purify sins. As water flows down a slope, as months roll into year, similarly the prayer is for the students coming from all quarters and for Brahma to rest in him, be known to him and to be known by him through and through. Further, the prayer for prosperity dealt with in this context of knowledge is for the sake of wealth as wealth is needed for rites and rites are meant for diminishing the accumulated sins — on the exhaustion of these, the knowledge becomes revealed. Samriti says, Just as one sees oneself on the clear surface of a mirror, so knowledge arises for the man on the exhaustion of sins.

Bhuh, Bhuvah, Suvah are the three vyahrtis and Maha i.e. Brahma is the fourth. It is self and the other gods are limbs. 'Bhuh' is this world, 'Bhuvah' is the intermediate space and 'Suvah' is the other world. 'Maha' is the sun and through the sun does all the world flourish. Then 'Bhuh is fire, 'Bhuvah' the air and 'Suvah' the sun and 'Maha' the moon and through the moon all the luminaries flourish. Again 'Bhuh' is the Rig Ved; 'Bhuvah' the Sam Ved and 'Suvah' the Yajurveda. 'Maha' is Brahma as by Brahma, indeed, are all the vedas nourished. 'Bhuh' is 'prana', 'Bhuvah' the 'apana' and 'Suvah' is 'vyana'. Maha is 'food' as by food are all the vital forces nourished. Then these four are four fold. The vyahrtis are divided into four groups of four each. He, who knows these, knows Brahma, to whom all the gods carry presents i.e. who is worshipped by all gods. So the other deities viz. those of 'Bhuh', 'Bhuvah' and 'Suvah' are the limbs of Brahma as identified with the vyahrti called 'Maha'. Just as a 'Saligram' is in the case of Vishnu, so the cavity of heart is being prsented as the place for the direct realisation of and the meditation on Brahma of which the vyahrtis are the limbs as when Brahma is meditated on there, it is directly realised as possession of such attributes are being realised through knowledge etc., and the way to realisation of self-identification with all has to be stated.

In the heart, there is space and in the space lives the person, who is realisable through knowledge and who is immortal and effulgent and this is the path of Brahma. He becomes established in Fire, in Air, in Sun and in Brahma which is Maha. He gets sovereignty; he attains the Lord of mind, he becomes the ruler of speech, the ruler of eyes, the ruler of ears and the ruler of knowledge. Over and above all these, he becomes Brahma, which is embodied in space, which is identified with the gross and the subtle and has truth as its real nature, which revels in the vital forces, under whose possession, the mind is a source of bliss, which is enriched with peace and is immortal. Since Brahma is all pervasive, it is the lord of all the minds; indeed it thinks through all the minds. A man, who meditates thus, attains him. Moreover, it becomes the ruler of all the organs of the speech, the eyes, the ears and of intellect. The idea is that he being the self of all, becomes possessed of the respective organs through identification with the organs of all beings.

Now the very Brahma, which has been presented for meditation as 'Hiranyagarbha', identified with the vyahrtis, another meditation identifying it with the group of five things beginning with the earth, is being narrated. Because of the similarity of the number five, they are equated with the metre called 'Pankti', thereby everything becomes identified with 'Pankti' and a sacrifice too is identified with 'Pankti' because 'Pankti' has five feet (with five letter is each), and as per vedas, the sacrifice is equated with 'Pankti'. As a result, all things beginning from the worlds and ending with. 'The Atma', that are thought of as reduced to 'Pankti' are thereby virtually imagined to be a sacrifice and through the sacrifice one becomes Prajapati, who again is identified with all that is equated with

'Pankti' and then is shown how all this universe consists of 'Pankti' (five factors). The earth, sky, heaven, the primary quarters and the intermediate quarters — these constitute the groups of five in the context of the worlds — fire, air, sun, moon, stars — these constitute the group of five deities. Water, Herbs, Trees, Space and Atma are five natural things. Here the 'Atma' implies the cosmic gross body beause this is in context of natural things and this expression is used to imply the two groups of five worlds and the five deities as well.

After identifying meditation on Brahma with the vyahrtis, a meditation on the same Brahma, conceived of as a five fold identity is followed. Now we seek to enjoin a meditation on 'OM', which is involved as a factor in all meditations for though 'OM' is a mere word, it becomes a means for the entertainment of the Supreme Brahma or of 'Hiranyagarbha' in accordance as it is meditated on with the idea of the Supreme Brahma or of 'Hiranyagarbha'. Just as an image is a symbol of Vishnu, so is 'OM' verily a symbol of Brahma. In accordance with the vedas 'The illumined soul attains either of the two through this one, means alone viz 'OM'. 'OM' is Brahma, 'OM' is all this. 'OM' is well-known as a word of imitation i.e. concurrence. Moreover, they make them recite with the word, 'OM'. They commence singing samas with 'OM', uttering the words 'OM', soon they recite the sastras. Brahmins approve with the word 'OM'. Agnihotra sacrifice is done with 'OM' and ultimately it is said that all this is 'OM', purport is that since the activities which are undertaken with the utterance of 'OM' become fruitful, 'OM' should be meditated upon as Brahma.

From the statement that knowledge alone leads to the attainment of sovereignty, it may follow that the duties enjoined by vedas and samrities are useless. In order to avoid such a contingency, the duties are being presented here, so that they may be shown as contributory to the attainment of human goals. For this purpose, righteousness and learning and teaching are to be practised. Truth and learning and teaching are to be practised. Austerity, learning and teaching are to be resorted to. Control of the outer organs and learning and teaching are to be practised. Control of the inner organs and learning and teaching are to be resorted to. The fires are to be kept up ; Agnihotra is to be performed ; guests are to be adored ; social good conduct is to be adhered to ; progeny is to be together; procreations are to be carried on ; and grandsons are to be raised. Learning and teaching are mentioned in all the contexts in order to imply that these two are to be carefully practised even by one, who is engaged in all these duties, for the comprehension of meaning is dependent on study and the supreme goal, emancipation, is dependent on the understanding of the meaning and teaching is for the preservation of that memory and for the increase of virtue. Therefore, one has to entertain a love for learning and teaching. Satyam (truth) alone is to be practised. One, whose speech consists of truth is one whose name is Satyavaca. Learning and teaching verily constitute 'tapah' and 'austerity'. Therefore, they alone are to be followed. Further, mantras are there for the sake of self-recital (Jap) and from the context it follows that the self-recital is for the sake of development of knowledge for the present topic is concerned with knowledge and no other purpose apears to be implied. Moreover, it is considered that knowledge arises in one whose mind is purified by self-recital. For instance 'I am the invigorator of the tree (of the world), my fame is high like the ridge of a mountain. My source is the pure Brahma, I am like that pure reality of the self, which is in the sun. I am the effulgent wealth. I am possessed of a fine intellect and am immortal and undecaying'. Thus was the statement of Trisanku after the attainment of realisation. This statement was for the sake of expressing the fact that he had reached fulfilment just like Vamdeva. The idea is that the traditional text in the form of the 'mantra' as visualised by Trinsanku with the eyes of a seer, reveals the knowledge of the self. And it is understood that the self-repetition of this 'mantra' is calculated to lead to knowledge. It is also clear that the visions of the seers, with regard to the self etc., become revealed to one, who engages thus in the obligatory duties enjoined in the vedas and samritis, who is devoid of selfish motives and who hankers after the realisation of the Supreme Brahma. Thus before the realisation of Brahma, the duties inculcated in the vedas and samritis are to be performed regularly as it is meant for creating proper tendencies in a man as in accordance with the samritis, he eradicates sin through austerities and attain immortality through knowledge ; the knowledge of the self draws easily as one who has the proper mental disposition and whose mind is purified. Moreover, there is the fact of the earlier treatment of the rites etc. Hence, it is known that duties are calculated to lead to the dawn of knowledge through the eradication of sins accumulated in the past and vedas too say so crossing over death through rites etc. one attains immortality through meditation.

The instructor further imparts instructions to the students to speak the truth ; practise righteousness; make no mistake about study, do not cut off line of progeny to teachers etc., there should be no inadvertence about truth; there should be no mistake about protection of yourself ; do not neglect propitious activities and not to be careless about learning and teaching. The duties towards the gods and manes must be performed. The mother, father and teacher are to be worshipped as gods. The activities undertaken by good people as are ordained by vedas, should be resorted to only. Here good people means Brahmins and not Kshatriyas and others. Whatever is given should be given with modesty. While doing these duties, if at any time, there is doubt with regard to the 'Karmas' (rites and duties) inculcated by vedas and samritis or with regard to conduct, consisting in customary behaviour, then one should behave as the Brahmins behave or should apply the text in the ways as shown before viz. in vedas and samritis.

For the sake of distinguishing between knowledge and 'Karma' i.e. scriptural rites and duties, we enter into a consideration of the question as to whether the supreme goal (emancipation) results from 'Karmas' alone or from 'Karmas' aided by knowledge, or from 'Karmas' and knowledge in combination or from knowledge aided by Karmas or from knowledge alone. Since the emancipation is the result of Karmas alone and a man well-versed in vedas and samritis is competent for 'Karmas', preferably as taught by the Brahmins who have masterd vedas and samritis along with the purport of the upanisadas regarding the knowledge of self etc. for attaining salvation. After knowledge, the practise is must and it is here that 'Karmas' come into play. The aim of the vedas is to impart instruction in respect of human goals, the vedic texts, which are devoted to the communication of knowledge, engage themselves in the revelation of knowledge under the belief that a man has to be liberated from the world. Ignorance, which is the cause of the world, can be eradicated through knowledge only. Further, the Karmas are multifarious. Agnihotra etc. are not the only Karmas, there also exist such practices as celebacy, austerity, truthfulness, control of external and internal organs and non-injury, which are familiarly associated with the other stages of life, besides such practices as concentration, meditation etc. — all of which are best calculated to serve as means for the origination of knowledge, since they are unadulterated with sinful actions. Even for one, who has accepted the life of a householder, there will surely be a cessation from Karma after the rise of knowledge and after the renunciation of everything on the maturity of knowledge — when one feels no need for any 'Karma' in accordance with the indication in vedas etc. are much at pains to enjoin Karmas' etc., for the 'Karmas' such as Agnihotra as also the practice of celibacy etc. undertaken in the past lives, become helpful to the rise of knowledge, because of which fact some are seen to be non-attached to the world from their very birth, while others are seen to be engaged in 'Karma', attached to the world and averse to enlightenment. In the case of those, who have become detached, owing to tendencies created in past lives, it is desirable only to resort to other stage of life. Further, there is no such rule that knowledge arises from the mere elimination of the obstructions alone and not from the grace of God or the practice of austerity, meditation etc. as non-injury, celibacy are ways to enlightenment and hearing, thinking and meditating are the direct causes of it. Therefore, people in all the stages of life can aspire for knowledge and that the supreme goal is attainable through knowledge alone.

Then the belief is that the knower of Brahma attains the highest. Brahma is truth, knowledge and infinite. He, who knows that Brahma is existing in the intellect, which is lodged in the supreme space in the heart, enjoys, in identification with the all knowing Brahma, all desirable things simultaneously.

From Brahma, which is this self, has produced space; from space emerged air; from air was born fire ; from fire water was created; from water came earth; from earth are born the herbs;

from herbs are produced food; from food may born man. The man is the product of essence of food. Of him is the head, self etc. Brahma is Brahma because he is the greatest and then as per the verdict that, 'Any one, who knows that Supreme Brahma, becomes Brahma indeed', clearly shows the attainment of Brahma itself by the knower of Brahma. Even though Brahma is one's self, it can remain unattained through ignorance and the discovery of the self is through knowledge and after attaining knowledge, on the instructions of the scriputres, one gets enlightenment leading to realisation of self or Brahma. Since Brahma is surpassingly subtle, there is nothing else whether subtle or screened or remote or past, present or future, which can be knowable to it. Therefore, Brahma is omniscient as is said 'Though he is without hands and feet, still he runs and grasps, though he is without eyes, still he sees, though he is without ears, still he listens'. He knows the knowable and of him there is no knower. He is the first great person. Just because Brahma's nature of being the knower, is inseparable and because there is no dependence on other accessories like the sense-organs Brahma though intrinsically identical with knowledge, is well known to be eternal. He, who has known Brhama thus, he enjoys all without any exception i.e. all enjoyable things i.e. all desirable things and not sons, heaven, wealth etc. alone. That very fact has been described as in identification with Brahma. Thus the man of knowledge having become Brahma, enjoys as Brahma, all the desirable things simultaneously; and he does not enjoy in sequence the desirable things that are dependent on such causes as merit etc. and such sense-organs as the eyes etc. as does an ordinary man identified with the worldly self; which is conditioned by limiting adjuncts and which is a reflection of the Supreme self like that of the sun on water. The purport of the text is 'The knower of Brahma attains the highest', occurring in the Brahmin portion. It has been earlier said that Brahma is truth, knowledge and infinite. Then the question arises how it is truth, knowledge and infinite. In this connection, it may be indicated that there are three kinds of infinitude — from the standpoint of space, time and objects. Such as sky is unlimited from the point of view of space, for it is not limited in space. But the sky is not infinite as regards time or as regards other objects since it is a product. Brahma is not thus limited in time like the sky, since it is not a product. For, a created thing is circumscribed by time, but Brahma, is not created. Hence it is infinite from the point of view of time as well. Similarly, too, from the point of view of objects, it is non-different from every thing. A thing that is different, acts as a limitation to another. But when the intellect gets occupied with something, it becomes detached from something else. That idea, because of which another idea becomes circumscribed, acts as a limit to the latter idea. Such as the idea of cowhood is repelled by the idea of horsehood; hence horsehood debars cowhood and idea of cowhood becomes delimited. That limitation is seen in the case of distinct objects. Brahma is not differentiated in this way. Hence it has infinitude even from the stand point of substances. Now since Brahma is the cause of everything, he is non-different from everything. Brahma is, therefore, verily the cause of all things — time, space etc. Ultimately, in his competence for 'Karma' and knowledge does the pre-eminence consist, because man alone, who is desirous of results and possessed of learning and capacity, is qualified for rites and duties as also for knowledge, by virtue of his ability, craving for results and non-indifference to results. This is proved by the evidence of vedic text, 'In man alone is the self most manifest, for he is the best endowed with intelligence'. He speaks what he knows, he sees what he knows; he knows what will happen tomorrow; he knows the higher and the lower worlds ; he aspires to achieve immortality though mortal things. He is thus endowed with discrimination while other beings have consciousness of hunger and thirst only. The intention here is to make that very human being enter into the inmost Brahma through knowledge. But his intellect, that thinks of the outer particular forms, which are not selves, as selves cannot without the support of some distinct object, be suddenly made contentless and engaged in the thoughts of the inmost indwelling self. The text takes the help of a fiction that has an affinity with the identification of the self and the perceived body and leading thereby the intellect inward, of that human being, who is such and who is a modification of the essence of food, this is verily the head that is well known.

All beings that rest on the earth are born verily from food; they live on food and in the end they get merged in food. Food was verily born before all creatures. Therefore, it is called the medicine for all. So food was born before creatures. Therefore, creature are born of food, being born, they grow by food, and since it is eater and it eats the creatures, it is called food. Compared with this self made of food, there is another inner self, which is made by air. That is also verily of human form. Of this 'Prana' is the head, 'Vyan' the right side, 'Apana' the left side, space is the self, the earth is the tail that stabilizes. Since food was born before all, it is worshippable by all. So outer food is Brahma and the inner is self as the rice is within husk, so self is within Brahma but is separated from him and adopts another body and again ends up in Brahma when again sown. Compared to other functions that are in the periphery, the one that exists in the middle is the self. As per vedas, 'The middle of these limbs is verily their soul, means the deity of the earth and this deity supports the physical vital force, since this deity is the cause of its stability according to another vedic verdict, 'That deity favours by attaching the 'Apana' in a man'. Else the body would ascend upwards because of the function of the vital action 'Udana' then would be falling down because of its weight. Therefore, the deity of the earth is the stabilizing tail of the vital self. The senses act by following the vital force in the mouth, all human beings and animals that are there act similarly, since on the vital force depends the life of all creatures, therefore, it is called the life of all. Those, who worship the vital force as Brahma, attain the full span of life. Since on the vital force depends the life of all, it is called the life of all and this is indeed, the embodied self. As compared with this vital body, there is another internal self constituted by mind, fire etc. perform the act of breathing — become active through the functioning of the vital force 'anuparanam', after the self that is constituted by air, that is to say, the gods perform the vital functions by becoming identical with that which possesses the power of sustaining life. The human beings and animals become active through the function of breathing. Hence it is not simply by possessing the limited self in the form of the body built up by food, that creatures become dowered with selves. What then, human beings and others are endowed with their selves by virtue of possessing a vital body within each physical body, which former is common to, and pervades, each physical body as a whole, is that all creatures are possessed of their selves by virtue of being provided with the bodies beginning with the mental and ending with the blissful, which successively pervades the preceding ones and which are made up of the elements counting from akash that are the creations of ignorance. So also are they blessed with theirselves by the self that is common to all, self-existent, the source of space etc. everlasting, unchanging, all pervading, defined as truth, knowledge and infinite and beyond the five sheaths, and by implication, it is also said that this is the self of all in the real sense, and the senses act by following the activity of the vital force as according to vedas, 'Life lasts so long as the vital force resides in the body'. Therefore, those, who, after detaching themselves from this external, personal, physical self, meditate on the inner, common vital self as Brahma with the idea 'I am the vital force that is the self of all beings and their life', being the source of life get verily the full space of life in this world i.e. they do not meet with any accidental death before the ordained span of life.

One is not subjected to fear at any time if one knows the bliss that is Brahma, failing to reach which Brahma, as conditioned by the mind, words, along with the mind, turn back. Of that preceding vital one, this mental one is verily the embodied self. As compared with this mental body, there is another internal self constituted by valid knowledge. By that one is this one filled up. This one as aforesaid, has verily a human shape. It is humanly shaped in accordance with the human shape of the earlier one. Of him faith is verily the head; concentration is the self (trunk); the principle called Mahat (new born) is the stabilising tail. Further, knowledge actualises a sacrifice, and it executes the duties as well, as the gods meditate the first born Brahma, conditioned by knowledge. If one knows the knowledge, Brahma, and if one does not err about it, one abandons all sins in the body and fully enjoys all enjoyable things. Of that preceding mental one, this cognitive one is verily the embodied self. As compared with this cognitive body, there is another internal self constituted by bliss. By that one is this one filled up. This one, as aforesaid, has verily a human shape. It is humanly shaped in accordance with the human shape of the earlier one. Of him joy is verily the head, enjoyment is the right side, hilarity is the left side, bliss the self (trunk), Brahma is the tail, that stabilises.

Also knowledge actualises a sacrifice, for a man of knowledge executes it with faith etc. Hence knowledge is presented as a doer in the expression, 'Since everything is accomplished by knowledge, it is reasonable to say that the cognitive self is Brahma and all gods Indra etc. meditate on Brahma, which is the first born since it was born before all or because all actions presuppose it.' Hence through the worship of Mahat (Brahma), they become possessed of knowledge and glory and if one has eschewed all ideas of identity of the physical selves etc. with his own self and goes on thinking of the knowledge — Brahma only as his self — what will happen thereby is all sins in the body shall get abondoned as all sins are verily caused by the identification of oneself with the body. So having abondoned the body itself, all sins, which arise from the body, which are caused by the identifiction of oneself with the body and becoming identified with the knowledge Brahma, one fully enjoys, through the cognitive self itself all the desirable things that are there in the knowledge, Brahma. Self cannot be attained by the self itself in as much as there is no division within the self and Brahma is the self of the attainer. The self is that which has been described as "Not this, not this". This follows that if anyone knows Brahma as non-existent, he himself becomes non-existent. But the fact that Brahma does not exist, cannot arise with regard of Brahma, which is directly perceived as the self made of bliss and possessed of such limbs as joy for its head and so on. Besides, it is unjustifiable to refer separately to Brahma as the stablising tail in 'Brahma is the stabilising tail'. Since joys etc., which are the fruits of rites and meditation are nearer to the self, it is logical that they should be within the cognitive self, for the blissful self, revived by the impression of joy etc., is perceived in dream to be dependent on the cognitive self. The possession of any worldly thing or enjoyment gives only momentary happiness since the result of past deeds that bring about those particular modifications of the mind, are unstable. That being so, in proportion as that mind becomes purified through austerities that dispel indolence, and also through meditation, continence and faith, so much do particular joys attain excellence and gain in volume in that calm and free mind, that is the source of joy for one becomes happy by coming in contact with that source of joys permanently. It follows, therefore, that there exists that one, non-dual Brahma, as the farthest limit of the negation of duality called up by ignorance and this Brahma supports the duality like a tail. Now the question arises whether after departing from here, does any ignorant man go to the other world or does he not ? Alternatively, does any man of knowledge, after departing from here, reach the other world or does he not ? The answer is that he (the self) wished, 'Let me be many, let me be born'. He undertook a deliberation. Having deliberated, he created all this that exists. That Brahma, having created that, entered into that very thing and having entered there, it becomes the formed and the formless, the defined and the undifined, the sustaining and non-sustaining, the true and untrue. He becomes non-existing indeed and remains dissociated from the human objective viz. liberation. He, who perchance, knows Brahma as non-existent, as opposed to that if he knows that Brahma, which is the basis of all diversification and the seed of all acitivity, though in itself it is devoid of all distinctions, does exist. Then the knower of Brahma considers him as existing. For instance, it is well-known that a pot comprehended as a thing that man can deal with, is true, while anything of an opposite nature is false. Thus by a part of reasoning, there may arise here also an apprehension of the non-existence of Brahma. Therefore, it is said, 'If anyone knows that Brahma does exist', what will happen to him. Because of that realisation of existence, the knowers of Brahma, know this one — who has this realisation, as existing — identified with the self that is absolutely real — by virtue of his having become one with the Brahma that exists. So if a man thinks, 'Brahma is non-existent', then that man, because of his faithfulness to the entire righteous path consisting of the scheme of castes, stages of life etc., becomes non-existent in as much as that path is not calculated to lead him to Brahma. Hence this athiest is called unrighteous in the world. As opposed to such a man, if anyone knows that 'Brahma does exist', then he, because of his faith, accepts properly the righteous path comprising the scheme of castes, stages of life, etc., and leading to the realisation of Brahma. Therefore, the good people know this one as treading the righteous path and so Brahma is to be accepted as surely existing. But Brahma being the cause of space etc. is equally common to the man of knowledge and the ignorant. Therefore, it may be suspected that the ignorant man too reaches Brahma. Contrarily, if the ignorant man fails to reach Brahma, though it is the common source of all, then the attainment of Brahma by an enlightened man, may as well be doubted. From hearing, 'If one knows Brahma does exist', the doubt arises as to whether it exists or does not exist. From that by implication crops up Brahma exists or it does not, or since Brahma is impartial, whether does the unenlightened man reach him or not ? Even if Brahma is equal to all, its non-attainment in the case of the enlightened man can be suspected as much as in the case of unenlightened one and hence question arises, 'Does the man of knowledge attain or does he not'? Apropos of this, existence is being first spoken of. It remains to be explained as to what kind of truth is meant in the assertion that was made thus 'Brahma is truth, knowledge, iinfinite'. It is said Brahma's truth is affirmed by speaking of its existence, for it has been asserted that the existing is true. Therefore, the very affirmation of existence amounts to an avowal of reality. Since Brahma is the cause of space etc., it is not a fact that Brahma does not exist. Further, since all the products issuing from Brahma such as space etc., are perceived, it is a matter of common experience in this world that any thing from which something is produced, does exist, as for instance, seed, earth etc., which are the causes of a sprout, a pot etc., so Brahma does exist, since it is the cause of space etc., and no effect is perceived in this world as having been produced from a non-entity. If such effects as name and form had originated from a non-entity, they should not have been perceived since they have no reality. But they are perceived. Hence Brahma exists. Should any effect originate from a non-entity, it should remain soaked in unreality even while being perceived. But facts point otherwise. Therefore, Brahma exists. Vedas also say, 'How can a thing that exists, come out of a thing that does not exist'. This points out logically the impossibility of the creation of something out of nothing. Therefore, it stands to reason that Brahma is verily a reality. Brahma's desires are truth and knowledge by nature, and they are pure by virtue of their identity with Brahma. Brahma is not impelled to action by them. But Brahma ordains them in accordance with the results of actions of the creatures. Therefore, Brahma has independence with regard to desires. So Brahma has no want and this follows also from the fact of Brahma's non-dependence on any other means.Further, Brahma has no dependence on accessories etc., as others have, whose desires are not identified with themselves but are dependent on such causes as righteousness, and require the extraneous body and senses as their instruments. They exist because they are non-different from itself. Also Brahma becomes many, not like the man getting a son to multiply but when name and form existing latently in the self get manifested, they evolve — by retaining their intransic nature as the self under all conditions — in time and space, which are inseparable from Brahma. Then that evolution of name and form is the appearance of Brahma as the many. In no other way is it possible for the partless Brahma to become either multiple or finite, as for instance, the finitude and plurality of space are surely the creations of extraneous factors. Hence the self becomes multiple through these alone for no such subtle, disconnected and remote thing exists as non-self, in the past, present or future, which is different from the self and separated from it by time or space. Therefore, it is only because of Brahma that name and form have their living under all circumstances, but Brahma does not consist of them. They are said to be essentially Brahma, since they cease to exist when Brahma is eliminated and conditioned by these two limiting adjuncts, Brahma becomes a factor in all empirical dealings involving such words as knower, knowable and knowledge, as also their implications etc.

The association of the self with the cavity of the internal organ causes the knowledge of Brahma, for the internal organ has proximity, to the self and the nature of illumination. Just as pot etc. are perceived, when in contact with light, so also the self is perceived, when in contact with the light of intellectual conviction. It can, therefore, be said that the self is lodged in the cavity of the intellect which is the cause of its experience. So that very Brahma itself, which is the cause of space and which, after creating the effect, has entered into the creation, as it were, is perceived, within the cavity of intellect, as possessed of such distinction as being a seer, a hearer, a thinker, a knower etc. That indeed, is its entity. Hence Brahma, as the cause of this phenomenon must exist and because it exists, it should surely be apprehended as such.

In the beginning of the creation, all this was but the unmanifested Brahma. Not that absolete non-existence is meant for the existent cannot come out of non-existent. The standing for the manifested world possessed of the distinctions of name and form in the beginning, before creation, was that Brahma could be called unmanifested. From that unmanifested, indeed, that which is distinguished by manifested name and form was born, to the effect entirely separated from that just as a son is from the father. That which is called unmanifested, itself, created itself. Since this is so, therefore, that Brahma itself is called the self creator or since Brahma itself created everything by virtue of its being everything, therefore, that very Brahma, which is the cause from the standpoint of virtue as well, is called merit. At all events whether the meaning be merit or it be the self creator, that cause which brings one into association etc., with a result is familiarly known in the world as merit. That is possible onlv if there is an eternal consciousness acting as the cause. Hence from the well-known fact of merit, it follows that Brahma exists. Brahma also exists because it is a source of joy. As that which is known as the self-creator, is verily the source of joy too. Then the sources of joys are there like sweet and sour things, which are well-known to be so in the world. After getting a thing of joy, one becomes happy. A non-entity is not seen in this world to be a cause of happiness. In as much as those Brahmins, who have realised Brahma, are seen to be as happy as one is from obtaining an external source of joy — though infact, they do not take help of any external means of happiness, make no effort, and cherish no desire — it follows, as a matter of course, that Brahma is indeed, the source of their joy. Hence there does exist that Brahma, which is full of joy and is the spring of their happiness.

Brahma also exists as actions like inhaling and exhaling are seen. The body of a living being, exhales through that function of the vital force called 'prana' and inhales through the other called 'apana'. Thus are the body and senses, in their association, seen to perform their vital and organic functions. Thus coming into association for serving a common purpose is not possible unless there is a sentient being, which is not a part of this conglomeration. For such is not the case anywhere else. Therefore, that Brahma, for whose purpose there are such activities of the body and senses, as exhaling etc., does exist and the happiness of the people is caused of that itself. This is how Supreme self indeed enlivens people in accordance with their merits.

That Brahma also exists as the cause of fear and fearlessness of the men of ignorance and knowledge respectively. Fearlessness comes as a result of taking refuge in something that exists, whereas fear cannot cease by resorting to something that does not exist. Anything possessed of attributes can alone be expressed in words and anything possessed of attributes is mutable, whereas Brahma is changeless, it being the source of all modifications. Hence it is inexpressible. That being so, it is a nest, a refuge and is the opposite of that it is without support. When a man becomes established in his true nature, then he does not see anything else, does not hear anything else, does not know anything else. Someone gets afraid of someone else but it is not logical that the self should be afraid of the self. Inspite of the existence of the cause of fear, there are Brahmins to be found, who are free from all quarters. This would be injustifiable if Brahma, the protector from fear, were not there. Therefore, from the fact of noticing their fearlessness, it follows that Brahma exists as the source of their, intrepidity. One reaches fearlessness, when one does not perceive anything else and does not create any difference in the self, then he attains fearlessness. On the contrary, in the state of ignorance, one sees in the self something presented by nescience like the vision of a second moon seen by a man suffering from the eye-disease called 'timira' and in Brahma, he perceives even a slight hole — since the perception of difference is the cause of fear — it means that even if he sees the slightest difference there because of that seeing of difference, fear crops up for this soul, that perceives difference. So the self alone is the cause of fear to the self in the case of an ignorant man. Accordingly, the man, who does not realise the reality, that is the self, which is one and undifferentiated, is surely unenlightened, though he may be learned. Anyone, who considers oneself destructible, becomes struck with fear at the very sight of a destructive agency. A destroyer, in the ultimate analysis, can be so, only if it is itself indestructible. Now, if there be no cause of destruction, there should be no such fear in the destructible as issues from a perception of a destroyer. The whole world, however, is seen to be stricken with fear. Therefore, from the perceived fact of fear, in the world, it follows that there does exist a terrifying thing which is by nature an indestructible agent of destruction, because of which the world shudders.

It is out of the fear for the Brahma that the wind blows, sun rises, fire, Indra and death run. Suppose there is a youngman — good, learned, strongly built and energetic — and there is a cart full of wealth lying before him. This will be one joy for him. Then he acts according to the arisings of desires and their satisfaction with the wealth available. But then arises the fear of Brahma, what after the accomplishment of worldly joys. This fear is there even amongst gods and that Brahma, the source of fear, is thus a bliss. Then what is there to be assessed about bliss is that bliss can be studied from the point of view of whether it arises from the contact of subject and object, as is the case with worldly happiness or whether it is natural. The worldly bliss attains excellence owing to a concurrence of external and internal means. The bliss thus attained is instanced here as an approach to the bliss that is Brahma, for through this familiar bliss can be approached the bliss that is comprehensible by an intellect free from objective thought. Even worldly bliss is a particle of bliss that is Brahma, which becomes transmuted into impermanent worldly bliss, consequent on knowledge becoming covered up by ignorance, and ignorance becoming successively thicker according as the individuals starting with 'Hiranyagarbha', think diversely of this bliss under the impulsion of the result of their past actions and in conformity with their past contemplations and under the influence of contact with accessories like objects etc. That very bliss, which is visualised by one, who is learned, versed in vedas and free from passions, appears diversely as increasing more and more — a hundred fold each time in the plans starting with that of man-Gandharvas till the bliss of 'Hiranyagarbha', Brahma is reached, in accordance with the attenuation of ignorance, desire and action. But when the division of subject and object, created by ignorance, is eliminated by enlightenment, then there is only the intransic, all pervading, bliss that is one without the second.

Further, he that is here in the human person, and he that is there in the sun, are one. He, who knows this, attains, after desisting from this world; this self made of food; attains this self made of the vital force ; attains this self made of mind; attains this self made of intelligence; attains this self made of bliss. The bliss of his is directly experienced everywhere by one, who is versed in vedas, free from sins and unsullied by desires. Hence it is understood that these three qualities are the means for attaining the bliss. Of these, vedic learning and sinlessness are invariable (in all the plans) whereas the desirelessness increases, and hence the last is known to be the best means.The bliss of Brahma, experienced on the perfection of desirelessness and also open to the direct vision of one, who follows the vedas, is a particle or bit of the supreme bliss, in accordance with the vedic text, 'On a particle of this very bliss other beings live'. This bliss of Brahma is a particle of that supreme bliss that is natural, from which it has separated like spray from the sea and into which it merges again. In the supreme bliss, there is no bifurcation of the joy and the enjoyer, since it is non-dual. He that is here in the human person, and he that is there in the sun, are one. He, who knows thus, attains, after desisting from this world, this self made of food; attains this self made of the vital force ; attains this self made of mind; attains this self made of intelligence and attains this self made of bliss. It may in the end be said in regard to the existence or otherwise or Brahma that from the reasonings which justify the phenomena of creation, acquisition of joy, functioning of life, reaching a state of fearlessness and experience of fear, it follows that Brahma does exist as the cause of those space etc. there are also other questions relating to attainment or non-attainment of Brahma by the enligtened man and the unenlightened man. Of these, the last question is 'Does the enlightened man attain or does he not'? The answer to this shall cover the middle question too. Anyone, who is a knower of this kind, who, having descended all ideas of superiority and inferiority, knows Brahma, described earlier in this manner 'I am the non-dual truth, knowledge and infinity'. He, lit after departing, desisting without expecting anything from this world — the totality of things seen and unseen is verily indicated by the term 'this world' without expecting anything from that world, attains this body built up by food, as explained already. Then he attains this body constituted of vital force, undivided and inside the body built up by all the food, made of mind, made of intelligence and made of bliss. Then he reaches the state of fearlessness in the unperceivable, bodiless, inexpressible, and unsupporting self. The knower of Brahma thus attains the highest; becomes Supreme self through its knowledge as knowledge eradicates ignorance and is the means for the attainment of self.

The enlightened man is not afraid of anything after realising that bliss of Brahma failing to reach which, words turn back along with the mind. Him, indeed, this remorse does not afflict. 'Why did I not perform good deeds and why did I perform bad deeds'? He, who is thus enlightened, strengthens the self with which these two are identical; for it is he, indeed, who knows thus, that can strengthen the self, which these two really are. This is the secrét teaching. The bliss that is free from the relation of subject and object, is natural, eternal and indivisible. The man of knowledge, having known that bliss, is not afraid of anything, for there remains no cause of fear. There certainly does not exist anything, distinct from that man of knowledge, of which he can be afraid for it has been said that, when anyone creates, the slightest difference in the Brahma, through ignorance, then one is subject to fear. But since for the enlightened man, the cause of fear, which is the effect of ignorance, has been removed, it is proper that he has no fear of anything. But when death approaches, remorse comes in the form, 'Why did I not perform good deeds'. Similarly, repentence in the form, 'Why I prohibited things', come to a man of no knowledge from fear of affliction in the form of falling into hell etc. The omission of good and commission of the bad donot torment a man who is enlightened as they do the ignorant man.

Since Brahma that is truth, knowledge, and infinity, brought about this creation starting with space and ending with the body made of food, then, it entered into it and seem to be possessed of distinction because of this fact of entry, therefore, one should realise, 'I am that very Brahma which is the bliss that is distinct from all creation and is possessed of such characteristics as invisibility'. In the case of one, who knows thus, good and bad deeds do not bring about rebirth. After this, is to be taught concentration, which is helpful to the knowledge of Brahma, as also such meditations with regard to food etc., which have not been dealt with so far here that knowledge is imparted by father to a son.

Bhrigu, the well-known son of Varuna, approached his father with the request to teach him Brahma. Varuna told him that food, vital force, eye, ear, mind, speech — these are the aids to the knowledge of Brahma. He said that crave to know well that from which all these beings take birth, that by which they live after being born, that towards which they move and into which they merge, that is Brahma. He practised concentration. Varuna also said that food etc. are the doors to the realisation of Brahma and that its definition is, 'That from which all these beings take birth etc'. That indeed is incomplete for Brahma was not directly pointed out there, otherwise Brahma, in its true nature, should have been indicated by saying, 'This Brahma is of this kind, to the son, who was desirous of knowing'. He knows food as Brahma, for food is endowed with the aforesaid characteristics. But how from food these beings are born and having born, they live by food and they move towards and enter into food. Hence it is reasonable that food is Brahma. He, having practised concentration in this way and having known the food as Brahma, from its characteristics as well as by reasoning, approached his father Varuna over again, being under boubt, with formal request to teach Brahma. He also knew the vital force as Brahma as from vital force spring all the beings and having come into being, they live through the vital force; they move towards and enter into the vital force. Having known thus, he again approached his father to teach him Brahma. Varuna again asked him to concentrate. Bhrigu knew the mind as Brahma as from the mind indeed spring all the beings. Having been born, they are sustained by mind and they move towards and merge into the mind. Having known that, he approached his father again and made the same request to teach him Brahma. Varuna again asked him to concentrate. Then Bhrigu knew knowledge as Brahma, for from knowledge, spring all beings and having born they are sustained by knowledge and then they move towards and merge in knowledge. Having known that. Bhrigu again approached for being taught Brahma and Varuna again asked him to concentrate. Bhrigu knew bliss as Brahma as all beings originate from bliss. Having been born, they are sustained by bliss; they move towards and merge in bliss. This knowledge realised by Bhrigu and imparted by Varuna starts from food itself and ends with Supreme bliss, established in the cavity of heart. He, who knows thus becomes firmly established; he becomes the possessor of food and the eater of food and he becomes great in progeny, cattle and the lustre of holiness and great in glory. Thus becoming pure in mind through concentration and failing to find the definition of Brhama in its fullness, in the selves composed of the vital force etc., Bhrigu penterated inside by degrees and with the help of concentration alone realised the innermost bliss that is Brahma. Therefore, anyone, who is desirous of knowing Brahma, should undertake concentration of the internal and external organs as the most excellent practice of austerity. Now standing inside from the story, the upanisada states the purport of the story in its own words, 'This then is the knowledge, which was realised by Bhrigu, imparted by Varuna, which commencing from the self constituted by food, culmimats in the supreme, non-dual bliss that is lodged in the cavity that is the supreme space within the heart'. Anybody else too, who realises the bliss that is Brahma by entering through this very process and through concentration alone as his and — that man, too in consequence of his knowledge gets established in the bliss that is the Supreme Brahma, that is to say he becomes Brahma itself. Moreover since Brahma is realised through the portal of food, one should not deprecate food first as one would not cavil at his teacher. One, who has know Brahma, his vow is that he should not deprecate food. The vital force is verily food and the body is the eater of food. The body is fixed on the vital force. The vital force is lodged in the body. Thus the body and the vital force are both foods and one food is lodged in another ; gets firmly established. He becomes a possessor and an eater of food. He becomes great in progeny, cattle and the lustre of holiness and great in glory. His vow is also that he should not discard food. Water too is food, fire is the eater of food. Fire is established in water and water resides in fire. Thus again one food is lodged in another food. He, who knows thus that one food is lodged in another food, gets firmly established. He becomes a possessor and an eater of food. He becomes great in progeny, cattle, lustre of holiness, and great in glory. His vow again is that he should make food plentiful. Earth is food; space is the eater of food. Space is placed in earth. Earth is placed in space. Thus one food is lodged in another food and he, who knows thus gets firmly established. His vow is that he should not refuse anyone come for shelter. Therefore, one should collect plenty of food by whatsoever means he may and one should collect food for the further reason that they say, 'Food is ready for him' because he offers cooked food in his early age with honour; he offers food in his middle age with medium courtesy, food falls to his share in his middle age with medium honour and he offers food in his old age with scant esteem as in old age, food falls to his share with scant consideration. He, who knows it gets established. There is also the vow for one, who meditates on earth and space. Now is being started a process of meditation on Brahma, means the preservation of what has been acquired; Brahma is to be meditated on as existing in speech; in the form of preservation. Yoga means the acquisition of what is not in possession.Though these acquisition and preservation occur so long as exhaling and inhaling function, still they are not brought out by the mere fact of living. They are caused by Brahma. Therefore, Brahma is to be meditated on as existing in exhalation and inhalation in the form of acquisition and preservation. Since work is done by Brahma, Brahma is to be meditated on as existing in the hands in the form of work, as movement in the feet and as discharged in the anus. Brahma is similarly to be meditated on in rain and in all existing forms, including energy in lightning. He is to be worshipped as fame in hearts, light in stars, as procreation, immortality and joy in the generative organ, as everything in space. One should meditate on Brahma as the support; thereby one becomes supported and meditating him as great, one becomes great, worshipped as exalted makes him exalted; meditating a medium of destruction makes the adversaries that envy such as one dies and so do the enemies whom this one dislikes.

He, who knows thus, attains, after desisting from this world, this self made of food. After attaining this self, made of food. Then attaining this self made of vital force; then attaining this self made of intelligence; then attaining the self made of bliss and roaming over these worlds with command over food at will and command over all forms at will, he continues singing the same song. 'Oh ! Oh ! Oh! I am the food, I am the food, I am the food, I am the eater, I am the eater, I am the eater, I am the unifier, I am the unifier, I am the unifier, I am Hiranyagarbha, the first born of this world consisting the formed and the formless; I am (as Virat) earlier than the gods; I am navel of immortatlity. He who offers me thus as food, protects me just as I am, I, food as I am, eat him up, who eats food without offering. I defeat the entire universe'. Our effulgence is like that of the sun. He who knows thus gets such results. Starting from the self constituted by food, and by degrees reaching the self, constituted by food, he sits singing on this song. And so our effulgence is ever-shining like the sun.This is the knowledge of the supreme self inculcated in the above narration. To him come the aforesaid fruit, who, like Bhrigu, masters the above mentioned upanisada through practice of great concentration after the acquisition of control over the inner and outer organs, dispassionateness, imperturbability and concentration.

9

Aitareya Upanisada

The Aitareya Upanisada forms the 4th, 5th and 6th chapters of the second Aranyaka of Aitarya Brahmana. This upanisada is concerned only with knowledge of the self, whereas the earlier portion deals with Varuna, associated with meditation. The highest result that is achievable through 'Karma', associated with meditation, was concluded with the meditation on 'Uktha' (prana). It was said that Brahma that is truth is called 'Prana'; this is the only deity and all the gods are but manifestations of this 'Prana'. Attaining identity with this 'Prana', one becomes united with the gods. Some people believe that the highest human goal consists in the merger in the deity, that this is emancipation, that this is attainable by the means of a combination of meditation and 'Karma', as described and that this is nothing higher than this with a view to refuting them and enjoining the knowledge of the absolute self, it is said that in the beginning this was but the absolute self alone. He, who knows 'Vidya' (knowledge) and 'Avidya' (rites etc.) together attains immortality through 'Vidya' by crossing over death and through 'Avidya' by doing 'Karma' indeed should one wish to live here for a hundred years. When the supreme knowledge is achieved, there can be no idea of results and so no action is possible. It is, however, wrong to say that the knowledge of self comes to the man engaged in 'Karma' and that it is associated with 'Karma' and so on, as action is inconceivable in one, who has the knowledge of Brahma as his self, comprised in the realisation, 'I am the Supreior Brahma in which all desires are fulfilled and which is above all the worldly short-comings and who has no idea of results because he feels no need for anything to be got for himself from actions done or so to be done by him'.

Renunciation consists in mere cessation from activity. The feeling of want follows from ignorance and is not inherent in any object for the fact of feeling of want towards an object is in evidence in all beings. Moreover, one acts through speech, mind and body, when one is impelled by thirst for desired results and it is said, 'He desired "Let me have a wife" and these are desires. Sons, wealth etc. that constitute the five-fold 'Karma' are comprised within desire'. Five factors for Karmas are wife. Son, divine wealth (meditation), human wealth and rites. Now since domestic life is indeed by desire, 'This indeed is desire', both these are desires. Renunciation is mere absence of well-established relationship with sons etc., arising from desire and not as the mere moving away from that domestic life and so the inactive man of realisation cannot continue in the domestic life itself. Some householders, shy of begging alms and afraid of ridicule, advance the argument that in as much as a mendicant, desirous merely of maintaining his body, is seen to subject himself to regularisation about begging, there can be continuance in the domestic life even for that householder, who has become freed from both kinds of desires with regard to ends and means, but who has to depend as mere food and raiment for the maintenance of the body. But it is not so as when there is no clinging to any particular house of one's own,then follows begging alone as a matter of course, in the case of one, who has no inclination for turning to his own and who seeks for food and raiment under the mere impulsion of maintaining the body. From the fact that a fresh injunction of renunciation, despite its emergence as a matter of course, in the case of a man of illumination, is met with, it becomes evident that it is obligatory for the man of illumination. And monasticism is obligatory even for the illumined soul that hankers after emancipation. Therefore, he, who knows thus, becomes self controlled, eater etc. Kaivalya Upanisada says that 'Some attained immortality not by 'Karma', not by 'progeny,' not by wealth but by renunciation'. Manu samriti too says 'After attaining knowledge, one should have recourse to inactivity and he should continue in that order of life (sanyas) which is conducive to the attainment of Brahma.

According to shastras 'From the domestic life one should resort to that of the forest-dweller (recluse) and then embrace monasticism'. Alternatively, one should embrace monasticism from the stage of the celibate, or the householder's or the recluse. Even for one, who has embraced the householder life, monastecism is desirable as a disciplinary means for the realisation of self. It is, however, proved that for the knower of the self, there can be neither wantonness nor engagement in any other duty apart from renunciation.

In the beginning 'OM' was the absolute self alone and there was nothing else whatsoever that winked. It then thought, 'Let me create the worlds', and having visualised thus, he created these worlds viz. one beyond heaven (ambhar), with heaven as its support and sky (marice), the earth (mara) and the world below (apaha). Starting with space, he created in due order the cosmic egg and then created the worlds (ambhar etc.) After having created the worlds, he thought of creating the protectors of the worlds. Then having gathered a lump of the human form from the water itself, he gave shape to it with head, hands, etc. from water itself and from the five elements in which water predominated. He then deliberated with regard to 'Virat' human form. Then his mouth parted and from the mouth, speech emerged, from speech caused fire, from nostrils came out the sense of smell and from the sense of smell, came air. Then the two eyes parted and from the eyes emerged the sense of sight and from the sight came the sun. Then ears parted, from which came the sense of hearing and from the sense of hearing came the directions. Then skin emerged and from skin came hair i.e. the sense of touch associated with hair and from the sense of touch caused the herbs and trees. Then heart took shape and from the heart issued the internal organ (mind) from which came the moon. Then naval parted, from navel came out the organ of ejection and from the organ of ejection issued death. Then seat of the procreative organ parted ; from that came the procreative organ and from that came out the water. Thus in all cases the seat of organs, the organs and the deity — these three emerged in succession. These deities, which have thus been created, fell into this vast ocean. He subjected the virat human to hunger and thirst. They requested the creator to provide an abode for them, where they could stay and eat food. The idea here is that even the attainment of the state of merger in the deities viz fire and others, which is explained earlier, and which is the result of the combined practice of meditation and 'Karma' even this is not adequate for the removal of the sorrows of the world. Therefore, for the eradication of all worldly miseries, one should realise the Supreme Brahma as the self of one's own as also of all beings. It, therefore, follows that, 'This, that is the knowledge of the oneness of Brahma and the self, is the path, this is the 'Karma', this is Brahma and this is truth'. The god then brought a cow for them but it was not considered adequate. Then he brought a horse, which too was not considered adequate. Then he brought a man. They said 'This one is well formed; man indeed is a creation of God himself'. To them he asked for entereing into there respective abodes. Then they also became free from misery and asked all gods to enter into the dwellings such as speaking, hearing etc. Fire entered into mouth taking the form of organ of speech; air entered into nostrils taking the form of sense of smell; sun entered into eyes as the sense of sight; directions entered into ears becoming the sense of hearing; herbs and trees entered into the skin in the form of hair i.e. sense of touch ; the moon entered into heart in the shape of mind; death entered into navel in the form of apana i.e. the vital force that presses down ; water entered into the limb of generation in the form of semen. When gods had thus found their abodes, hunger and thirst, being without abodes, asked God to provide some abode to them. God told them that since they were only feelings, they could not possibly eat food without being supported by some conscious being, therefore, he made them sharers among those gods. Whatever allotment, consisting of oblation etc. is assigned to any deity, he made them sharers in that very portion. Even today, for whichsoever deity, are oblation — such as porridge, cake etc. is taken up — hunger and thirst become sharers with that deity.

God then thought, those, then are the senses and the deities of the senses and thought of creating food for them. He deliberated with regard to water and from the water evolved a form and the form that emerged was verily food. This food, that was created, turned back and attempted to run away. He tried to take it up with speech, but did not succeed and if he had succeeded then one could have become contented merely by talking of food. Then he tried to grasp that food with the sense of smell. Again he did not succeed. He then wanted to take up food with the eyes but did not succeed. Then he wanted to take up with ears, but could not succeed. Then he wanted to take up with the sense of touch; with the mind; with procreative organ etc. but could not succeed. Then he wanted to take up with 'apana' and took it up. This is the devourer of food. That vital energy which is well-known as dependent on food for its subsistence is this vital energy called 'apana' the indrawing energy of air through the cavity of mouth. He took up food thus. Therefore, this 'apana' air is the seizer of food i.e. the devourer of food. The vital energy that is well-known as dependent on food, for its susbistence in this one, which is the vital energy called 'apana'. Then he thought how he could enter in the body through speech, nose, ear, eyes etc. Then who shall he be. Having thus made the existence of the congress of the senses and their deities dependent on food, like the existence of a city, its citizens and its rulers, he thought like the ruler of the city. While cogitating thus, how without him, the master of the city could there be? So he thought that he should be Supreme Lord, the ruler like a king without a city the witness of whatever has been done or not done as also their results and the enjoyer. But then he thought that after entering into the combination of the body and the organs, he did not witness the fruits of utterances etc., made by speech etc., just as a king, after entering a city, observes the omissions and commissions of the officers, then nobody would understand or think of him. Having reasoned thus, he thought of how he shall enter. There are two ways of entrance into this composite thing — the lower of the food and the head. He thought he should not enter from lower part and it should be the entry for his servant, who would act on his behalf. He then thought of entering through the head and entered just like a human being, who performs what he thinks. He then entered through that door known as the cleft-entrance, which is delightful. There are three abodes for him — the three states of dream. Then cleft, this very end, having made a hole at the farthest point where the hair is parted, entered the world i.e. the conglomeration of body and organs. Now he having born and having entered into the body as the individual soul manifested the beings he realised this very 'Purusha' as Brahma, the most pervasive thus: 'OH ! I have realised this, that is the real nature of myself'. He was given the name as 'Idandra' or 'Indra' for the gods are verily fond of indirect names.

The purport of the above narration is the reality that is the creator, preserver and destroyer of the universe and is transcendental, omniscient, omnipotent and all-knowing, created in due order this entire universe beginning with space, without the help of any substance other than himself. Then he himself entered into all bodies possessed of vital force etc. for the sake of realising his own self, and having entered there he realised directly, his own self in its reality 'I am this Brahma.' Therefore, he is the only one self in all the bodies and there is none besides. And so everybody else too, should realise thus: 'He is my self', 'I am Brahma' and so on. Without the help of anyone he created this universe, gathering up the human size from water, he gave it shape from his brooding. parting with mouth etc., created all organs, all deities, hunger and thirst. Thus the deity, who is omniscient, and omnipotent and is a great conjurer, created all this like a magician.

The imagination of difference among God, the individual soul and the Supreme self can be traced to the erroneous idea as 'It is' or 'It is not' with regard to the eternal and unconditional version of that entity in which all the variations of speech and mind (the name and form) get unified. He, who entertains any desire of fancying that it exists or does not exist; that is one or is many; that it has attributes or has not; that it knows or knows not; that it is active or is not; that it is fruitful or is fruitless; that it has a seed or is seedless; that it is happiness or misery; that it is inside or outside; that it is void or not or that it is different from me or that I am different from it. In this conneciton a story is related. An idiotic person, who committed some guilt was told 'Fie on you ! You are no man'! Because of his stupidity he approached somebody to get the conviction that he was a man and told him 'Tell me who I am' the later said, 'I shall make you understand by degrees' and then after proving that he was not a motionless thing and so on, he concluded with, 'You are none other than a man'. That first man told him that he, who started to enlighten him had become silent. He asked how can he, who does not understand himself to be a man when told, 'You are none other than a man' understand himself to be a man even when told 'You are a man'. Therefore, the process to be followed in enlightening about the self is as it is set forth in the scriptures and nothing else as even scripture which started imparting knowledge about the nature of the self, stopped after declaring 'Not this, not this'. Just as it was done in the story after negating all that was other than man. Then this self, the perceiver of everything in Brahma so long as one does not realise thus this self, one transmigrates under the influence of ignorance, desire and action by rotating again and again through the regions of the gods, animals and men, that range is from Brahma to a clump of grass. While transmigrating thus, one rejects the body assumed earlier, and giving it up, accepts another and continues thus without a break in the current of birth and death as though in a river, with a view ultimately to generate detachment.

In man, the soul is conceived first. That which is this semen is extracted from all the limbs as their vigour. He holds that self of his in his own self and when he sheds it into his wife, then he procreates it. That is its first birth. This very man performs such 'Karmas' as sacrifice etc. owing to his self-identification with ignorance, desire, and action; then he reaches the lunar region after passing from this world through smoke and the rest in succession and then, when the fruits of his actions, become exhausted, he reaches this world to become food after passing in succession through rain etc. In that man, the transmigrating soul, is first conceived in the form of semen after passing through the essence of food etc. This is being stated that one takes birth in that form this self (that is the man) offers this self of his, that is the semen, to that self of his that is the wife. It becomes non-different from the wife just as much as her own limb is. Therefore, the foetus does not hurt her. She nourishes this self of his that has entered her womb by avoiding taking such things as are injurious to the foetus and by accepting such food as is favourable to it. So the nourisher becomes fit to be nourished. The wife bears that embryo (before the birth). The father protects the son from the very start after birth, thereby he protects his own self for the sake of the continuance of these worlds and thus is the continuance of the worlds ensured. That is the second birth of the self but these are for the continuance of the worlds and not for emancipation. So this self of the son is deputed by the father for the performance of virtuous deeds and the other self of the father of the son having got his duties fulfilled and having advanced in age, departs and takes birth again. That is the third birth.

This fact, was stated by the seer, even while lying in the womb. 'I came to know of the birth of all the gods.A hundred iron citadels held me down. Then like a hawk, I forced my way through by dint of the knowledge of the self'. Vamdeva said this while still lying in the mother's womb.He, who had known thus had become identified with the supreme and attained all desirable things even here and having then ascended higher up after the destruction of the body, he became immortal in the world of the self.

There are Brahmins of the modern times, who crave for emancipation, hanker after the knowledge of Brahma and realise that the achievement of the identity with the self of all follows from the disciplines for the knowledge of Brahma as revealed by the vedas through the succession of teachers like Vamdeva and very well known in the councils of the knowers of Brahma. Then these Brahmins becoming desirous of desisting from the impermanent world of ends and means, inclusive of being born as limited soul ask one another, thus while engaged in deliberation. Which is this self that we worship as the self and which of the two is self. Is it that by which one sees and by which one hears, smells, speaks and by which one takes the sweets and the sour and which again is that one organ that has become diversely differentiated? It is this heart or intellect and mind that were stated earlier. It is sentience, rulership, secular knowledge, presence of mind, retentiveness, sense-perception, fortitude, thinking, genius, mental suffering, memory, ascertainment, resolution, life activities, hankering, passion, and such others. All these verily are the names of consciouness and when it does the fucntions of living, it is called the vital force. Then there is one inferior Brahma, this is Indra, Prajapati and all other gods and the five elements viz. earth, air, space, water and fire; all big creatures and the tiny ones that are the procreators of others and referable in pairs — to wit those that are born of eggs, of wombs, of moisture and of earth viz horses, cattle, men, elephants and all the creature which fly and those which donot move. All these are impelled by consciouness; all these have consciousness as the giver of their reality; the universe has consciousness as its eye and consciousness its end. Consciousness is Brahma too. The entity thus dealt with when freed from all distinctions created by the limiting adjuncts, is without stain, without taint, without action, one without the second to be known as 'Not this, not this' by the elimination of all attributes and it is beyond all words and thoughts. That very entity, which is the omniscient God because of the association with the limiting adjunct of very pure intelligence — and is the ordained of the common seed of all the unmanifested universe, assumes the name of the inner controller by virtue of being the guide. That entity itself assumes the name of 'Hiranyagarbha', who identifies himself with cosmic intelligence which is the seed of the manifested world. That entity itself gets the name of 'Virat', 'Prajapati', who has as his limiting adjunct the gross cosmic body born first within the cosmic egg and it comes to be known as the deities, fire etc. by assuming their respective limiting adjuncts viz. speech etc., born from the egg. Samriti says, 'Some call this very entity fire; some call it Manu ; and some Prajapati; some Indra; while others call it 'Prana'; and still others the eternal Brahma, etc.

Through the self that is consciousness, he ascends higher up from this world and granting all desires fulfilled in that heavenly world, he becomes immortal. Vamdeva and others knew thus the Brahma, as described, through the self that is consciousness through that very conscious self by which the seers of old became immortal. Similarly, this enlightened too through this self that is consciousness ascending higher up from this world, and attaining all the desires, in that heavenly world, becomes immortal.

10

Chhandogyopnisada

In Chhandogyopnisada, various methods of worship have been narrated. Also there is narration of soul and God. The method of narration is old and is at some places symbolic only. The worship can be done by remembering his names, thinking of his names and devotion to his names. Singing the name of God, i.e., 'OM' is called 'Udgeetha'. 'OM' means one, who protects and he is 'Udgeetha' too. The basic thing is earth. Earth's substance is water; water's substance are foodgrains and herbs etc; herbs etc. are the susbtance of mankind; man's substance is the power of voice and voice's susbtance is praise of God; praise of God is the susbtance of Samved and to praise the God by singing and then the susbstance of all is the name of God, which is the last resort for any being.

By our voice, we praise God and by our life we sing that praise of God. The combination of life and voice leads to worship of God and by worship of God, the human being gets closer to God. Anyone, who worships God by singing voice, putting life in it, attains fulfilment of his desires and ultimately the salvation. In senses all good and bad vices exist but if God is praised by singing and by life, then all such vices disappear and one gets absorbed in God.

11

Ishavashyopanisda

All the upanisadas exhaust themselves simply by determining the true nature of the self and the Gita and the scriptures dealing with Moksa (Salvation) have only this end in view. Accordingly 'Karmas' have been enjoined by assuming such qualities for the self as multiplicity, enjoyership etc. and impurity, sinfulness etc. which commonsense takes for granted. The verses in upanisadas remove one's natural ignorance about the self through the revelation of the true nature of the self and thereby, produce the knowledge of the oneness of the self, which is the means for the uprooting of sorrows, delusion, etc. incidental to the beings' existence.

ॐ दिशा वास्यमिद सर्वं यत् किचं जगत्यां जगत्

तेन त्यकतेन भुंजीथा मा गृंधः कस्यस्विद्धनम्।। (ईशा-1)

(Whatever is available on the earth, is covered by God. One should protect oneself through detachment from wealth as it does not remain with anyone).

One should consider self as supreme truth and get detached to all that he finds in the universe — the wife and sons, wealth and the world, as one is competent to renounce these through 'Karma'. After all, all these worldly things donot belong to anyone and rather than involving oneself in these belongings, one should make efforts to know the self. It is because of the correct 'Karma' only that one can live for hundred years. The life is inanimate and so without any vices. Human being eats and drinks with a view to keep all his senses operational; by protecting all senses, one maintains life too and by life one worships God. On analysing 'Udgeetha', (उद्गीथा), we find that it comprises of उत्+गी+थ meaning thereby that the life is raised above 'उत', voice is 'गी' and foodgrains (eatables) are 'थ'। The entire life rests on foodgrains. Therefore, 'Udgeetha' is to get ready to sing and continue in life i.e. in existence. For the purpose of singing the praise of God, one has to first arrive upon the metre in which it is sung; then decide the position of sitting in which the praise is to be sung and then one should think of one's aim of singing i.e. the pleasures of this universe or the attainment of salvation. When one praises God on concentration, one gets awakening and gets absorbed in God. In praising God by voice and life, one have to use eyes to see the vedic mantra, hear the mantra being sung by ears and concentration of mind to think of God only without allowing the mind to waver and think of anything else and in this way one shall get absorbed in God.

Ishwar is one, who is almighty and indivisible and the visible universe too is full within Himself. This universe is born out of the full almighty God. Although present in the universe and in each individual being, he is one whole and not divisible. He is the soul of this universe, which is his body. All in this universe are born out of Him, continue because of Him and ultimately join Him. One should, therefore, accept Him existing in this universe and continue his actions as ordained by Him. We are living for the sake of others, being good to others, and for doing all good deeds. In this way human being is always busy doing his jobs and is never idle and except for continuing one's performance, one has no other way of living. Now this performance can be good or bad. For bad performance, one has to fall in the channel of transmigration from one specie to another and for good performance, one gets absorbed in the almighty and thus gets rid of the transmigration. This universe is full of attractions leading to bad deeds and the human being on birth is all truth and even though he wants to continue to be true, he is misled by the attractions of the universe and fall prey to bad deeds. One, therefore, has to keep oneself above these attractions and in this way continue living in this universe.

Since God is one and indivisible and invisible, the human

being cannot see Him by his eyes, cannot hear His voice and cannot have any feeling of His existence by his senses because he is above all these things. Even the air, electricity and other fast powers cannot reach Him. Human beings are born in this universe and continue here as ordained by the almighty called the destiny.

One, therefore, has to learn about Him after the birth and those who do not try to know Him, keep themselves in dark; then mental and physial faculties do not develop properly and thus continue living in the life and world of ignorance. Even the education, which does not teach about existence of the almighty, is no education because with that type of education, one will not be able to differentiate between good and bad, true and untrue, Dharma and Adharma.

Learning about God is the real education. If one has known God, one has known everything. For this purpose one has to know one-self and the existence of God within oneself. After this only one shall start feeling as a part of the almighty.

If anyone says that he knows the God fully then he is mistaken. What he knows and what is known of gods is also a little knowledge about him. Therefore, whatever is known by anyone about God, he has to further devote himself to Him so that he reaches above any shape of God, as God is without any shape and one should not boast of having known God in a particular shape. One should, therefore, go on thinking about Him, have belief in Him but never boast of having known Him. Boasting of having knowledge about God is mere pride and at the same time, one should not think that God is not there. It is, on the contrary, sufficient to say that he is almighty. One, therefore, have to have faith in Him thinking that he is eternal, very minute, and unseeable, without having any pride about that thinking. One can know Him by constantly thinking about Him. By constant thinking and devoting to Him, one gets awakened and if one still continued thinking after attaining awakening, one gets Him. If one is able to reach Him in this life, then it is alright, otherwise this life is wasted and it is difficult to have the specie of human being again. Therefore, to have best use of this life is to go on thinking about Him and fully devoting to Him.

God only has created this universe, he created fire, etc and then it was thought that the creation of the universe is because of the gods like fire etc.These gods then started being proud of their existence and this fact came to the knowledge of God. God warned them but they could not realise their mistake nor could they know that their warner was God himself. They asked fire (Agni), who he was. Agni went to him and told him that it was Agni. He asked about her power and then Agni told that she could burn the entire universe. God placed a straw before her and asked her to burn it. Agni could not burn the straw even after applying her full force. Agni went back saying that she could not know him. Then gods sent Air (Vayu) to check up who he was. Vayu went to him. He asked about her power and Vayu told that she could blow away everything in this universe. God placed a straw before her and asked her to blow it. But even with full force she could not blow the straw. Vayu left that place and told the gods that she could not know him. Then the gods went to Indra and requested him to check up who he was. He went to God but God disappeared from there. We came to know from this that Agni and Vayu are the two forces only but whatever force they have, is that of God himself. Indra too, could not know him. Indra, however, met Uma, a shining and well-dressed lady and asked her about God. Uma can also be treated as the shining power of sun. Uma told Indra that it is Brahma (God) only and he should devote himself to Him only. In this way Agni, Vayu and Indra could know Him closely.Out of these three too, Indra had known Him first. So he is more powerful than other gods and the creation of the universe is only indicative of his force. In this universe, there are various beings, human beings being the best out of them. But they are attracted towards the luxuries of this universe. This attraction is by senses to have satisfaction and the senses are monitored by mind. Therefore, mind has to be controlled and put in devotion of God. It should always think of God, remember God and devote himself to God only. By doing this, one's soul (atma) gets closeness to Him and ultimately gets absorbed in Him. Upnisada means closeness or the self realisation, devotion, knowledge of Brahma and knowing the difference between the soul and the God. The Guru then told that he had narrated the upnisada, the existence of God, knowledge of God and the devotion to God, remembering Him and thinking of Him leads to salvation, has also been told to him.

In the universe, one should devote himself to God, be tolerant, and lead a simple and pious life. Control the senses by controlling the mind first. Then comes the performance in this universe. It should be regular as per one's Dharma. Such a person becomes eligible for Bhagwad bhakti, through the knowledge of God.